SENTENCE SENSE

Houghton Mifflin Company • Boston

Dallas   Geneva, Illinois   Palo Alto   Princeton, New Jersey

SENTENCE SENSE

A Writer's Guide

EVELYN FARBMAN

Greater Hartford Community College

ACKNOWLEDGMENTS

p. 299   "Laughter: The Ageless Prescription for Good Health," by John M. Leighty. Reprinted with permission of United Press International, Copyright 1987.

p. 305   "Events for Disabled Athletes of Both Sexes Increasing at Olympics," by Ross Atkin. Reprinted by permission from *The Christian Science Monitor* © 1988 The Christian Science Publishing Society. All rights reserved.

Cover design by Hannus Design Associates, Richard Hannus.

Printed in the U.S.A.

Library of Congress Catalogue Card Number: 88–81329

ISBN: 0–395–38004–9

ABCDEFGHIJ-H-9543210-898

Contents

To the Instructor   **xi**

PART ONE   GRAMMAR   **1**

Chapter   1   An Overview of the Whole Sentence   **3**

Writing   4

Growing Sentences — A Comparison   5

Return to your writing   9

Chapter   2   Verbs   **11**

Writing   12

Doing and Being Verbs   13
Single-Word Verbs and Verb Strings   14
Split Verbs   18
Time (Tense)   21
A Verb's Four Forms   24
Irregular Verbs   29
Non-Verb Forms   34
Combining Sentences by Compounding Verbs   35

Return to your writing   37

Chapter   3   Subjects   **39**

Writing   40

"Who or What (Verb)?"   41
Placement   42
Nouns and Pronouns as Subjects   43

Simple Subjects   45
Combining Sentences by Compounding Subjects   46

Return to your writing   48

Chapter 4   Completers and Modifiers   49

Writing   50

"(Subject + Verb) Whom or What?"   51
Words That Act as Completers   52
Recognizing the Difference between Completers and Subjects   53
How Modifiers Work   54
Single-Word Modifiers   55
Prepositional Phrase Modifiers   57
Combining Sentences by Compounding Completers or Modifiers   59

Return to your writing   62

Chapter 5   Embedded Thoughts   63

Writing   64

From Independent to Dependent Clause   65
Recognizing Dependent Clauses   67
From Verb to Verbal   70
Recognizing Verbal Phrases   72
Combining Sentences by Embedding Thoughts   74
Combining Sentences by Compounding Embedded Thoughts   77

Return to your writing   79

Chapter 6   Capitalization and Punctuation   81

Observation of writing   82

Capital Letters   83
Period   85
Question Mark   85
Exclamation Point   85
Comma   86
Colon   91
Semicolon   91
Quotation Marks   93
Parentheses   94

Return to your observation of writing   97

Chapter 7   Combining Sentences   99

Writing   100

Compounding Whole Sentences   101
Sentence Combining Summary   102

Return to your writing   105

PART TWO   USAGE   107

Chapter 8   Sentence Fragments   109

Writing   110

Incomplete Verbs   111
Disconnected Prepositional Phrases   112
Disconnected Verbal Phrases   113
Disconnected Dependent Clauses   115
Review and Practice   118

Return to your writing   122

Chapter 9   Run-on Sentences   123

Writing   124

Spotting Run-on Sentences   125
Correcting Run-on Sentences   126
Summary of Solutions   132
Avoiding Run-on Sentences   133
Review and Practice   138

Return to your writing   143

Chapter 10   Final -*ed*   145

Writing   146

Recognizing Final -*ed*   147
Using the Final -*ed* in the Simple Past Tense   149
Using the Final -*ed* in the Perfect Tenses   151
Using the Final -*ed* with Verbs in the Passive Voice   152

Using the Final *-ed* in Past Participles That Act as Modifiers   153
Avoiding Incorrect *-ed* Endings   155

Review and Practice   158

Return to your writing   162

Chapter 11   Final *-s*   163

Writing   164

Recognizing Final *-s*   165
Using Final *-s* on Plural Nouns   167
Using Final *-s* for Present Tense Verbs   170

Review and Practice   178

Return to your writing   182

Chapter 12   Subject-Verb Agreement   183

Writing   184

Subject-Verb Agreement in the Present Tenses   185
Subject-Verb Agreement with *Was* and *Were*   187
There Is, There Are, There Was, and *There Were*   189
Modifying Phrases or Clauses between Subject and Verb   190
Indefinite Pronouns as Subjects   193
Who, Which, and *That* as Subjects   196
Compound Subjects   197

Review and Practice   200

Return to your writing   206

Chapter 13   Pronouns   207

Writing   208

Recognizing Pronouns   209
Finding a Pronoun's Antecedent   211
Choosing between Subject and Object Forms of
    Personal Pronouns   212
Making Pronouns and Antecedents Agree   218

Review and Practice   224

Return to your writing   228

Chapter 14   Spelling   229

Writing   230

Changes Before an Added Ending   231
Possessive Nouns   236
Words That Sound Alike   240
Spelling Chart   247
Review and Practice   251

Return to your writing   259

Chapter 15   Consistency   261

Writing   262

Finding and Using Parallel Elements   263
Making Verb Tenses Consistent   266
Making Pronoun Point of View Consistent   269
Review and Practice   272

Return to your writing   275

PART THREE   WRITING   277

Chapter 16   Techniques for Writing   279

1. Freewriting   281
2. Clustering   282
3. Limiting a Topic   283
4. Writing Topic Sentences for Paragraphs   284
5. Giving Examples and Explanations   288
6. Using Specific Language   290
7. Making Paragraph Breaks   292
8. Using Transitional Expressions   293
9. Writing Thesis Statements for Essays   295

Chapter 17   Topics for Writing   297

1. An Official and a Personal Account   299
2. A Round Robin Story   300
3. A Character Sketch   301

4. A Description of a Significant Place   302
5. A Definition of an Emotion   303
6. A Controversial Stand   304
7. A Summary   304
Guide for Finding Another Dozen Assignments   309

PART FOUR   TESTS   311

Chapter 18   Pretests and Mastery Tests   313

Pretests for Chapters 8–15   315
Mastery Tests for Chapters 8–15   339

Answer Key   362
Index   403

To the Instructor

In selecting and organizing material for *Sentence Sense,* I have had two goals. The first has been to provide beginning college writers with several approaches to improving their writing skills. The second has been to offer instructors flexibility in using the text's resources.

ORGANIZATION AND APPROACH

The organization of *Sentence Sense* enables instructors to mix and balance exercises and writing practice to suit the needs of their classes. Part One, "Grammar," shows students how sentences work. By manipulating the parts of working sentences, students learn to recognize underlying patterns in the English language. Part One offers a vocabulary for recognizing and discussing sentence regularities, using terminology that reflects my experience of what students understand best. Most of the terminology is traditional, but a few less familiar generic terms such as *completer, modifier,* and *embedded thought* simplify the explanations of how sentences work. Part Two, "Usage," tackles error, concentrating on those errors that are most likely to prejudice readers against inexperienced writers. Part Three, "Writing," offers a collection of techniques and topics for writing practice. The techniques address issues that commonly arise in the writing process, and the topics focus on the discovery and use of evidence, laying groundwork for the transition from personal to academic writing. Part Four, "Tests," contains tests for use as needed with the chapters in Part Two.

- Part One provides a sequenced introduction to sentence analysis. Studying sentence patterns enables students to make informed choices and puts them in charge of their own writing. Part One provides background for Part Two.

- Each Part Two chapter looks closely at a convention of standard English and offers explanations, examples, and exercises to help students master that convention. Chapters are independent of each other so that they may be assigned as needed.

- The writing techniques and topics offered in Part Three encourage students to use writing as a way to generate thoughts and to reflect on their implications. Techniques and topics can be assigned at any time.

• The *pretests* in Part Four clarify students' needs for the corresponding chapters, and the *mastery tests* help to evaluate students' progress. Instructors may take advantage of the perforated pages to remove the tests for distribution as needed.

FEATURES

• The **flexible format** of *Sentence Sense* is adaptable to collaborative learning settings, and the complete answer key allows students to use the text for self-paced work. Parts One and Two can be assigned for work outside of class, freeing classroom time for writing, revising, and editing activities.

• **Writing assignments** at the beginning of each Part One and Two chapter encourage students to write regularly, with grammar and usage issues anchored in their writing. Students return to this writing assignment after completing each chapter to revise their work in the light of what they've learned.

• **A large number and variety of exercises** offer breadth of practice. Exercises are in both sentence and paragraph form, and initial explanations are as brief as possible, emphasizing application over explication of concepts. Sentence combining exercises appear throughout Part One; this early introduction to compound structures simplifies later work on parallelism and subordinated forms.

• Complete **answer key**, at the back of the book, provides answers to the exercises in the text and to the pretests in Part Four.

• **Incorrect sentences are kept to a minimum.** Even in Part Two, where the avoidance of error is the focus, the exercises are not usually error-based. Wherever possible, students are asked to produce transformations from one standard form to another.

• **Extensive ancillary program** for instructors includes an *Instructor's Resource Guide, Test Package, Transparency Package,* and software for instructors' and students' use. Details are presented in the *Instructor's Resource Guide.*

ACKNOWLEDGMENTS

I am grateful to the following reviewers. Their comments and suggestions have helped in shaping *Sentence Sense.*

Pasquale Angelo   Edinboro University of Pennsylvania
Tom Anselmo   New York City Technical College
Shirley Bell   University of Arkansas, Monticello
Rita Bova   Columbus State Community College, Ohio

Henry Castillo   Temple Junior College, Texas
Fay Chandler   Pasadena City College
Patricia E. Connors   Memphis State University
Jane Tainow Feder   New York City Technical College
Carolyn Gordon   Cuyahoga Community College (Metropolitan Campus), Ohio
Sandra Sellers Hanson   LaGuardia Community College, New York
Peggy Harbers   Nashville State Technical Institute
Roslyn J. Harper   Trident Technical College, South Carolina
Priscilla Haworth   Elon College, North Carolina
Gary Hottinger   Quinebaug Valley Community College, Connecticut
William Kamowski   Eastern Montana College
Jane Maher   Nassau Community College, New York
Marilyn Martin   Quinsigamond Community College, Massachusetts
Robert A. McQuitty   Northeastern State University, Oklahoma
Christian Noordhoorn   Oakland Community College (Highland Lakes Campus), Michigan
Michael Orlando   Bergen Community College, New Jersey
Judith F. Pett   North Hennepin Community College, Minnesota
Nancy Rayl   Cypress College, California
Joyce Schenk   El Camino College, California
Nina Theiss   Santa Monica College, California
Audrey Williams   Valencia Community College (West Campus), Florida

John Carey, Luz Raquel Cruz, Andrew DiSilvestro, Barry McClean, and Talitha Moon contributed written works so that the book could be enlivened by student voices. Mary Seelye and Marvin Farbman wrote passages that I adapted for several exercises and tests. Many others have helped in indirect yet essential ways. Their names would fill pages, but I want to offer particular thanks to my students for reminding me daily of what this book is about, to my editors for coordinating countless details, and to Herschel and Daniel Farbman for maintaining household good humor and sharing ever wider perspectives.

E.F.

SENTENCE SENSE

PART ONE

Grammar

Chapter 1

An Overview of the Whole Sentence

An overview is the view you get when you stand back to look at a whole thing rather than at its separate parts. It is a passenger's view from an airplane — a view that makes it hard to recognize particular buildings but shows the patterns of the roads in the neighborhoods.

This chapter offers an overview of the English sentence. Because you speak English, you already understand many things about the way English sentences work. Here you'll see the four parts of the sentence working together, and you'll have an opportunity to use each part and come to your own conclusions. In Chapters 2 through 7, you'll be given definitions and explanations of the four sentence parts. These explanations will build on what you have already thought about. The details will become clear when you focus on each sentence part in these chapters. In this overview, though, think about the patterns the parts make as they fit together into whole sentences.

Writing

On scrap paper, jot down ideas about how it feels to write. Here are some questions that may start you thinking: How tightly are you holding your pen or pencil? How do your shoulders feel? What do you think about when you face the blank page? How is writing different from talking? You may answer some of these questions, or simply write down any thoughts that come into your head when you consider how the act of writing affects you. Turn these observations into four or five sentences, and copy them onto a fresh sheet of paper.

GROWING SENTENCES — A comparison

Sentences grow.

These sentences grow.
Sentences on this page grow.
Starting from seeds, sentences grow.

Sentences grow easily.
Sentences grow before your eyes.
Sentences grow to develop sturdy shapes.
Sentences grow until they seem to gather
a momentum of their own.

Sentences grow branches.
Sentences grow new branches.
Sentences grow branches of words.
Sentences grow branches unfolding fresh ideas.
Sentences grow branches that may blossom with
unexpected possibilities.

Starting from seeds, these sentences grow easily
before your eyes until they seem to gather a
momentum of their own. To develop sturdy
shapes, sentences grow new branches of words,
unfolding fresh ideas that may blossom with
unexpected possibilities.

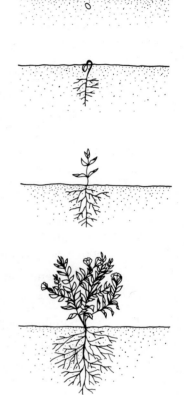

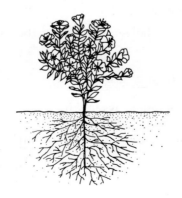

SENTENCES GROW FROM SEEDS

In the sentences below, look at the words with one line underneath them. What do all these words have in common? Now look at the words with two lines underneath. What do these words have in common with each other?

Sentences grow.

Love deceives.

Someone is painting.

Kenisha must have forgotten.

Were they hiding?

The seed of a sentence is a **subject** and a **verb.** In this book we identify subjects by underlining them once. We underline verbs twice. Chapter 2 focuses on verbs, and Chapter 3 focuses on subjects.

Look at the words in boxes below. What do they have in common? As you think about this question, compare these sentences with the sentences given above as examples.

Sentences grow branches .

Love deceives people .

Someone is painting graffiti .

Kenisha must have forgotten Donnell .

Were they hiding anything ?

Sometimes a third part may join the subject + verb seed to complete the sentence's idea. A box is used to mark a **completer** in this book, and Chapter 4 examines what completers do.

In the sentences below, notice how the subjects, verbs, or completers grow in meaning when descriptive words or groups of words are added.

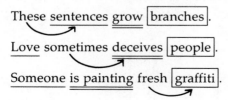

These sentences grow branches .

Love sometimes deceives people .

Someone is painting fresh graffiti .

Kenisha must have forgotten Donnell (since the summer).

Were they hiding anything (of value)?

The words marked with arrows are **modifiers.** In this book we use arrows to point to the words that the modifiers describe. Some modifiers are single words; others are groups of words, which we hold together with brackets ⟨ . . . ⟩. Chapter 4 shows how modifiers work.

Comparing a sentence to a growing plant displays some of the ways the sentence works. Starting from the seed of a subject + verb, a completer may join these parts to complete the sentence's idea. Modifiers may sprout from a subject, a verb, or a completer and describe any of these words in more detail. Understanding the four sentence parts will help you develop your ideas clearly in writing.

The following exercise will help you see what you already know about the four sentence parts: subject, verb, completer, and modifier. (You will find suggested answers for the Applications in this book in the Answer Key.)

APPLICATION.   Finish each of the following sentences. In sentences 1–4, add one word in each space. The word you add will be a **subject.**

1. _____ cracks jokes at unexpected moments.

2. At the bank this morning, _____ had everyone in stitches.

3. Even _____ relaxed and laughed at that one.

4. _____ will keep you from taking yourself too seriously.

In sentences 5–8, add one word in each space. The word you add will be a **verb.**

5. Martha's foul shots _____ not very good today.

6. Her posture _____ a lot of work too.

7. The coach _____ some extra time with her last night.

8. He _____ her a fancy new trick.

In sentences 9–12, add one word in each box. The word you add will be a **completer.**

9. You should see this ⌐_____⌐.

10. After all, it is ⌐_____⌐.

11. Would you prefer [   ] for dinner?

12. Eric and I had very good [   ] at that new restaurant last week.

In sentences 13–16, add a word or group of words in the space to finish the sentence. Each word or group of words you add will be a modifier or will finish a modifier already started for you.

13. You are painting that wall very _____.

14. Do you always paint ⟨with _____⟩?

15. The _____ color over the sink is an improvement.

16. I bought some _____ paint last week for the kitchen.

Return to your writing

Find the sentences you wrote at the beginning of this chapter. Read them aloud. Pick one sentence and see if you can identify a subject, verb, completer, or modifier. The following chapters in Part One will offer you chances to look more closely at words and groups of words performing these four sentence functions, each one contributing to the growth of a whole sentence.

Chapter 2

Verbs

A sentence contains two essential parts, a verb and a subject. Recognizing the verb is the key to analyzing a sentence. Further, knowing how verbs work allows you to make intelligent choices among verb forms as you write.

In Chapter 2, you will learn that

- verbs usually begin the section of a sentence that tells what someone is *doing* or *being*. (Fabian talks to himself. He is often alone in the car.)
- verbs can be combinations of a main verb plus one or more auxiliaries. (I could understand only a little of the speech.)
- verbs split apart in a question or negative statement. (Can you hear me now? The window should not be open.)
- verbs give clues about the time of an event. (Yesterday he ran down the street. Today he is running on the grass.)
- verbs can appear in four different forms: base, simple past, present participle, and past participle.
- irregular verbs do not follow the usual pattern in their four forms.
- sentences can be combined by compounding their verbs.

Writing

Think about a TV show you saw, a story you read, or an incident at school in the past week. Remember what happened, who did what, and why. Try to recall what was interesting or funny or exciting. On scrap paper, jot notes about what happened in the show, story, or incident.

1. Arrange your ideas into a paragraph describing the events as they happened *in the past*. Rewrite your paragraph on a fresh sheet of paper. For example:

   In history class yesterday, I got mad. The videotape we were watching irritated me because the narrator kept trying to force his opinion down our throats. . . .

2. Now change the time of your paragraph. Tell the story as if it were happening right now. Cross out the words that place the events in the past, and above them write words that place the events in the present. The example sentences above would look like this:

   today   am getting   are

   In history class ~~yesterday~~, I ~~got~~ mad. The videotape we ~~were~~

   irritates   keeps

   watching ~~irritated~~ me because the narrator ~~kept~~ trying to force

   his opinion down our throats. . . .

Many of the words you've crossed out and changed are verbs.

DOING AND BEING VERBS

A verb usually begins the section of a sentence that tells what someone or something is doing or being.

Someone or Something	Doing
Finally Sir Edmund Hilary	<u>arrived</u> at the peak of Mount Everest.
Clouds	<u>were rolling</u> far below.
He	<u>breathed</u> carefully through his mask.
His oxygen supply	<u>was running</u> low.
	Being
Hilary	<u>had become</u> the first foreign conqueror of the mountain.
This	<u>was</u> a great moment for international exploration.
However, for Tenzing Norkay, the Sherpa guide, it	<u>was</u> simply another trip up the ancient and holy slopes.

The words with two lines under them are the verbs of the sentences above.

APPLICATION 1.   Create sentences below by imagining and writing down what each person or thing is doing or being.

Example: Some of the pebbles by the road *seem to shine in the light.*

1. The last people in the line _____.

2. General Sherman _____.

3. My mother-in-law's neighbor _____.

4. The paint on the door of the truck _____.

5. One bowl of pea soup _____.

APPLICATION 2.   In the sentences below, use a slash mark (/) to indicate the place where the doing or being part of each sentence begins.

Example: The new restaurant / attracts hundreds of customers each evening.

1. The traffic at the supermarket intersection is out of control.

2. We should call the traffic commission.

3. Someone from out of state is building a new set of condominiums on the corner.

4. That sixty-unit complex might be completed by next winter.

5. Then the congestion will become even crazier.

TIP FOR FINDING VERBS: Look at the first group of words in the doing or being section of the sentence.

SINGLE-WORD VERBS AND VERB STRINGS

A verb may be just one word.

The moon's cycle, not the sun's, governs the tides. Therefore, low tide comes at a later time each day.

Often, however, a verb is a string of words made of a *main verb* with one or more *auxiliaries* in front of it.

The tide was changing at 10:30 yesterday morning. It should be turning today at about 11:10 A.M. We probably could have waited until noon for our fishing trip.

The **main verb** identifies the event that the sentence is reporting. The **auxiliaries** tell more about the time or conditions of the event, and they always come before the main verb. The **verb string** is the combination of auxiliaries and main verb, which act together to play the role of verb in a sentence. In the following exercises, the verbs are analyzed and marked like this:

single-word verb = sv

main verb = mv

auxiliary = x

Verbs in the simple present or simple past tense consist of just one word.

> $\overset{sv}{I \underline{sing}}$ beautifully in the shower every day, but $\overset{sv}{I \underline{sang}}$ better than ever
>
> yesterday.

Verbs that emphasize the continuation of an event include some form of *to be* as an auxiliary (*am, is, are, was, were, being*).

> $\overset{x}{I} \overset{mv}{\underline{am\ singing}}$ in the shower now, but $\overset{x}{I} \overset{mv}{\underline{was\ feeling}}$ hoarse before.

Verbs that emphasize the completion of an event include some form of *to have* as an auxiliary (*have, has, had*).

> $\overset{x}{Chris} \overset{mv}{\underline{has\ sung}}$ that song once too often. $\overset{x}{I} \overset{mv}{\underline{had\ warned}}$ him about it several
>
> times before the argument.

Verbs that express a future event include the auxiliary *will* or *shall*.

> $\overset{x\ \ x\ \ \ mv}{He \underline{will\ be\ singing}}$ a different tune soon; $\overset{x\ \ mv}{you \underline{will\ see}}$.

Verbs may include several other auxiliaries to express shadings of time or condition. These additional auxiliaries are *do, does, did, can, could, should, would, may, might, must.*

> If only $\overset{x\ \ \ \ x\ \ \ \ \ mv}{Chris \underline{could\ have\ stopped}}$ his howling, $\overset{x\ \ \ \ \ x\ \ \ \ \ mv}{I \underline{might\ have\ told}}$ him about
>
> the phone call from home. $\overset{x}{I} \overset{x}{\underline{do}}$ not $\overset{mv}{\underline{criticize}}$ him very often, though. It
>
> $\overset{x}{\underline{would}} \overset{mv}{\underline{spoil}}$ his fun.

APPLICATION 3.   Consider each underlined verb below. Analyze its parts: put "sv" above any single-word verb, "mv" above any main verb, and "x" above any auxiliary. The first verb is done for you.

> Sometimes on a very clear day you $\overset{x}{\underline{can}} \overset{mv}{\underline{see}}$ things beyond the horizon.
>
> Yesterday, for instance, just after the noon sun <u>had peaked</u>, a strange island
>
> <u>appeared</u> on the horizon. We <u>were pointing</u> to it in amazement when Mr.

Gummidge explained that what we were seeing was actually the shadow of a real island thirty miles away. The sun's rays were casting a reflection into the air, and this shadow island was floating several hundred feet above the real one, just high enough for visibility over the earth's curve. If you look carefully, you will see that mirage today. I will show you where to look.

In fact, we did watch for the mirage today, but we could see nothing unusual. We must have been straining our eyes because by suppertime you could have put a watermelon in front of us and we would have called it a mirage.

The following words may be used as auxiliaries within verb strings:

Forms *of* to be	Forms *of* to have	Forms *of* to do	Others
am, is, are	have, has	do, does	can, will, shall
was, were	had	did	could, would, should
be, being, been			may, might, must

The words in the shaded area of this chart may sometimes act as single-word verbs:

sv   sv   sv

I am your brother. You have the same kind of eyes as I do.

The rest of the auxiliaries in the chart work only in verb strings:

x mv   x x x mv

Everyone will be happy. They must have been expecting something.

Learn the auxiliaries in the chart. They will help you to find verb strings.

APPLICATION 4.   Return to Application 2. Draw two lines under the verb in each sentence. Sometimes the verb is a single word and sometimes it is a verb string.

Many auxiliaries can shrink into shorter forms called *contractions*.

I'm looking forward to this evening with Arny's boss. After supper we'll watch the game unless she'd prefer to play cards.

Here are some common contractions.

COMMON CONTRACTIONS

Auxiliary	Short Form	Example of Contraction
am	'm	I am = I'm
are	're	you are = you're
is *or* has	's	Emma is = Emma's
have	've	they have = they've
had *or* would	'd	we would = we'd
will *or* shall	'll	he will = he'll

Notice that the apostrophe (') replaces missing letters.

APPLICATION 5.   Rewrite each of the following sentences, contracting the auxiliaries. Then put two lines under each verb. Be sure to include the contracted auxiliaries as you underline.

Example: I have returned to my old job at last. *I've returned to my old job at last.*

1. We are sending Jenny to day care now. _____

   _____

2. She is enjoying most of it, but she has been getting into fights. _____

   _____

3. I would have spoken to the teachers, but Jack has convinced me that she will get over it soon. _____

   _____

4. I am watching Jenny go through some of the same stages that I have been through myself. _____

_____

5. She has taught me a lot about parts of my childhood that I had forgotten.

_____

_____

TIP FOR FINDING VERBS: Look for auxiliaries. If you find one, look for a main verb accompanying it. Remember that auxiliaries sometimes appear in contractions.

SPLIT VERBS

In a question or a negative statement, the verb splits into two parts.

In a question, the subject splits the verb apart.

Some of the union members <u><u>are voting</u></u> for the strike.

<u><u>Are</u></u> some of the union members <u><u>voting</u></u> for the strike?

In a negative statement, the word *not* splits the verb.

Some of the union members <u><u>are</u></u> not <u><u>voting</u></u> for the strike.

Sometimes the word *not* contracts and attaches itself to the first part of the split verb:

Some of the union members <u><u>aren't</u></u> <u><u>voting</u></u> for the strike.

APPLICATION 6.   Turn each of these sentences into a question and then into a negative statement. Put two lines under the verb string in every sentence.

Example: The nurses <u><u>have been</u></u> off duty for six hours.

Question: *<u><u>Have</u></u> the nurses <u><u>been</u></u> off duty for six hours?* _____

Negative: *The nurses <u><u>haven't</u></u> <u><u>been</u></u> off duty for six hours.* _____

1. The hospital will incur the risk of lawsuits.

Question: _____

Negative: _____

2. In that case, the mayor could intervene.

   Question: _____

   Negative: _____

3. He's meeting with his legal advisers now.

   Question: _____

   Negative: _____

When you turned the statements above into questions or negative statements, you split the verbs between the first auxiliary and the rest of the verb string. But what happens when the verb is a single word? You have to change a single-word verb to a verb string before you can split it. For this purpose, add the auxiliary *do, does,* or *did.* Then split the string to make the question or negative statement:

> *do train*
> Those people ~~train~~ tigers.

Question: Do those people train tigers?

Negative: Those people do not train tigers.

> *does train*
> Sandra ~~trains~~ tigers.

Question: Does Sandra train tigers?

Negative: Sandra does not train tigers.

> *did train*
> Sandra ~~trained~~ tigers several years ago.

Question: Did Sandra train tigers several years ago?

Negative: Sandra did not train tigers several years ago.

Notice in the examples above that if the single-word verb ends in *-s* or *-ed,* it drops that ending as it enters the verb string. Chapters 9 and 10 explain this shift. For now, practice adding *do, does,* or *did* and then splitting the new verb string.

APPLICATION 7.   Replace each single-word verb below with a verb string starting with *do,* *does,* or *did.* Next, turn each sentence into a question and then into a negative statement. Finally, put two lines under the complete verb in every sentence.

Example: Your check ~~comes~~ *does come* today.

Question: *Does your check come today?*

Negative: *Your check does not come today.*

1. We get a bonus every six months.

   Question: _____

   Negative: _____

2. We waited for two weeks between checks last month.

   Question: _____

   Negative: _____

3. The business office operates more efficiently this year.

   Question: _____

   Negative: _____

The verb *to be* often behaves differently from other verbs. When a form of *to be* stands alone as a single-word verb, it doesn't need to split to form a question or a negative statement. It simply moves to the beginning for a question, or adds *not* for a negative statement:

Dinosaurs were warm-blooded.   Were dinosaurs warm-blooded?

Their bones are like birds' bones.   Their bones are not like birds' bones.

APPLICATION 8.   Turn each of these sentences into a question and then into a negative statement. Put two lines under the verb in every sentence.

Example: I am fond of leftovers.

Question: *Am I fond of leftovers?*

Negative: *I am not fond of leftovers.*

1. The cookout and the party were very successful.

   Question: _____

   Negative: _____

2. Mom was ecstatic about your friends.

Question: _____

Negative: _____

3. There is enough pie left for tomorrow.

Question: _____

Negative: _____

TIP FOR FINDING VERBS: Turn each sentence into a negative statement. The word *not* will come before the main verb and after the first auxiliary. (When a form of the verb *to be* stands alone as a single-word verb, it is an exception; it will come right before the word *not*.)

TIME (TENSE)

A verb gives clues about the time of an event.

When Ricardo <u>was making</u> flan, he <u>used</u> a couple of the eggs that we <u>had brought</u> from the farm. There <u>is</u> only one left, and we <u>have finished</u> all the other food in the house, so we <u>will have</u> a very small supper.

The verbs in the sentences above can be spread out on a time line like this:

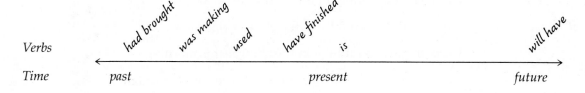

Verbs	*had brought*	*was making*	*used*	*have finished*	*is*	*will have*
Time	*past*			*present*		*future*

APPLICATION 9.   Read the passage below, noticing how the underlined verbs express the time of each event. Put each verb on the time line at the end of the passage. The first verb is done for you.

The groundhogs <u>are invading</u> my garden again. Last spring I <u>built</u> a tall fence. I <u>had buried</u> chicken wire all around the border the year before, but they <u>got</u> over or under or through that. So I <u>spent</u> a lot of money and two whole days of labor on a heavy new fence. But now that the lettuce <u>has turned</u>

crunchy and sweet, the groundhogs <u><u>are</u></u> back. They <u>must have found</u> a secret way into the garden, because there <u><u>are</u></u> no holes in the fence or in the ground. It <u><u>is becoming</u></u> obvious that the groundhogs <u><u>are</u></u> here for good, and that I <u>will be sharing</u> my vegetables with them in spite of my efforts.

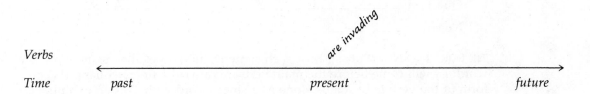

Verbs

Time   *past*   *present*   *future*

A verb usually changes to show time differences.

Channice <u><u>is working</u></u> on the same paper she <u><u>worked</u></u> on last week. She <u><u>works</u></u> on it a little bit every day.

APPLICATION 10.   In the sentences below, notice the words or groups of words that give you clues about the time of the action. Then concentrate on the section of each sentence that comes before the word *shower*. Draw two lines under any time clues in that part of the sentence. The first one is done for you.

I <u><u>sing</u></u> beautifully in the shower every day.

I sang beautifully in the shower once upon a time.

I will sing beautifully in the shower after the game.

I am singing beautifully in the shower right now.

I was singing beautifully in the shower this morning.

I will be singing beautifully in the shower until midnight.

I have sung beautifully in the shower all my life.

I had sung beautifully in the shower for hours before breakfast.

I will have sung beautifully in the shower for hours by that time.

The words with double lines under them are the verbs of the sentences above. They show the time changes built into the verb *to sing*. Notice that the verb is sometimes a single word and sometimes a verb string. These forms showing different times are often called **tenses.**

APPLICATION 11.   Change the time of each sentence below by changing the verb to express the time shown in parentheses. Cross out the old verb and write in its changed form.

Example: In a town nearby, ordinary people ~~learn~~ *learned* to walk on beds of hot coals. (past)

1. A teacher introduces several techniques of special meditation. (past)

2. While the students are practicing their techniques, the teacher monitors their breathing rates. (past)

3. After four training sessions, the students gather around a shallow mound of glowing charcoal. (future)

4. One by one, the members of the class stride unhurt over the coals. (future)

5. Each class will attract several doubters who will amaze themselves by succeeding as fully as the true believers. (present)

TIP FOR FINDING VERBS: Change the time of each sentence. Look carefully at the words that change form. Many of them will be verbs.

A VERB'S FOUR FORMS

Verbs appear in four forms: *base, simple past, present participle,* and *past participle.*

Before we define each form, study these examples. Fill in the blanks in the last half of the chart, following the pattern of the first half:

Name of Verb	Base Form	Simple Past Form	Present Participle	Past Participle
to watch	I can **watch**. I **watch**.	I **watched**.	I am **watching**.	I have **watched**.
to wait	I can **wait**. I **wait**.	I **waited**.	I am **waiting**.	I have **waited**.
to try	I can **try**. I **try**.	I **tried**.	I am **trying**.	I have **tried**.
to laugh	I can **laugh**. I **laugh**.	I **laughed**.	I am **laughing**.	I have **laughed**.
to yell	I can **yell**. I **yell**.	I _____.	I am **yelling**.	I have _____.
to dance	I can _____. I _____.	I **danced**.	I am _____.	I have **danced**.
to wink	I can **wink**. I **wink**.	I **winked**.	I am _____.	I have _____.
to stop	I can **stop**. I _____.	I _____.	I am **stopping**.	I have **stopped**.

Study the chart again. Which forms can stand alone as single-word verbs? Which ones act as main verbs in verb strings? Draw your own conclusions before going on to the explanations of each form below.

The *base* form comes directly from the name of the verb.

> to watch: **watch**
> to wait: **wait**

The base form can combine in a verb string with any of these auxiliaries:

Auxiliaries	*Examples of Verb Strings*
can, will, shall	can watch, will watch, shall watch
could, would, should	could wait, would wait, should wait
may, might, must	may try, might try, must try
do, does, did	do laugh, does laugh, did laugh

The fireworks <u>will scare</u> Saeed, so probably we <u>should go</u> home.

He <u>may object</u>, but after all, he <u>does need</u> some sleep.

APPLICATION 12.   Complete the verb strings below by adding the base form of the verb named below the line.

Perhaps I ___*could move*___ to Albany, but first I *must* _____to my

                 to move   to talk

niece, who *would* _____ me good advice. My parents

                    to offer

might _____ unhappy about the distance; they really

          to feel

do _____ on me, and I *should* _____ that seriously.

    to depend   to consider

Used without any auxiliary, the *base* form expresses present or recurring time. Verbs using this form are in the *simple present tense*.

Under warm air, water <u>evaporates</u> faster than under cold air. The minerals in the water <u>remain</u> behind, so south sea waters <u>contain</u> a higher concentration of salt than northern seas <u>do</u>.

Notice that in some cases, the base form adds an -*s*. Chapter 11 explains how this -*s* ending works.

APPLICATION 13.   Complete the following sentences in the simple present tense by adding the base form of the verb named below the line.

Those clowns ___*perform*___ an incredible juggling act. They

                    to perform

_____ for two volunteers from the audience, and then they

   to ask

_____ a couple of clubs clumsily back and forth in front of the vol-
   to pass

unteers, who _____ that this is just another goofy game. Then the
                  to believe

clowns _____ clubs one by one until nine clubs _____
          to add   to twirl

smoothly around the dizzy volunteers, who _____ in a moving cage
                                              to huddle

while the people in the crowd _____ with glee.
                                  to whistle

The *simple past* form of *regular verbs* is the base form + *-ed*:

> watch: **watched**
> wait: **waited**

It works without any auxiliary and expresses past time. Verbs using this
form are in the *simple past tense*.

> The spider webs <u>collected</u> dew and <u>sparkled</u> when the wind moved them.
> The light <u>grew</u> on them slowly, and no animal <u>disturbed</u> them.

Notice that one simple past verb above (*grew*) does not end in *-ed*. We'll examine the exceptions to the *-ed* ending rule when we study *irregular verbs* later
in this chapter. Chapter 10 explains more about how the *-ed* ending works.

APPLICATION 14.   Complete the following passage in the simple past tense by adding the
simple past form of the verb named below each line. All the words you add
will end in *-ed*.

The children _____*stayed*_____ in the water so long that their lips
                  to stay

_____ blue. They _____ across to the island where Felicia
   to turn   to race

_____ a beaver last week. We _____ to them several times,
   to spot   to call

but they never _____ us. The children _____ eventually,
                   to answer   to return

in their own sweet time, and then they _____ us as we
                                             to ignore

_____ them about taking risks in the water. While we
   to lecture

_____, they just _____ themselves around the fire and
     to sputter   *to warm*

_____ with silent pride.
     to grin

The *present participle* is always the base form + *-ing.*

> watch: **watching**
> wait: **waiting**

It combines with a form of the auxiliary *to be* (*am, is, are, was, were, being, been, be*) in a verb string that expresses a continuing action. Verbs using this pattern are in the *progressive tenses.*

> Two storm systems <u>are converging</u> on the island. This morning school-teachers <u>were bringing</u> blankets to the shelter. The trucks <u>will be arriving</u> soon for emergency assignments.

APPLICATION 15.   Finish the following sentences using progressive tenses by adding the present participle of the verb named below the line.

> Your supper ____*is waiting*____ for you in the kitchen. I *was* _____
>   *to wait*   *to expect*
> you to show up tonight. The stuffed clams *are* _____ on the table
>   *to sit*
> now. I *was* _____ them all last night. While the clams
>   *to cook*
> *were* _____, I made the sauce. Our house *will be* _____ of
>   *to bake*   *to smell*
> garlic for weeks.

The *past participle* usually looks the same as the simple past form.

> I watched. I have **watched**.
> I waited. I have **waited**.

It can be combined with a form of the auxiliary *to have* (*have, has, had*) to express a completed action or one that has continued into the present time. Verbs using this pattern are in the *perfect tenses.*

> Marty <u>has cooked</u> me dinner twice since Saturday. When he <u>had finished</u> last night's cleanup, he <u>joked</u> that by the time my leg <u>has healed</u>, he <u>will have weaned</u> me from junk food entirely.

APPLICATION 16.   Finish the following sentences using the perfect tenses by adding the past participle of the verb named below the line.

> We _____ *have worked* _____ without a break all week. My sister
> _____ (to work)
>
> *has* _____ me several times to quit, and I always
> _____ (to beg)
>
> *have* _____. But last night when she visited me, I
> _____ (to refuse)
>
> *had* _____ from fatigue. She *has* _____ me into taking a
> ____ (to collapse)   ____ (to talk)
>
> vacation next week. Fortunately, the new trainees *will have* _____ us
> ____ (to join)
>
> at the plant by then.

A past participle can also be combined with a form of *to be* to express the *passive voice,* a sentence structure in which the subject is not performing the action of the sentence.

> The tree <u>was damaged</u> by the wind.
>
> Our house <u>was not harmed</u>, though.

The subjects above are *tree* and *house,* and neither the tree nor the house is doing anything. Both are simply sitting there passively, having something done to them. Notice how a past participle and a form of the auxiliary *to be* (*am, are, is, was, were, being, been, be*) are combined to form a verb string in each sentence below.

> The umpire's call <u>was drowned</u> out by the clamor of the fans.
>
> The camera crew <u>is amazed</u> by the enthusiasm. This play <u>will be remembered</u> for years.

APPLICATION 17.   Complete the following passive-voice verb strings by adding the past participle of the verb named below the line.

These masks _were painted_ by your children. But in the process, paint
                _{to paint}

was _____ all over the floor. I _am_ _____ to make the most
    _{to spill}   _{to expect}

of a small budget. Your contributions for new paint _will be_ _____
                                                              _{to appreciate}

very much.

IRREGULAR VERBS

Many English verbs are *irregular*: their simple past and past participle forms are unpredictable.

The verbs you've been working with in Applications 12 through 17 have been **regular** verbs, which move through their four forms in a regular way, adding either *-ed* or *-ing* to the base. But **irregular** verbs do not fit that pattern. Although their present participles always end in the usual *-ing*, you can't count on the *-ed* endings for the simple past and past participle forms.

The verb *to be* is the most irregular of all.

You are patient with me when I am in trouble.

Many times I have been glad that you were nearby.

This verb, whether it acts as an auxiliary, a main verb, or a single-word verb, appears in more forms than any other verb. Here are examples of its eight forms:

Base	Simple Present	Simple Past	Present Participle	Past Participle
I can **be**	I **am**	I **was**	I am **being**	I have **been**
	You **are**	We **were**		
	She **is**			

Most verbs appear in their base form for the simple present tense, but the verb *to be* does not. Instead it uses three different simple present forms. Further, the simple past tense of this verb has two forms. Chapter 12 will explain how to decide which form to use in each of these tenses. The following application will help you see what you already know about choosing the forms of the verb *to be.*

APPLICATION 18.   Complete the following paragraph by adding the correct form of the verb *to be* in each blank.

Nowadays I _____*am*_____ a careful person, but once I _____ pretty reckless. I used to think nothing could ever happen to me. Then came the day when my son and I _____ going to the beach in the old truck. You _____ not going to believe how fast I _____ going, so I won't even tell you. Before I knew it, the truck _____ on two wheels. I glanced over at my little boy and suddenly slowed down to a sedate pace. Ever since then, I have _____ a model driver. I see now that even if I _____ immune to danger, he _____ not, and that has changed my style of living. I can never _____ quite so foolhardy again.

The other irregular verbs have only four forms.

No other verb is as irregular as *to be,* but some may be unfamiliar to you. Below is a list of some of the common irregular verbs. Look it over, marking and memorizing any forms that you don't already know.

COMMON IRREGULAR VERBS

Base	Simple Past	Present Participle	Past Participle
be	was, were	being	been
become	became	becoming	become
begin	began	beginning	begun
bet	bet	betting	bet
bite	bit	biting	bitten
blow	blew	blowing	blown

COMMON IRREGULAR VERBS (continued)

Base	Simple Past	Present Participle	Past Participle
break	broke	breaking	broken
bring	brought	bringing	brought
buy	bought	buying	bought
catch	caught	catching	caught
choose	chose	choosing	chosen
come	came	coming	come
cut	cut	cutting	cut
dig	dug	digging	dug
do	did	doing	done
drink	drank	drinking	drunk
drive	drove	driving	driven
draw	drew	drawing	drawn
eat	ate	eating	eaten
fall	fell	falling	fallen
feed	fed	feeding	fed
feel	felt	feeling	felt
find	found	finding	found
freeze	froze	freezing	frozen
get	got	getting	gotten
give	gave	giving	given
go	went	going	gone
grow	grew	growing	grown
have	had	having	had
hear	heard	hearing	heard
hit	hit	hitting	hit
hurt	hurt	hurting	hurt
keep	kept	keeping	kept
know	knew	knowing	known
lay	laid	laying	laid
lead	led	leading	led

COMMON IRREGULAR VERBS (continued)

Base	Simple Past	Present Participle	Past Participle
leave	left	leaving	left
lend	lent	lending	lent
lie	lay	lying	lain
lose	lost	losing	lost
make	made	making	made
pay	paid	paying	paid
put	put	putting	put
read	read	reading	read
ride	rode	riding	ridden
ring	rang	ringing	rung
rise	rose	rising	risen
run	ran	running	run
say	said	saying	said
see	saw	seeing	seen
set	set	setting	set
shake	shook	shaking	shaken
sing	sang	singing	sung
sit	sat	sitting	sat
speak	spoke	speaking	spoken
steal	stole	stealing	stolen
swear	swore	swearing	sworn
swim	swam	swimming	swum
take	took	taking	taken
teach	taught	teaching	taught
tear	tore	tearing	torn
think	thought	thinking	thought
throw	threw	throwing	thrown
wear	wore	wearing	worn
win	won	winning	won
write	wrote	writing	written

APPLICATION 19.   Complete the following paragraph, using the simple past form of each indicated verb. Write only one word in each space.

From Thanksgiving onward, the wind _____*blew*_____ through the streets
to blow

and alleys and _____*froze*_____ the puddles of dirty dishwater that the tenants
to freeze

_____ out there every night. Winter _____ tensions to the
to throw   to bring

neighborhood, because most of the money the people _____ at work
to make

_____ for heat. With what was left, they _____ the rent
to go   to pay

and _____ what food they could. Prices _____ every few
to buy   to rise

months. Those who _____ their jobs between Christmas and June
to keep

_____ the lucky ones. The rest _____ anxious and danger-
to be   to lead

ous lives; some _____, some _____ shady businesses, and
to steal   to run

others just _____ down to wait till spring. Those of us who
to lie

_____ up in such alleys _____ capable of reading stories in
to grow   to become

people's faces — messages and meanings that the rich never _____
to see

at all.

APPLICATION 20.   Review the paragraph you've completed in Application 19. Above each verb you've inserted, write a verb string combining *has* or *have* with the past participle of each verb. Some of the past participles will be spelled the same as the simple past forms, but others will be different. The first sentence will look like this:

has blown

Example: From Thanksgiving onward, the wind *blew*_____ through the
to blow
has frozen
streets and alleys and *froze*_____ the puddles of dirty dish-
to freeze

water . . .

NON-VERB FORMS

A participle must be in a verb string in order to behave as a verb. Without an auxiliary, a participle plays a non-verb role in its sentence.

> **Arriving** home late, Priscilla <u>rushed</u> into the kitchen.

> She <u>was thinking</u> about the **burnt** potatoes.

Remember that **participles** are *parts* of verb strings. They need auxiliaries to do a verb's work. If a participle has no auxiliary in front of it, look elsewhere for the sentence's verb.

When the word *to* stands in front of the base form of a verb, it creates an *infinitive*. An infinitive plays a non-verb role in its sentence.

> **To know** him <u>is</u> **to love** him.

> I <u>want</u> **to bring** him with me at Christmas.

The infinitive serves as the name of a verb. It can play several roles in a sentence. However, if a base form has the word *to* in front of it, look elsewhere for the sentence's verb.

APPLICATION 21.   Draw two lines under the verb in each sentence below. Avoid the non-verb forms.

1. Baking bread keeps Tillie in touch with her old customs.
2. She loves to get up early on Saturday mornings.
3. Kneading the dough, she was thinking about her past.
4. We wake to the smell of the rising loaves and the fresh-ground coffee.
5. I don't want her to move into a house of her own.

TIP FOR SEPARATING THE NON-VERB FORMS FROM THE VERB FORMS: A base form with *-ing* on the end can act as part of a verb only if it is in a verb string. A base form with *to* in front never plays the role of verb.

Chapter 5 explains these non-verb forms in more detail.

COMBINING SENTENCES WITH COMPOUND VERBS

A subject can take more than one verb.

I sat right down and cut my toenails.

Compounding is the process of joining similar parts. Joining two separate verbs to go with one subject results in a **compound verb**. The words that can join verbs are *and, but, yet, or, nor.* These words are **conjunctions**.

Population growth will slow down **and** may stabilize by the year 2110.

Sometimes conjunctions work in partnership with other words, as in

either . . . or . . .	*neither . . . nor . . .*
both . . . and . . .	*not only . . . but also . . .*

One study **not only** predicts a steady 10.5 billion total population for several decades **but also** describes a new distribution of people throughout the world.

When more than two verbs are compounded, the conjunction may appear between only the last two, and the others are separated by commas.

In contrast to families in the Third World, families in the industrialized nations bear fewer children, move more frequently, **and** feel less bound to their home communities.

APPLICATION 22.   Combine each set of sentences by compounding the verbs using the conjunction shown in parentheses.

Example: We watch for a clue. We wait for a clue. (and) *We watch and wait for a clue.*

1. Mosquitoes can buzz through the screen. But mosquitoes can't bite through the screen. (but not) _____

   _____

2. She tries to help. She fails to help. (yet) _____

   _____

3. Your dog eats my garbage. If not, he scatters it all over the yard. (either . . . or) _____

_____

4. Tara bought herself a digital watch. She also learned how to play the video game on it. (not only . . . but also) _____

_____

5. The movie surprised the children. It delighted the children. It instructed the children. It amused the children. (, , , and) _____

_____

Return to your writing

Read aloud the paragraph you wrote at the beginning of this chapter. Which of the words you crossed out and changed were not verbs? Which ones were? Look for auxiliaries, and wherever you find one, check to see if a main verb follows. Where you're not sure of a verb, turn the sentence into a negative statement and use *not* as a flag that waves in the middle of your verb. Underline all your verbs. Have you used any compound verbs? Trade papers with a classmate, and check each other's work. Whenever you disagree, explain your reasons. Raise questions and get a tutor or teacher to answer them.

Chapter 3

Subjects

In a sentence, every verb needs a subject. Once you have found a verb in a sentence, you can identify its subject if you know the typical relationships between verbs and subjects. Recognizing the subjects of your sentences makes it easier for you to clarify and develop your ideas in writing.

In Chapter 3, you will learn that

- the subject answers the question "Who or what ⟨verb⟩?"
- the subject in a statement usually comes before the verb, except in questions; the subject in a question is usually between the two parts of the split verb.
- the role of subject is often played by a noun (sometimes a pronoun can stand in the place of a noun).
- the simple subject is a subject stripped of all the words that describe it.
- sentences can be combined by compounding their subjects.

Writing

Recall an experience from your past (for instance, the time you met someone important to you, the first time you left home, an accident, a surprise, or an adventure). Concentrate on just one incident. Picture yourself as you were then, and try to remember how you felt. Recall the people and things around you, the smells, the sounds, the weather, and so on. On scrap paper, jot down all that you can recall about that incident.

1. Arrange what you've written into one paragraph, selecting the details you think are most important. Use the word *I* at least five times in your story, and rewrite the paragraph on a fresh piece of paper.

2. Now imagine that someone else is telling this same story about you. Cross out *I* wherever you've used it, and write in either your name or *he* or *she*. Make all other changes necessary for the story to sound as though someone else is telling it. When you're through, the first two sentences might look like this:

   Monica   *she*   *her*
   When ~~I~~ was ten, ~~I~~ met ~~my~~ grandparents from Italy for the first
   She   *she*
   time. ~~I~~ was so excited and scared about their coming that ~~I~~

   could hardly eat for a week in advance.

Many of the words you've crossed out and changed are subjects.

"WHO OR WHAT ⟨verb⟩?"

Once you've found the verb of a sentence, you can identify the subject by putting the question "Who or what?" in front of the verb.

Bronson <u><u>hates</u></u> jazz.

In this sentence, *hates* is the verb. You ask, "Who or what hates jazz?" The answer is *Bronson*, so *Bronson* is the subject.

<u>Enchiladas</u> <u><u>aren't</u></u> always hot. (What aren't hot? **Enchiladas**)

A <u>friend</u> of mine in San Diego <u><u>makes</u></u> them without peppers. (Who makes them? **friend**)

Even your picky <u>niece</u> <u><u>would eat</u></u> that kind. (Who would eat them? **niece**)

(You) <u><u>Bring</u></u> her over on Friday for the big test. (Who brings her? **you**)

Notice that the last sentence is a command in which the subject is not stated but is understood. Asking "Who or what ⟨verb⟩?" reveals that the subject must be *you*:

(You) <u><u>Give</u></u> me a bite. *(You)* <u><u>Don't put</u></u> chili sauce on it.

APPLICATION 1. Put two lines under the verb in each sentence below. Then find the subject by asking "Who or what ⟨verb⟩?" Underline each subject once. The first sentence is done for you.

The African Stone <u>Game</u> <u><u>doesn't look</u></u> complicated. Even children can learn the basic moves. However, practice can humble even the most confident players. Strategy is only part of the key to mastery of the game. The other part is memory. Some expert stone game veterans have developed incredible powers of observation and recall. The stone piles change constantly from move to move, and yet those gnarled old men know the number of stones in each pile at all times. If they are ever puzzled, they never show it. Their speed can baffle beginning players, and yet it can inspire them, too. Come with me tonight and see for yourself.

PLACEMENT

In most statements, the subject comes before the verb.

You have been dreaming about socks again.

That has some deep significance.

In most questions, you can find the subject after the first part of a split verb.

(Remember that to split a single-word verb, you must add *do, does,* or *did.*)

Have you been dreaming about socks again?

Does that image have some deep significance?

When *am, is, are, was,* or *were* stands as a single-word verb, it doesn't split for a question, but it does move to the front of the subject in a question:

That is a good luck sign. Is that a good luck sign?

You are superstitious. Are you superstitious?

APPLICATION 2.   Turn each of the following statements into a question. Then, in both the statement and the question, underline the verb twice and the subject once.

Example: Marcia has lost her patience. *Has Marcia lost her patience?*

1. She's slamming doors all over the house. _____

   _____

2. The porch door screen just fell off. _____

   _____

3. You could talk to her about her temper. _____

   _____

4. She is eager to please you. _____

   _____

5. You have a calming influence on her. _____

   _____

NOUNS AND PRONOUNS AS SUBJECTS

A subject is often a *noun*. Sometimes a *pronoun* can stand in the place of
a noun.

A noun labels or names a person, a place, a thing, or an idea. The words in
italics below are nouns:

The *message* came from *Harold Durum* in *Illinois,* where the *sky* is broad and
the *farmers* cherish their *freedom.*

A pronoun is a word that takes the place of a noun.

he   *it*
Gary can't find his polka-dotted *shoelace* because ~~G̶a̶r̶y̶~~ dropped ~~the shoelace~~
behind the *bathtub* in the *dark.*

The pronoun *it* takes the place of the noun *shoelace* and refers to an earlier
mention of that same noun. The pronoun *he* replaces and refers to *Gary.* Some
other pronouns that replace and refer to nouns are *they, them*, she, her*,* and
him*.

he   *them*
Those *shoelaces* cost *Gary* $3.50, and ~~G̶a̶r̶y̶~~ washed ~~the shoelaces~~ every night.
They   *him*
~~The shoelaces~~ meant a lot to ~~G̶a̶r̶y̶.~~

Several other pronouns don't have to refer to the words they replace because
everyone knows what they stand for:

I, me* = the person speaking

we, us* = the people speaking

you = the person or people listening

The pronouns with an asterisk (*) beside them cannot be used as subjects.
Chapter 13 examines pronouns in more detail.

APPLICATION 3.   Write a subject for each sentence below, using a noun. Then write another sentence whose subject is a pronoun that refers to that noun. Finally, underline all verbs twice and all subjects once.

Example: Those _egg rolls_____ taste awful with ketchup. _They have plenty_
_of spice already._____

1. However, _____ needs a little extra flavor. _____
_____

2. _____ loves spicy dishes and searches for them on every menu.
_____

3. _____ knows only a few restaurants capable of satisfying her.
_____

4. My _____ once cooked a great Indian meal for her. _____
_____

5. His _____ has been the theme of her stories ever since. _____
_____

APPLICATION 4.   In the sentences below, underline the verbs twice, and then identify the subjects by asking "Who or what ⟨verb⟩?" Put one line under the nouns or pronouns that answer that question. Do not mark any other nouns or pronouns in the sentences.

For many American Indians, words had tremendous power. According to Indian beliefs, a singer could cause a change in nature or in people through the words of a song. A poet was renewing the vitality of the earth itself as he told the story of the beginning of the world. A song could heal a wound, or a chant could encourage the growth of crops. The word, whether in song or in tale, was considered sacred. It existed even before the gods did. Don't be surprised, then, if contemporary Native American writers use language with great reverence. They may speak English instead of the languages of their ancestors, but word power still guides many of them in their daily lives.

SIMPLE SUBJECTS

When a subject is stripped of all the words that describe it, the *simple subject* is left.

The <u>girls</u> <u><u>laughed</u></u>.

The tough <u>girls</u> <u><u>laughed</u></u>.

The rowdy, tough <u>girls</u> <u><u>laughed</u></u>.

The rowdy, tough <u>girls</u> in the roller derby <u><u>laughed</u></u>.

The rowdy, tough <u>girls</u> in the roller derby on TV <u><u>laughed</u></u>.

In each of these sentences, the simple subject is *girls.* The simple subject is only one word.

APPLICATION 5.   Put two lines under the verb in each sentence below. Then put one line under each simple subject.

1. The whales are racing.

2. The black and white whales are racing.

3. The black and white whales in the aquarium are racing.

4. The black and white whales behind the wall in the aquarium are racing.

5. Everybody loves a lover.

6. Everybody in this crowd loves a lover.

7. Everybody in this crowd of sentimental Frank Sinatra fans loves a lover.

8. Your answer reassured me.

9. Your quick and simple answer reassured me.

10. Your quick and simple answer to my question about the deadline for registration reassured me.

In the sentences above, notice the following words: *in, of, about, for.* These four words are examples of **prepositions** (discussed in more detail in Chapter 4). The first noun or pronoun that appears after one of these words *cannot* be the simple subject:

The kids ~~in my family~~ <u>love</u> the African Stone Game.

The <u>pattern</u> ~~of the stones~~ <u>is</u> always <u>changing</u>.

APPLICATION 6. Put two lines under each verb below. Cross out the groups of words beginning with *in, of, about,* or *for.* Then put one line under each simple subject.

Example: This winter, the baseball <u>gloves</u> ~~in the basement~~ <u>became</u> moldy.

1. Farley's advice about the care and treatment of leather must have been ignored.

2. Some of the gloves in the bin were spoiled completely.

3. Still, a few of them were worth rescuing.

4. That smelly reconditioning oil for leather has restored Aaron's favorite one.

5. The rest of the players weren't so lucky.

Chapter 4 describes in more detail how modifiers expand subjects, and Chapter 12 offers more practice with sentences in which groups of words come between the simple subject and the verb. Throughout the rest of this book, the word *subject* refers to the *simple subject,* the one-word subject without any modifiers.

COMBINING SENTENCES WITH COMPOUND SUBJECTS

A verb can take more than one subject.

The <u>padlock</u> **and** <u>chain</u> on his refrigerator door <u>speak</u> louder than words.

Compounding is the process of joining similar parts. Joining separate subjects to go with one verb results in a **compound subject**. The words that can join subjects are *and, but, yet, or, nor.* These words are **conjunctions**.

<u>Sugar</u> **and** <u>insulin</u> <u>are</u> always <u>changing</u> their levels in human blood.

Sometimes these conjunctions work in partnership with other words:

either . . . or . . .	*neither . . . nor . . .*
both . . . and . . .	*not only . . . but also . . .*

Not only <u>sweets</u> **but also** <u>starches</u> <u>may stimulate</u> the pancreas to produce excess insulin, which reduces the blood sugar level.

When more than two subjects are compounded, the conjunction often appears between only the last two, and the others are separated by commas.

<u>Muffins</u>, <u>potatoes</u>, **and** <u>spaghetti</u> <u>are converted</u> to sugar during digestion.

A brief <u>spurt</u> of energy after eating, a sudden <u>attack</u> of fatigue, **and** then sustained low <u>spirits</u> <u>can follow</u> eating orgies.

APPLICATION 7.   Combine each set of sentences by compounding the subjects, using the conjunction in parentheses.

Example: The consumer price index can measure the activity of a nation's economy. The balance of trade figure can measure the activity of a nation's economy. (and) *The consumer price index and the balance of trade figure can measure the activity of a nation's economy.*

1. The press is watching for a clue. The police are watching for a clue. (and)

   _____

2. Mosquitoes bother us all night long by the lake. Blackflies bother us all night long by the lake. (and) _____

   _____

3. Your dog eats my garbage. If not, your cat eats my garbage. (either . . . or . . .) _____

   _____

4. Tara has not bought a digital watch. Her boyfriend hasn't bought one either. (neither . . . nor . . .) _____

   _____

5. The movie delighted the children. The music delighted them. The popcorn delighted them. The soda delighted them. (, , , and) _____

   _____

   _____

Return to your writing

Read aloud the paragraph you wrote at the beginning of this chapter. Which of the words you changed were subjects of their sentences? Which weren't? How can you tell? Underline all your verbs twice and your subjects once. Trade papers with a classmate, and check each other's work. Whenever you disagree, give reasons for your opinions. Take your questions to a tutor or teacher.

Chapter 4

Completers and Modifiers

A subject + verb combination may need a word or group of words to complete the meaning of the sentence. In addition, a sentence is usually expanded with modifiers that clarify the meaning of the sentence. Recognizing completers and modifiers helps you to understand how sentences work so that you can straighten out tangles more easily as you revise your own written sentences.

In Chapter 4, you will learn that

- a completer answers the question "⟨Subject + verb⟩ whom or what?"
- nouns, pronouns, and describing words can act as completers.
- modifiers add to or limit a word's meaning.
- a modifier can be a single word.
- prepositional phrases always act as modifiers.
- sentences can be combined by compounding their completers and modifiers.

Writing

Take a few minutes to observe the room around you. Notice specific objects, the light, the space, and the atmosphere of the place. Look closely for details, including those that seem unimportant at first, like a shadow on the wall or the rumble of the air conditioner. Jot your observations on a piece of scrap paper, and then organize the observations into groups. You might, for instance, have one group of observations of things you can see in the room and another group of things you can see through the window.

1. Use the groups of observations to help you write a paragraph that conveys a picture of the room. Start your first sentence with these words: "When I walk into ⟨name of room⟩, the first thing I notice is . . ." Go on from there. Then rewrite your paragraph on a fresh piece of paper.

2. Look at your first sentence and draw a box around the word or phrase that you've written after "the first thing I notice is . . ." This is probably a completer. In the next two sentences, look for words that describe other words. These are probably modifiers. Draw arrows from the modifiers to the words they describe.

"⟨SUBJECT + VERB⟩ WHOM OR WHAT?"

Once you've found the subject and verb of a sentence, you can check to see if the sentence has a *completer* by asking "whom or what?" after the verb.

Bronson hates jazz.

In this sentence, *hates* is the verb and *Bronson* is the subject. You ask, "Bronson hates whom or what? The answer is *jazz*, so *jazz* is the completer. Here are some others:

Enchiladas aren't always hot. (Enchiladas aren't what? **hot**)

My friend in San Diego makes them without peppers. (Friend makes what? **them**)

(You) Believe me. (Remember from Chapter 3 that the subject of a command is **you**, so for this sentence the question is "You believe whom?" **me**)

After one bite of his enchiladas, your prejudice against Mexican food would vanish instantly. (Prejudice would vanish whom? Prejudice would vanish what? There is no answer, so there is no completer in this sentence.)

APPLICATION 1.   Identify each subject and verb below. Then ask, "⟨Subject + verb⟩ whom or what?" to see whether there is a completer. Mark the parts like this: subject   verb   completer .

Quilting is an ancient craft. Before the settlement of the New World, women in Europe and Asia had established a rich tradition of quilt stitchery. But in the isolated and poor communities of the American frontier, a new quilting style evolved. This was patchwork. The thrifty and ingenious pioneers didn't discard their worn-out clothing. Fabric was simply too precious to waste. Instead, they cut their old clothes into scraps and stitched them into quilt tops. At quilting bees, women shared their patchwork patterns, gave names to them, and moved the quilting craft into a new era.

WORDS THAT ACT AS COMPLETERS

A completer can be a noun, a pronoun, or a word that describes the subject.

The rowdy girls were making ⌈trouble⌉. (noun completer)

The cop finally arrested ⌈them⌉. (pronoun completer)

Behavior like that is ⌈crazy⌉. (completer describes the subject)

A noun names a thing, person, place, or idea. A pronoun takes the place of a noun and makes it possible to avoid repeating that noun. Chapter 13 discusses pronouns in more detail. The kind of completer that describes the subject is a **modifier** as well as a completer. The latter part of this chapter explores modifiers in more detail.

APPLICATION 2.   Identify each subject and verb below and then ask, "⟨Subject + verb⟩ whom or what?" to find each completer. Mark the parts like this: subject   verb   ⌈completer⌉. At the end of each sentence, note whether the completer is a noun, a pronoun, or a word that describes the subject.

Example: The whales in the aquarium are learning ⌈tricks⌉. *noun* _____

1. Apparently they're enjoying themselves. _____

2. In just a minute Soo-Yean will call their names. _____

3. The whales can answer her. _____

4. She has been training them for months. _____

5. The seal show is popular, too. _____

6. Yesterday's act was the best ever. _____

7. The aquarium is attracting tourists for the first time. _____

8. You really would enjoy the show. _____

9. The afternoon is the best time to go. _____

10. The crowds have always been much noisier in the mornings. _____

RECOGNIZING THE DIFFERENCE BETWEEN COMPLETERS AND SUBJECTS

Don't confuse completers with subjects.

It's important to see the difference between nouns or pronouns acting as subjects and those acting as completers.

At birth, a <u>baby</u> <u>has</u> three hundred and thirty | bones |.

The verb is **has**. "Who or what has?" **baby** = subject.
"Baby has whom or what?" **bones** = completer.

During growth, many small <u>bones</u> <u>fuse</u>.

Verb = **fuse**. "Who or what fuse?" **bones** = subject.
"Bones fuse whom or what? no answer; no completer.

Only two hundred and six <u>bones</u> finally <u>support</u> an adult's | body |.

Verb = **support**. "Who or what support?" **bones** = subject.
"Bones support whom or what?" **body** = completer.

To analyze a sentence, always look first for the verb (see Chapter 2 for more help). Then find the subject by asking "Who or what ⟨verb⟩?" Finally, check to see whether there is a completer by asking, "⟨Subject + verb⟩ whom or what?" The subject usually comes before the verb, and a completer usually comes after the verb.

APPLICATION 3. Identify all verbs, subjects, and completers below. Every verb has a subject; not every subject and <u>verb will</u> have a completer. Mark them like this: <u>subject</u>   <u>verb</u> | completer |.

Until fairly recently, few <u>societies</u> <u>used</u> | paper | as money. Coins were sturdier for circulation in a busy market. More important, they contained precious metals; the coins had value and people trusted them. Paper was another story. It was fragile, it was vulnerable to fire and flood, and it was merely a symbol of something valuable. Each bill represented a promise of a certain amount of silver or gold, and people have been suspicious of promises throughout human history. However, in the eighteenth century, the French government issued paper currency in large quantities, and the French people accepted it.

Other countries adopted the custom, and paper money spread rapidly. Now people all around the world pass it back and forth every day.

HOW MODIFIERS WORK

A *modifier* adds to or limits a word's meaning.

Modifiers describe other words, making the meaning of those words more specific. Modifiers answer the following questions about the words they modify:

What kind? Which one(s)? How many or how much? Whose?

When? Where? Why? How? To what extent? Under what conditions?

Watch how this sentence becomes more specific as modifiers are added to it:

Basic sentence: Women earn salaries.

(How many women?) Many women earn salaries.

(Which women?) Many women ⟨in the civil service⟩ earn salaries.

(What kind of salaries?) Many women in the civil service earn good salaries.

(When?) Many women in the civil service earn good salaries ⟨after their first few promotions⟩.

APPLICATION 4.   Answer the question beneath each line by adding or completing modifiers for the words to which the arrows point.

Basic sentence: People love movies.

1. _____ people love movies.
   how many?

2. _____ people love movies.
   which?

3. People ⟨from _____⟩ love movies.
   which?

4. People _____ love movies.
   when?

5. ⟨Because of _____⟩, people love movies.
   why?

6. People love movies _____.
   how much?

7. People love movies ⟨in _____⟩.
   where?

8. People love _____ movies.
   how many?

9. People love _____ movies.
   whose?

10. People love movies ⟨about _____⟩.
    what kind?

SINGLE-WORD MODIFIERS

A single word may play the role of modifier.

Some busybodies cause serious trouble. (**Some** answers "Which busybodies?" and **serious** answers "What kind of trouble?")

That creep constantly lies. (**That** answers "Which creep?" and **constantly** answers "When?")

Sometimes several words, each one acting separately as a single word, can modify the same word:

He has never felt a generous human impulse. (**Never** answers "When?," **a** answers "How many impulses?," and **generous,** and **human** answer "What kind of impulse?")

Note that when a verb's modifier splits the verb in two, as in the case of *never* in the example above, the arrow points to the main verb.

APPLICATION 5.   Draw arrows from each single-word modifier to the word it modifies.

1. Those fancy new forecasts amuse me.

2. Yesterday the reporters confidently predicted snow.

3. Today they expect light rain.

4. They change every hour's forecast.

5. I am ignoring those fickle daily predictions.

6. My cows can usually interpret the changing weather pretty accurately.

7. They sit still and face the humid wind.

8. My sinuses are becoming very reliable barometers.

9. Now I do not need any weather reports.

10. No scientific gadgets can beat my fine intuition.

There are two kinds of single-word modifiers: *adjectives* and *adverbs*. An *adjective* modifies a noun or a pronoun.

Do you remember the yellow tulips we had last year? (The adjective **yellow** modifies the noun **tulips**.)

Tall and majestic, they filled the yard with color. (The adjectives **tall** and **majestic** modify the pronoun **they**.)

An *adverb* modifies a verb, an adjective, or another adverb. Adverbs often end in *-ly*.

I thought Jean acted strangely at the last meeting. (The adverb **strangely** modifies the verb **acted**.)

She was completely silent, with her head bowed and her hands in her lap. (The adverb **completely** modifies the adjective **silent**.)

Usually she has a lot to say, though often she speaks very softly. (The adverb **very** modifies the adverb **softly**.)

PREPOSITIONAL PHRASE MODIFIERS

A prepositional phrase begins with a *preposition* and ends with an *object*.

In the prepositional phrases below, the asterisks mark the prepositions and the circles mark their objects, which are usually nouns or pronouns.

Please open that door ⟨beside* you⟩.

Thank goodness we put that fan ⟨by* the window⟩.

We really needed it ⟨during* the night⟩.

We'd have been miserable ⟨without* it⟩.

Notice how the preposition in each sentence shows a relationship between the object and the word that the phrase modifies. Prepositions often show space or time relationships (as in the first three examples above), but sometimes they show other kinds of relationship (as in the fourth example above).

Here is a chart of some words that often act as prepositions.

COMMON PREPOSITIONS

Usually Space Relationships		*Examples*
above	down	
across	from	beyond* Dallas
against	in	around* town
along	into	beside* the tracks
among	off	toward every stoplight
around	on	under the bridge
at	over	on these trips
behind	past	in her steady good humor
below	through	
beneath	to	
beside	toward	
between	under	
beyond	up	
by	within	

COMMON PREPOSITIONS (continued)

Usually Time Relationships		Examples
after	since	until the last moment
before	until	during the train ride
during		

Other Relationships		
about	like	like mine
as	of	for her
except	than	about my best friend
for	with	from a small town
from	without	of some forgotten old adventures

Don't try to memorize this chart. Once you understand the relationships signaled by prepositions, you won't need charts like this anymore.

Between a preposition and its object there may be one or more single-word modifiers.

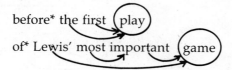

before* the first (play)

of* Lewis' most important (game)

APPLICATION 6.   Examine the prepositional phrases given as examples in the chart above. Some of them contain single-word modifiers. Draw an arrow from each single-word modifier to the word it modifies. Put an asterisk (*) after each preposition and circle the object of each preposition. The first three are done for you.

A prepositional phrase always acts as a modifier.

The roads ⟨beyond Dallas⟩ were in terrible shape. (where?)

I remember that bumpy street ⟨beside the tracks⟩. (which?)

You never stopped ⟨until the last moment⟩. (when?)

I certainly had doubts ⟨about my best friend then⟩. (what kind?)

No matter how many modifiers a prepositional phrase may contain, the phrase itself always acts as a unit that modifies some other word. For now, stop looking at what's inside the phrase and examine instead how the whole phrase works as a modifier.

APPLICATION 7.   In each sentence below, bracket the prepositional phrase. Each phrase, acting as a modifier, answers the given question about some other word in the sentence. Draw an arrow from the preposition to the word the phrase modifies.

Example: I'll take Aunt Betty ⟨around town⟩. (where?)

1. She has interests like mine. (what kind?)

2. She'll love the ice cream shop under the bridge. (where?)

3. She lives so intensely on these trips. (when?)

4. During the train ride, she didn't sleep a wink. (when?)

5. She was happily entertaining a homesick teenager from a small town.

   (which one?)

COMBINING SENTENCES WITH COMPOUND COMPLETERS OR MODIFIERS

A subject + verb can take more than one completer.

Completers can be compounded by the conjunctions *and, but, yet, or, nor*:
Every 3,000 miles, you should change the oil **and** the oil filter in your car.

A word can take more than one modifier.

Sometimes modifiers simply pile up near the word they modify:
You may need an adjustable long-handled filter wrench ⟨with a swivel joint⟩.

Copyright © 1989 Houghton Mifflin Company

At other times modifiers are connected by the same conjunctions that create compound subjects, verbs, and completers — *and, but, yet, or, nor*:

However, ⟨without tools⟩ **but** ⟨with a strong bare-handed grip⟩ you can unscrew the filter simply **and** quickly.

APPLICATION 8.   Combine each set of sentences by compounding the sentence parts in italics. Use the conjunctions given in parentheses.

Example: (completers) The conductor stopped the *blond man* in the aisle. He stopped the *tall mechanic* in the aisle. (and) *The conductor stopped the blond man and the tall mechanic in the aisle.*

Completers

1. We watch *the papers* for a clue. We watch *the network news* for a clue. (and)

   _____

2. That kind of arrogance impresses *Ben*. It doesn't impress *me*. (but not) __

   _____

3. Your dog always eats *my garbage*. If not, he eats *my flowers*. (or) _____

   _____

4. My father loves *your high little voice*. He loves *the sound of your big old tuba, too*. (and) _____

5. These jokes are not *new*. They are not *funny*, either. (neither . . . nor . . .)

   _____

Modifiers

6. I sing *beautifully* in the shower. I sing *freely* in the shower. (and) _____

   _____

7. Mosquitoes buzz *in the tent*. They don't buzz *in the cabin*. (but not) _____

   _____

8. Sylvia cooks spaghetti sauce *in a wok*. If not, she cooks it *over her grill*. (or)

   _____

9. Tricia expresses her feelings easily *with most people*. She doesn't express them easily *with children*. (but not) _____

10. Hannah wears socks to bed *in the winter*. She wears them *even on chilly nights in the summer*. (and) _____

Return to your writing

Read aloud the paragraph you wrote at the beginning of this chapter. Look for two more completers to box, and draw arrows from five modifiers to the words they modify. Bracket two prepositional phrases and draw arrows to the words they modify. Trade papers with a classmate and check each other's work. Don't be afraid to disagree; grammarians disagree all the time.

Chapter 5

Embedded Thoughts

Some groups of words that look like sentences are really dependent clauses. Some words that look like verbs are really verbals. A dependent clause or a verbal phrase can express a thought that is not able to stand on its own but has become embedded in a larger sentence structure. Understanding how thoughts become embedded will help you combine ideas and discover relationships among them through your writing.

In Chapter 5, you will learn that

- a clause is a group of related words containing a subject + verb.
- an independent clause is a clause that can stand by itself as a complete sentence (*Everyone can write*).
- a dependent clause is a clause that has given up its independence and can no longer stand by itself (*that everyone can write*).
- a phrase is a group of related words that does not contain a subject + verb combination.
- a verbal is a verb form that has lost its power to act as a verb in a sentence (*to write; writing; written*).
- a verbal phrase is a group of words containing a verbal and the verbal's completers or modifiers (*to write a clear essay*).
- sentences can be combined by embedding clauses or verbals.
- sentences can be combined by compounding clauses or verbals.

Writing

Think about something that irritates you (for example, your neighbor's radio playing at 2:00 A.M., the way a relative gives you advice you don't ask for, the smell of peanut butter cookies, the way your roommate leaves the milk on the table to spoil). How do you respond to that irritation, and why? What would you like to do about it? On scrap paper, jot notes on everything you can think of about the irritation you've chosen.

1. Arrange what you've written into one paragraph, selecting the details about which you feel most strongly. Start your first sentence with the words "I hate . . ." Then rewrite the paragraph on a fresh piece of paper.

2. Look through your paragraph and circle any of the following words: *because, unless, if, while, until, which.* Also circle any verb form ending in *-ing* without an auxiliary in front and any verb form with the word *to* in front. These words probably begin embedded thoughts.

FROM INDEPENDENT TO DEPENDENT CLAUSE

A *clause* is a group of words that contains a subject + verb. An *independent clause* can stand alone as a complete sentence. A clause beginning with a *dependent word* cannot stand alone but must be *embedded* in another sentence.

These are the most common dependent words.

DEPENDENT WORDS

after	than	where
although	that	whether
as	though	which
because	unless	whichever
before	until	while
how	what	who(m)
if	whatever	whoever
since	when	whose
		why

Here is an independent clause that can stand alone as a complete sentence:

Marriage is old-fashioned.

Watch what happens when a dependent word introduces this clause:

although marriage is old-fashioned

The clause still has a subject and verb, but the addition of the dependent word *although* makes the clause unable to stand alone. The broken lines underneath *marriage* and *is* indicate that the subject + verb can no longer act as the seed of an independent sentence. The word *although* also does something else — it prepares the newly dependent clause for embedding in some other sentence:

⟨Although marriage is old-fashioned⟩, I'm getting married in the morning.

The word *although* shows the relationship between the two clauses as it embeds one in the other. Other dependent words show different relationships between clauses:

⟨Because marriage is old-fashioned⟩, I'm going to live without it.

Cindy is always arguing ⟨that marriage is old-fashioned⟩.

Notice the comma in the first example, where a dependent clause comes at the beginning of a sentence.

APPLICATION 1.   Turn each sentence below into a dependent clause by using the dependent word shown in parentheses. Then embed the newly dependent clause in a larger sentence. If the dependent clause comes first in the sentence, put a comma at the end of the clause.

Example: You have a good education. (because)

Dependent clause: *because you have a good education*

Sentence with embedded clause: *You are earning a good salary because you have a good education.*

1. The weather irritates his joints. (when)

   Dependent clause: _____

   Sentence with embedded clause: _____

   _____

2. The soup was cooking. (while)

   Dependent clause: _____

   Sentence with embedded clause: _____

   _____

3. Oranges will be plentiful this year. (that)

   Dependent clause: _____

   Sentence with embedded clause: _____

   _____

4. The whole family will fit into the Honda. (how)

   Dependent clause: _____

   Sentence with embedded clause: _____

   _____

5. The spool of thread dropped into her mitten. (whether)

Dependent clause: _____

Sentence with embedded clause: _____

_____

RECOGNIZING DEPENDENT CLAUSES

Any clause introduced by a dependent word has been deprived of its independence and can function only by playing a role in a larger sentence.

A dependent word does two things: it turns an independent clause into a dependent clause, and it defines a role for that clause to play within a larger sentence:

While
∧ Zora Neale Hurston was writing during the Harlem Renaissance.

She may not have realized something.

That
∧ Her novel about Janie Starks would become an American classic.

The addition of the dependent words to the first and last sentences above turns them into dependent clauses. The dependent words also define the roles that the two newly dependent clauses can play in a larger sentence:

⟨While Zora Neale Hurston was writing during the Harlem Renaissance⟩, she may not have realized ⟨that her novel about Janie Starks would become an American classic⟩.

In this new sentence, the first clause acts as a modifier (answering the question "when?"), and the last acts as the completer ("She may not have realized what?").

You can think of an embedded clause as a unit within another sentence, acting in the way a single word might to play a role in a larger sentence:

Eden understands my thoughts.   Eden understands ⟨how I think⟩.

She'll come tonight.   She'll come ⟨before I even call⟩.

APPLICATION 2.   Find the dependent clauses that play the sentence roles and that answer the questions given in parentheses. Circle each dependent word and bracket each dependent clause.

Example: That slow, bent man ⟨(whom) they follow⟩ is Moses. (modifier, "Which man?")

1. Whatever you want is okay with me. (subject, "What is?")

2. I can't understand why you are so upset about the new benefits package. (completer, "Can't understand what?")

3. You must report to the union before the managers call you. (modifier, "When?")

4. You should address your comments to the woman whom you met yesterday. (modifier, "Which woman?")

5. The meeting that you will have with the negotiating team could make a difference to all of us. (modifier, "Which meeting?")

6. Where the meeting will be held has been kept a big secret. (subject, "What has been kept?")

7. One or two managers may explain how they feel. (completer, "Explain what?")

8. You can judge their sincerity by whether or not they look at you. (object of preposition *by*)

9. If I meet with the managers, they'll just argue with me. (modifier, "Under what conditions?")

10. They'll probably like you better because you're much calmer in these situations. (modifier, "Why?")

APPLICATION 3.   For further study, look again at the sentences in Application 2. Underline all subjects once and all verbs twice, using broken lines for the subjects and verbs of the dependent clauses. Box any completers for the subject + verb seeds of independent clauses. Don't worry about the completers within dependent clauses. When a dependent clause is a modifier, draw an arrow from the dependent clause to the word it modifies. The example sentence will look like this:

That slow, bent man ⟨(whom) they follow⟩ is Moses.

Often several dependent clauses are embedded in a single sentence.

⟨After Jan earned eight days of vacation time⟩, she took her handicapped nephew to Cinnamon Bay ⟨because he loved to swim⟩. (2 modifiers, "When?" and "Why?")

⟨When evening came⟩, she cooked ⟨whatever he wanted⟩ on the little camp stove ⟨that came with their rented tent⟩. (2 modifiers, "When?" and "Which?," and 1 completer, "She would cook what?")

APPLICATION 4.   Find the dependent clauses that play the sentence roles given in parentheses. Circle the dependent words and bracket the dependent clauses.

Example: ⟨(Although) everybody complains about it⟩, the subway still runs ⟨(when) the streets above are in gridlock⟩. (2 modifiers)

1. If I'm in a hurry, that's how I go places. (1 modifier, 1 completer)

2. Our subways are just noisier than the ones in Washington are because our equipment is older. (2 modifiers)

3. Unless you object, I'll send Mark home on the subway after the party is over. (2 modifiers)

4. Because he has spent so much time with me, he'll know where he should transfer to the other line. (1 modifier, 1 completer)

5. Whether he eats supper or not can be his choice since we'll have plenty of food here. (1 subject, 1 modifier)

APPLICATION 5.   For further study, look again at the sentences in Application 4. Underline all subjects once and all verbs twice, using broken lines for the subjects and verbs of the dependent clauses. Box any completers for the subject + verb seeds of independent clauses. Don't worry about the completers within the dependent clauses. Whenever a dependent clause is a modifier, draw an arrow from the dependent clause to the word it modifies. The example sentence will look like this:

⟨(Although) everybody complains about it⟩, the subway still runs ⟨(when) the streets above are in gridlock⟩.

Because a dependent clause contains a subject and a verb, it may look like a sentence. Sometimes a dependent clause is even longer than the independent clause in which it is embedded. A dependent clause, though, is not able to stand alone as a sentence.

FROM VERB TO VERBAL

A verb may become a *verbal*, ready for embedding, by the addition of the word *to* or by the loss of an auxiliary.

In each set of sentences below, the verb in the first sentence has become a verbal in the last one.

Emily can take out the garbage.

Emily wants **to take** out the garbage.

A full moon was glowing. The snow magnified its light.

The snow magnified the light of the **glowing** full moon.

Emily had discarded a letter. In the moonlight, she could read the address on the letter.

In the moonlight, Emily could read the address on her **discarded** letter.

Each set of sentences above illustrates a different kind of verbal. We'll look at the three kinds one at a time.

First kind of verbal: To + [base form of verb]
This is called an *infinitive.*

An infinitive may play several sentence roles:

To twitch at the moment of falling asleep is perfectly natural. (subject, "What is?")
Some people try **to control** this motion. (completer, "People try what?")
They lie on their stomachs **to suppress** the twitch. (modifier, "Why?")

An infinitive never acts as the verb of a sentence.

Second kind of verbal: [base form of verb] + *-ing* with no auxiliary in front
This is called a *present participle*, or in some cases, a *gerund*.

The present participle, when it stands without an auxiliary, may play the role of modifier:

Willie Loman was a **traveling** salesman. ("What kind?")

Sometimes the same verb form is used in one of the roles that a noun could play. Then it is called a gerund:

Losing his job pushed him beyond the brink of sanity. (subject, "What pushed?")

People focus on some basic elements of the American character by **reading** *Death of a Salesman.* (object of the preposition *by*)

Whether the *-ing* form acts as a modifier or plays a noun's role, if it is not preceded by a form of the auxiliary *to be*, it cannot work as the verb of its sentence.

Third kind of verbal: [past participle of verb] with no auxiliary in front

A past participle, standing alone without an auxiliary, plays the role of modifier:

Gandhi's **chosen** strategy of non-violent protest had its roots in Christian as well as Hindu doctrines. ("Which strategy?")

Educated in Britain, this young lawyer saw the connections between his own Indian traditions and the highest ideals of Western civilization. ("What kind of lawyer?")

Remember (see Chapter 2, p. 27) that with regular verbs, the simple past and the past participle forms look exactly alike, but that with irregular verbs the two forms may be different.

APPLICATION 6.   Circle the verbals in the sentences below.

Example: In spite of the announcement, the conductors decided (to stay).

Infinitive

1. Nobody likes to wait in lines.

2. This workshop demonstrates new ways to concentrate.

3. To survive on a minimum wage takes tremendous resourcefulness.

Present participle/Gerund

    4. Out of the corner of her eye, Anuja glimpsed a shooting star.

    5. Diving is not a good idea at this beach.

    6. The cleaner will trim that dangling piece of lace.

    7. Most students enjoy Ms. Burgess's teasing.

Past participle

    8. The ball flew right between the astonished umpire's knees.

    9. Frozen yogurt is becoming a fad in some cities.

    10. The unemployed flight attendants are bringing pots and pans to the airport.

APPLICATION 7.   For further study, look again at the sentences in Application 6. Underline all subjects once and all verbs twice. Box the completers. If a verbal is a modifier, draw an arrow from the verbal to the word it modifies. The example sentence will look like this:

In spite of the announcement, the <u>conductors</u> <u>decided</u> .

RECOGNIZING VERBAL PHRASES

A *verbal phrase* is a verbal plus its completers and modifiers.

Like the verb it came from, a verbal can take a completer and modifiers.

Boiling uses more energy than **frying** does. (verbals stand alone, without phrases)

⟨**Boiling** eggs ⟩ uses more energy than ⟨**frying** them ⟩ does. (verbals take completers, creating verbal phrases)

⟨**Boiling** an egg in the winter⟩ will heat your kitchen a bit. (verbal takes a completer and modifier, creating a verbal phrase)

An embedded verbal phrase functions as a unit, acting the way a single word might to play a single role in a larger sentence:

The water <u>is</u> ☐wonderful☐.   ⟨Swimming in your pool⟩ <u>is</u> ☐wonderful☐.

I'm <u>expecting</u> ☐friends☐.   1 m <u>expecting</u> ☐⟨to see my friends⟩☐.

APPLICATION 8.   Find the verbal phrases that play the sentence roles given in parentheses. Circle the verbal and bracket the whole verbal phrase.

Example: ⟨(Giving) concerts all over the country⟩ increases the popularity of rock groups. (subject)

1. Some rock singers like to go on tour. (completer)

2. They get a lot of money for appearing live on stage. (object of preposition *for*)

3. They become inspired in front of audiences cheering them on. (modifier, "What kind of audiences?")

4. A star surrounded by fans feels completely alive. (modifier, "Which star?")

5. Sometimes adults in the audiences will squabble like two-year-olds to get a good view of their idols. (modifier, "Why?")

APPLICATION 9.   For further study, look again at the sentences in Application 8. Underline all subjects once and all verbs twice. Box the completers of independent clauses (don't worry about a verbal's own completers). In sentences 3 through 5, draw an arrow from each verbal to the word it modifies. The example sentence will look like this:

⟨(Giving) concerts all over the country⟩ <u>increases</u> the ☐popularity☐ of rock groups.

Because a verbal comes from a verb, it behaves like a verb in several ways. It can take a completer and modifiers. It can also express time and imply action. But a verbal cannot be the verb of a sentence.

COMBINING SENTENCES BY EMBEDDING THOUGHTS

Several separate sentences can be combined into a more complex
sentence when one clause keeps its independence and the others are
embedded in it as dependent clauses.

Separate sentences:

> Lobbyists are paid by many private and public organizations.
>
> The organizations raise money from people.
>
> The people want their opinions to be taken seriously on Capitol Hill.

Separate sentences combined:

> Lobbyists are paid by many private and public organizations ⟨that raise
> money from people⟩⟨who want their opinions to be taken seriously on
> Capitol Hill⟩.

APPLICATION 10.   Combine each of the following sets of sentences, using the dependent
word(s) given in parentheses.

Example: I'm not sure I should tell you this story. It's about a little boy just
like yours. (since) *I'm not sure I should tell you this story since it's about
a little boy just like yours.*

1. The child rested on an old tree stump. He was lost on the mountain. (who)

   _____

2. The stump forked in a short branch. The branch's shape was like a chair.

   (whose) _____

   _____

3. The softness made the fork a perfect place for a nap. Thick moss provided

   the softness. (that) _____

   _____

4. He settled down and slept. A light rain started to fall. (until) _____

   _____

5. He woke up stiff and chilly. He realized that he was hungry. (when) _____

   _____

6. He didn't have a watch. He wondered what time it was. (because) _____

_____

7. He wasn't worried. He was only nine years old. (although) _____

_____

8. The rangers would find him soon. He could stay in the open. They could see him. (if, where) _____

_____

9. He started singing loudly. The moose at the nearby stream froze into stillness. She was both fascinated and afraid. (so that, because) _____

_____

_____

10. The sky cleared. The boy cut sticks with a knife. He carried a knife in his pocket. (as, that) _____

_____

Several separate sentences can be combined into a more complex sentence when the verb in one keeps its full powers and the verbs in the others become embedded verbals.

Separate sentences:

Recent polls show public concern about the influence of money in politics. Public concern is rapidly rising.
U.S. citizens spent $49 million on lobbyists in 1985.
The citizens were trying to sway congressional votes.

Separate sentences combined:

Recent polls show ⟨rapidly rising⟩ public concern about the influence of money in politics.
⟨Trying to influence congressional votes⟩, U.S. citizens spent $49 million on lobbyists in 1985.

APPLICATION 11.   Combine the following sets of sentences by changing the words in italics to embedded verbals or verbal phrases.

Examples: a. (embed a verbal only) That beach may not be open to the public much longer. It *is eroding.* <u>That eroding beach may not be open to the public much longer.</u>

b. (embed a verbal phase) The smaller beach *is hidden around the bluff.* It has higher and stronger dunes. <u>Hidden around the bluff, the smaller beach has higher and stronger dunes.</u>

1. The soldiers avoided the children. The children *were sleeping.* _____

_____

2. Talitha *was singing quietly to herself.* She approached the troops. _____

_____

3. Rosa and the twins shout in the crowd. The crowd *is rushing.* _____

_____

4. They *are laughing about the meeting.* They gesture with their hands. _____

_____

5. The steel *was polished.* It was sent to the die cutters. _____

_____

6. The sample *was engraved with the machinist's initials.* It went on display for a week. _____

_____

7. Please clean up Billie Sue's ice cream. It *is dripping.* _____

_____

8. We *are rushed by the deadline.* We're finally throwing out all Dad's old gadgets. _____

_____

9. Today I looked at my fender. It *is scratched.* _____

_____

10. I must have run into that car. It *was parked too close to my driveway.* _____

_____

_____

COMBINING SENTENCES BY COMPOUNDING EMBEDDED THOUGHTS

Several embedded thoughts can be compounded in a single sentence.

> Judy thought ⟨that the professor would have left⟩ but ⟨that the students would still be in the room⟩.

Since subjects, completers, and modifiers can be compounded, embedded thoughts that play these sentence roles can also be compounded by the conjunctions *and, but, yet, or, nor.* Remember that when two or more sentence parts of the same type are compounded, the conjunction usually appears between only the last two, and the others are separated by commas.

APPLICATION 12.   Combine each set of sentences by compounding the bracketed embedded thoughts. Use the conjunction shown in parentheses.

> *Example:*   I told you ⟨that last night I watched the news on television⟩. I told you ⟨that it really made me think hard⟩. *I told you that last night I watched the news on television and that it really made me think hard.*

1. Even the president agrees ⟨that tnese weapons are a waste of money⟩. He also agrees ⟨that they may spoil our negotiating position⟩. (and) _____

_____

_____

2. People are asking ⟨how we got to this point⟩. They are also asking ⟨why we didn't stop before now⟩. (and) _____

_____

3. You should lobby the legislators ⟨who are sympathetic⟩. You should lobby the ones ⟨who have strong arms-control pressure groups at home⟩. (or)

_____

_____

4. Politicians listen to people ⟨while any controversy is hot⟩. They listen ⟨when the news coverage is good⟩. They listen ⟨before an election rolls around⟩. (, , and) _____

   _____

   _____

5. ⟨Learning about the political system⟩ can give us hope. ⟨Recognizing our power⟩ can give us hope. (and) _____

   _____

6. Some people just don't have the energy ⟨to get involved⟩. They don't have the energy ⟨to make changes⟩. (or) _____

   _____

7. However, when I sit at home, I find myself ⟨getting depressed⟩. I find myself ⟨feeling even more tired⟩. (and) _____

   _____

8. As a result, I have decided ⟨to rest often⟩. I have decided ⟨not to give up⟩. (but) _____

   _____

9. ⟨Hoping for successes⟩, I keep trying. ⟨Failing often⟩, I keep trying. ⟨Making many small steps forward⟩, I keep trying. (, , yet) _____

   _____

   _____

10. Sometime ⟨after my senator returns from Washington⟩, I will start a petition drive. Sometime ⟨before summer vacation slows things down⟩, I will start a petition drive. (but) _____

    _____

    _____

Return to your writing

Read aloud the paragraph you wrote at the beginning of this chapter. Look at the words you circled, and check to see whether they introduce embedded thoughts. Bracket any other embedded thoughts you find. Trade papers with a classmate and check each other's work. Ask your tutor or teacher for help with questions.

Chapter 6

Capitalization and Punctuation

Writers use punctuation marks and capital letters to help readers interpret the structure of their sentences. Each mark has at least one purpose, and some have several, but no mark is ever used without a good reason.

Chapter 6 helps you understand when to use

- capital letters.
- periods.
- question marks.
- exclamation points.
- commas.
- colons.
- semicolons.
- quotation marks.
- parentheses.

Observation of writing

In the paragraphs below, circle all the capital letters and punctuation marks. Be sure you find each of the following marks:

.	period	;	semicolon
?	question mark	:	colon
!	exclamation point	" "	quotation marks
,	comma	( )	parentheses

We had agreed that we should go for a picnic on Saturday, August 15, but I wasn't sure where you were planning to take me. When you picked me up, you announced, "We'll go up to Marblehead to that park at the mouth of the harbor; do you know the one I mean?" I didn't, but it sounded good to me, and it was a beautiful summer day.

We arrived in Marblehead and parked in a sunny, hot parking lot. You had packed a lot into the trunk: a cooler filled with fried chicken, Pepsi, and ice; a bag containing cups, plates, and napkins; two beach chairs; and towels (though we didn't plan to swim). Beginning to wilt in the sun after the cool air of the air-conditioned car, we gathered the stuff and walked to the park. A short path led up a grassy hill. Suddenly, there below our feet was the harbor. Sailboats of all sizes and colors zipped around on the water. It seemed odd that so much activity should be so silent. The water was green near us but became blue farther away. A strong breeze cooled the top of the hill on which we sat, and the sun now felt pleasant rather than hot. What more could we ask for? You spread your arms and shouted to the horizon, "Thank heaven for weekends!"

CAPITAL LETTERS

Every sentence begins with a capital letter.

> A penny saved is a penny earned.
> People who live in glass houses shouldn't throw stones.

A proper noun begins with a capital letter.

> A **proper noun** names a specific person, place, thing, or idea. Proper nouns include people's names, titles, brand names, the names of languages and nationalities, and the names of days and months (but not seasons). For example:

Common Noun	Proper Noun
woman	Damaris
son	Julius
my **uncle**	Uncle Ernie
college **president**	President Bliss
a new **detergent**	Cloud Puff
my accounting **class**	Accounting 243
studying a **language**	studying Spanish
holiday	Labor Day
month	June
the **state**	Indiana

The pronoun *I* is always spelled as a capital letter.

> When I think of traveling, I always wish I could go to Borneo.

A capital letter begins the first, last, and any important word in the title of a book, magazine article, story, poem, movie, or other work.

> Have you read Paul Hoch's analysis of football, *Rip Off the Big Game*?

> Use capital letters only when you have a good reason to do so.

APPLICATION 1.   Capitalize letters only where necessary in the sentences below.

1. i know that canadians celebrate thanksgiving, but is their holiday also in november?

2. david was sitting in the corner of the restaurant, reading a science fiction book called *the green insects return.*

3. that new history class on presidents since 1945, history 602, is very popular.

4. i think you are supposed to plant all bulbs in the fall.

5. since last friday, she has spent more time studying german than anything else; her father is tutoring her.

APPLICATION 2.   Capitalize letters only where necessary in the passage below.

throughout history, people have treated the bodies of their dead with great respect. the ancient greek dramatist sophocles wrote a tragedy about antigone, who died rather than obey a rule that forbade her to bury the body of her brother. in modern times, evelyn waugh wrote a comic novel, *the loved one,* that pokes fun at the way funeral homes and cemeteries can exploit people's concern for decent burials. yet human beings are not the only creatures who feel the need to move the bodies of their dead to safe and quiet places. in sociology 101 last monday, dr. cummings lectured about burial customs among other species. when i signed up for sociology in the spring, i hardly expected to be studying animals. however, i find that it puts human rituals in perspective to know that many beasts, from the tiny birds swarming above the highway in october to massive african elephants grazing on a distant plain, will stop whatever they are doing to cooperate in hiding the remains of any members of their species who have died in open places.

PERIOD .

A complete sentence that makes a statement ends with a period.

> It's your turn now. Take a deep breath and blow.

Most abbreviations end with a period.

> Dr. Williams will meet you at the Oak St. office.

QUESTION MARK ?

A complete sentence that asks a question ends with a question mark.

> Have you been eating again? Does the coach know?

EXCLAMATION POINT !

A complete sentence that expresses unusual emphasis or great excitement may end with an exclamation point.

> You have been eating again! I'm telling the coach!

This mark is not used often. Usually a writer can express emphasis through the choice of words, using information to support an idea rather than relying on an exclamation point to create a general sense of high emotion. In writing, exclamation points are useful primarily for conveying the tone of informal conversations.

APPLICATION 3.   End these sentences correctly.

1. I told you not to smoke in front of the children
2. Did you know that children will mimic the bad habits of adults
3. Most adults who smoke began as teenagers
4. Why do different brands of cigarettes show different Surgeon General's warnings
5. You should see the one I read yesterday

APPLICATION 4.   The slashes (/) mark the breaks between sentences below. Put periods, question marks, exclamation points, and capital letters where they are needed.

watch out / the broken limb of the spruce tree is falling / thank goodness you got out of the way in time / don't you think we should cut that tree down / the electrician who lives on brand st was strolling by the other day and he noticed that the whole upper half of the tree is dead / sooner or later the branches will fall / it's a miracle that nobody has been hurt yet / besides, that spruce takes up the whole yard / wouldn't you like to have some space for tossing a ball with the kids / i love trees too, but maybe we could plant something slender and pretty, like a birch / that would please mrs lowe next door / she's always complaining that her house gets so little sun because of our big old tree / what do you think /

COMMA ,

A comma marks the breaks between items in a series.

They teased, begged, and flattered until I gave in.

Remember that when more than two items are compounded, the conjunction comes between the last two, and commas separate the others:

They appealed to my pride, to my faith in them, and to my generous instincts.

APPLICATION 5.   Add commas where necessary.

1. My family reunion will include two aunts two great-uncles and all six dogs.

2. My mother oldest brother and younger sister will be responsible for bringing most of the food.

3. A ham a huge salad baked sweet potatoes and watermelon will be my contribution.

4. In preparation, we painted two bedrooms refinished the floors replaced the light fixtures and installed screens.

5. Next week we will paint the bathroom the kitchen and both hallways.

A comma comes before the conjunction that compounds independent clauses.

> They joked around at my door, and then they won me over.
> The girls told me what good drivers they were, but the boys concentrated on washing the car windows.

The conjunctions that are used to compound independent clauses are *and, but, yet, or, nor, for,* and *so.*

APPLICATION 6.   Add commas where necessary.

1. Gary Farina won the state lottery and that was the end of his career as a roofer.

2. He had a successful business but he had always wanted to travel to South America.

3. He also wants to do more sailing so he is planning to join the crew of a boat headed for Venezuela.

4. He plans to go on to Colombia by car but he will miss sailing down the coast with the others.

5. Gary has hit the jackpot and can realize his lifelong dream yet he knows that he will think often about the friends he left behind in Massachusetts.

A comma marks the end of an introductory modifying phrase or clause.

> Since they'd waited all day, I couldn't refuse.
> After all, I owed them a favor.

Note that when a modifying clause comes after the independent clause, no comma is necessary:

> I was laughing to myself while they were talking to me.
>
> *but*
>
> While they were talking to me, I was laughing to myself.

A transitional expression at the beginning of a clause will be separated from the rest of the clause by a comma. In the sentences below, *finally* and *therefore* are transitional expressions.

> Finally, the water began to boil.
>
> Nobody noticed it for five minutes; therefore, several ounces evaporated.

APPLICATION 7.   Add commas where necessary.

1. After such a long winter Mary felt she could afford a trip to sunny Madeira.
2. She had saved more money than she had expected; therefore she could pay for her friend's fare as well.
3. She planned to leave first since her friend could not come until Monday.
4. During their visit to Madeira Mary took a long walk along the channels that carry irrigation water from the mountains to the terraced farms below.
5. Located off the coast of Africa Madeira is a Portuguese island.

A comma separates an interruption from the rest of a sentence.

An **interruption** is any word or group of words that is added to a sentence to offer extra information. It can be a whole clause:

> Marcel, **who was the oldest**, was a charmer.

The interruption can be a phrase:

> What they wanted, **of course**, was to borrow my car.

Sometimes the interruption is a single word:

> **Yes**, I did it again, **honey**. I loaned them the new car and the keys, **too**.

APPLICATION 8.   Add commas where necessary.

1. There are at least sixteen different kinds of tulips all members of the lily family available to the home gardener.
2. Tulip bulbs require cool climates however and do not do well in the South.
3. They owe their popularity to a great degree to their use in public gardens and parks.
4. These bulbs which are shaped like teardrops need to be planted 4 to 6 inches deep in the ground with the pointy end up.
5. Most American-grown tulip bulbs by the way come from Holland, Michigan.

A comma separates the exact words of a speaker from the rest of a sentence.

> "I must say," Marcel declared, "that you deserve your great reputation for kindness." I blushed and replied, "Enough sweet talk. Be back by five."

Notice that the first word of each quoted sentence is capitalized, even though, in the case of the last one, the mark before **enough** is a comma rather than a period. This is because the words being quoted create a sentence within a sentence.

APPLICATION 9.   Add commas where necessary in the sentences below.

1. "Well" he said "that certainly is a beautiful garden."
2. The last line of the poem I'm thinking of reads "And miles to go before I sleep."
3. Anita hissed "Stop crackling that paper."
4. The phrase "Fourscore and seven years ago" begins the Gettysburg Address.
5. "You'll probably need the dictionary" she said.

A comma separates items in an address or date.

> Come celebrate with us at 24 Morrill Avenue, Waterville, Maine, on Monday, June 18, 1990.

APPLICATION 10.   Add commas where necessary.

1. Zion National Park was established on November 19 1919, almost eighty years ago.

2. One can get information about lodging and activities by writing to Zion National Park Springdale Utah.

3. Carlsbad Caverns, an underground wonder located in southeastern New Mexico, was established as a national park on May 14 1930.

4. You can get information about walking tours and lantern trips by writing to Carlsbad Caverns National Park 3225 National Parks Highway Carlsbad New Mexico.

5. Sequoia National Park was established in California on September 25 1890.

SUMMARY OF COMMA USE

Use a comma

- to mark the breaks between items in a series.
- before the conjunction that compounds independent clauses.
- to mark the end of an introductory modifying phrase or clause.
- to separate an interruption from the rest of a sentence.
- to separate quoted words from the rest of a sentence.
- to separate items in an address or date.

Use commas only for the purposes described above.

APPLICATION 11.   Add commas only where they are needed in the following paragraph.

Aaron Copland one of the grand old men of American music came in with our century. He was born in Brooklyn New York on November 14 1900 and he began to study piano at the relatively late age of thirteen. He started compos- ing soon after. Unlike many struggling artists he met success early which is a little unusual since he was only nineteen when he published his first piece. Although his earliest works show the influence of his studies in Europe his later compositions are filled with American sounds. For example he built symphonies around folk tunes jazz rhythms and hymns. Perhaps the familiarity of these sounds has helped to make his music popular with people who don't usually listen to orchestral music. At the same time the clean and disciplined harmonies that link the horns and strings in his pieces have won Copland the reverence of music lovers. One critic said of him "Copland our own boy from Brooklyn is able to please the person in the back seat of the taxi and the driver too."

COLON :

A colon shows the reader that a list or an explanation follows.

> Here's what I want you to do: grab my bag, warm up the car, and take me to the station.
> There's one thing about you that makes me mad: the way you lose track of time when you work in the garden.

APPLICATION 12.   Add colons where necessary.

1. Tulips come in many varieties Mendel, Triumph Cottage, Dutch Breeders, and Late Doubles.

2. There is one important rule to remember always plant tulip bulbs in the sunny part of the garden.

3. Raising tulips is easy and requires just these few items bone meal, a trowel, and your choice of tulip bulbs.

SEMICOLON ;

A semicolon compounds two closely related independent clauses without a conjunction.

> Come with me; you'll be glad you did.
> There must be something I can do; I've been sitting here for an hour.

A semicolon compounds two independent clauses where the second clause begins with a *transitional expression*.

In the sentences below, **furthermore** and **however** are transitional expressions.

I'll show you the sights of my childhood; furthermore, we'll visit the alley where I learned to skate.

I thought we'd said enough about that; however, the look on your face tells me that you have something more to say.

Notice that a comma follows the transitional expression in the sentences above.

For more on transitional expressions (also known as *adverbial conjunctions*), see p. 135 and p. 294.

A semicolon separates items in a series when the items already contain commas.

As program director, she had several responsibilities: planning, budgeting, contracting, and hiring staff for the summer projects; managing the projects and supervising the staff; and, at the end of the summer, closing the offices, distributing remaining funds to agency departments, and writing final reports.

APPLICATION 13.   Add semicolons where they are needed in the sentences below.

1. We had planned to play basketball in the park this morning however, the rain is still falling.

2. Wait until the mail comes the letter might arrive today.

3. That new bicycle really helped Erica improve her time in the last race furthermore, she's been lifting weights lately.

4. The sap buckets on the maple trees are nearly overflowing therefore, this is going to be a good year for syrup.

5. Since we're moving this weekend, we'll need to do the following: send our change of address to the phone, electric, and gas companies get our security deposit from the landlord, return the keys to him, and remind him about the kitchen sink problem and let the babysitter know about our phone number.

Colons and semicolons are specialized marks. Use one only when a period or comma can't do the job.

APPLICATION 14.   Add colons or semicolons where they are needed in the following paragraph.

> In the twenty years between 1911 and 1931, second basemen dominated the National League roster of Most Valuable Players. Four men are responsible for this statistic Larry Doyle, who played for New York in 1912 Johnny Evers, who won for Boston in 1914 Rogers Hornsby, who won the award for St. Louis in 1925 and then for Chicago in 1929 and finally Frankie Frisch, who returned the prize to St. Louis in 1931. In the American League during the same period, only Eddie Collins of Philadelphia brought the prize back to second base his year was 1914. After that, second basemen nearly dropped off the MVP roster in both leagues in fact, only five men represented the position through the next fifty years. Here are the names of the scattered stars Charlie Gehringer (AL), Joe Gordon (AL), Jackie Robinson (NL), Nellie Fox (AL), and Joe Morgan (NL).

QUOTATION MARKS " "

Quotation marks identify the exact words of a speaker.

> Sheba was whispering, "That's not the way; turn left."
> "I know what I'm doing," Joan snapped.

Do not use quotation marks simply for emphasis; that's what underlining is for.

> This is your laundromat; please keep it clean.

> *not*

> This is "your" laundromat; please keep it "clean."

Quotation marks identify the title of a story, poem, or other short work.

> The first-person point of view in "The Lesson" blends humor with social commentary. The narration is entirely different in "Guests of the Nation."

The title of a long work (such as a book or movie) should be underlined. The title of a part (such as a story or chapter) of a long work should be in quotation marks:

> Vanessa Redgrave and Jane Fonda starred in <u>Julia,</u> the movie based on "Julia," a chapter in <u>Pentimento,</u> Lillian Hellman's autobiography.

On printed pages, slanted letters called **italics** replace underlining:

> <u>Julia</u> (handwritten or typed) = *Julia* (printed)

APPLICATION 15.   Use quotation marks where they are needed in the sentences below.

1. Name the character who said, Give me liberty or give me death.
2. Everything was going well, the mechanic said, until we reached sixty miles per hour.
3. Here come the blue jays was the last thing I heard her say before she stopped talking in her sleep.
4. In Flannery O'Connor's short story, A Good Man Is Hard to Find, a car accident has tragic results.
5. My *Modern Life* magazine came today; there is an interesting article in it called Love Triangles.

PARENTHESES ( )

Parentheses set off information that is not essential to the sentence.

> The price was low ($3.50), so I didn't mind paying.

Any extra information is an interruption (see commas, above), but parentheses are useful when the interruption is too long to be set off with commas, or when the writer wants to separate the information from the rest of the sentence more completely than would be possible with commas. The interruption might be a phrase:

I didn't go anywhere (except to the mailbox) until noon.

Sometimes the interruption is a whole sentence:

The roads (you'll be delighted to hear this) were completely dry by then.

APPLICATION 16.   Use parentheses where necessary in the sentences below.

1. What we need to do I know you don't want to hear this is throw this out and start again.

2. He brought so many supplies pencils, notebooks, tape recorders, even cups and spoons for coffee that we were ready within half an hour.

3. The paint job on Bev's car yellow and purple with swirls made me wonder what she is thinking about these days.

Quotation marks and parentheses always come in sets. When you mark the start of a quotation, the reader imagines a new voice entering. That new voice continues until you mark the end of the quotation. When you mark the start of an interruption, the reader will be looking for the end in order to see where the main sentence picks up again. Don't leave the reader hanging with only one half of either set.

APPLICATION 17.   Add quotation marks and parentheses where they are needed in the following paragraph.

We were just sitting down to our first decent meal in days when Ron walked by our table. I see you folks have an appetite for cholesterol, he teased. We laughed and shrugged, expecting him to walk on by. But he started poking at my plate, murmuring, Boiled cholesterol, cholesterol salad, fried cholesterol. Yum. I started to eat anyway. Ron is used to being ignored but he wouldn't let me ignore him now. He took hold of my fork and announced You should read this article. It will change your life. He handed me an old issue of some health food journal and pointed to the essay that had changed his life and was rapidly destroying my appetite: Can You and Your Serum Lipids Live in Peace? I carefully tore the essay out pages 56–58 and tucked one page under my collar as a bib, folding the others to use as napkins. Suicide! he yelled as he stormed away. We settled down and ate everything even the parsley believe it or not that was on our plates.

Return to your observation of writing

Look again at the paragraphs on page 82, in which you circled the capital letters and punctuation marks. Think about how the marks help you as a reader to understand the way in which groups of words work together. Now that you have studied the rules for using capital letters and punctuation marks, write beside each circled mark the reason for its use. In these paragraphs, you should find examples that illustrate the following number of different reasons.

Mark	*Number of Reasons for Using*
Capital letter	3
Period	1
Question mark	1
Exclamation point	1
Comma	6
Colon	1
Semicolon	2
Quotation marks	1
Parentheses	1

Trade papers with a classmate and check each other's work. Ask your tutor or teacher for help with questions.

Chapter 7

Combining Sentences

Before leaving the study of sentence structure behind, this chapter shows how whole sentences can be compounded. The chapter goes on to offer a summary of the sentence combining patterns you've learned throughout Part One:

- compounding sentence parts.
- embedding clauses.
- embedding verbals and verbal phrases.
- compounding whole sentences.

Writing

country	as	just	it
in*	the*	your*	accent
were	and	where	does
spirit	of	speech	heart
born	you	lives	

1. If these were the only words in the English language, how many sentences would you be able to create from them? You may use any of the words more than once if you wish, but don't add new ones and don't change any of the words. Write as many sentences as you can.

2. Compare the sentences you wrote with those of a classmate. Working together, try to compose just one sentence that uses *all* the words in the list. This time you may use each starred word twice, but use the others only once each. (The Answer Key shows one solution to this puzzle, but before you look it up, give yourselves a fair chance at composing a sentence of your own.)

COMPOUNDING WHOLE SENTENCES

Just as similar sentence parts can be compounded, whole sentences also
can be compounded.

> Remember that subjects can be compounded with other subjects, modifiers
> with other modifiers, and so on. (See pp. 35, 46, and 59.) In the same way, one
> whole sentence can be compounded with another whole sentence by a con-
> junction (*and, but, yet, or, nor*). When you are compounding whole sentences,
> two other conjunctions come into play: *for* and *so*. When you compound whole
> sentences, a comma before the conjunction marks the place where one clause
> ends and the next begins. When more than two sentences are compounded,
> the conjunction usually appears between only the last two, and the others are
> separated by commas.

APPLICATION 1.   Combine each of the following sets of sentences by using a comma and
the conjunction in parentheses to link one whole sentence with another.

> *Example:*   I sing beautifully in the shower. You whistle tunelessly in the tub.
>
> (and) *I sing beautifully in the shower, and you whistle tunelessly in the*
> *tub.*

1. Bud will be leaving by noon. I'll call my mother then. (so) _____

   _____

2. Baking bread every Saturday keeps Tillie happy. Eating it keeps her fat.

   (but) _____

   _____

3. If you're sure, go ahead. You may lose your chance. (or) _____

   _____

4. The boy who got lost on the mountain settled down on an old tree stump.

   He knew that he needed some rest. (for) _____

   _____

5. My father loves TV. My fiancée loves football. My sister loves politics. I

   love sleep. (, , , and) _____

   _____

SENTENCE COMBINING SUMMARY

You can combine sentences by compounding two or more sentence parts
that play the same sentence role.

A conjunction can connect subject with subject, verb with verb, completer with
completer, or modifier with modifier (see pp. 35, 46, and 59). In the example
below, the conjunction connects two verbs:

Those blues tunes haunt me. Those blues tunes don't change my mind.

Those blues tunes haunt me **but** don't change my mind.

APPLICATION 2.   Combine each pair of sentences by using *and* to compound the sentence
parts in italics.

1. Bronson *listens to dozens of records*. Bronson *imitates the playing of his idols*.

    _____

    _____

2. He's probably learning a lot just *from talking with Bill*. He's probably learn-
    ing a lot just *from watching Bill's rehearsals*. _____

    _____

3. *Bill* adopted Bronson in a good-natured way. The *drummer* adopted Bron-
    son in a good-natured way. _____

    _____

You can combine sentences by embedding one within another.

A dependent word takes away a clause's independence and prepares it for
embedding in an independent clause (see p. 65):

Those blues tunes haunt me. You play them on your trombone.

Those blues tunes haunt me **when** you play them on your trombone.

APPLICATION 3.   Combine each pair of sentences by embedding one clause in the other,
using the dependent word given in parentheses.

1. He might just make it. He's throwing his whole soul into it. (because) ____

    _____

    _____

2. His friends are supporting him in little ways. They're poking fun at him, too. (although) _____

_____

3. It's hard to believe that this is the same Bronson. He hated jazz six months ago. (who) _____

A verb can be reduced to a verbal and embedded in another sentence alone or as a verbal phrase (see p. 70):

Those blues tunes are haunting. They echo constantly through my brain.
Those **haunting** blues tunes echo constantly through my brain.   *or*
Haunting me, those blues tunes echo constantly through my brain.

APPLICATION 4.   Combine each pair of sentences by embedding the italicized words as verbals or verbal phrases.

1. Bronson loved that trombone immediately. It *was dented.* _____

_____

2. He*'s working at night now.* He's saving money to get it fixed. _____

_____

3. Bronson *is teased by his friends and family.* Bronson moves steadily toward his dream. _____

_____

You can combine whole sentences by compounding them.

A conjunction with a comma before it connects two independent sentences:

Those blues tunes are haunting me. I don't want you to stop playing.
Those blues tunes are haunting me, **but** I don't want you to stop playing.

APPLICATION 5.   Compound each pair of sentences by using a comma and the conjunction given in parentheses.

1. Bronson used to swear that jazz was nothing but noise. Look at him today. (but) _____

_____

2. I can't help laughing at his conversion. I think even he will laugh with me eventually. (and) _____

   _____

3. Meanwhile, he's enjoying his obsession. Let's leave him alone for now. (so)

   _____

Return to your writing

Find the subjects and verbs of all the sentences you wrote using the words on p. 100. How many different words did you use as subjects? How many different words did you use as verbs?

Obviously, a sentence is more than just a collection of words. The way the words relate to each other is what allows you to create and communicate meaning in language. The primary relationships within an English sentence are those among subject, verb, completer, and modifier.

PART TWO

Usage

Chapter 8

Sentence Fragments

A sentence fragment is a piece of a sentence; it is a group of words that is broken off from a complete sentence. A sentence fragment cannot do the work of a complete sentence because the fragment lacks an independent subject + verb combination. Recognizing sentence fragments and knowing how to correct them will help you eliminate them from your writing.

Chapter 8 helps you to

- know the difference between fragments and complete sentences.
- correct the four most common types of sentence fragment.

You may want to start your work on sentence fragments by taking the Pretest on p. 315.

Writing

Leaf through the newspaper and find an article about something on which you have an opinion. Don't limit yourself to front-page news. Scan the sports, entertainment, and human interest articles. Read the article you have chosen and jot down your responses to it. Look over your notes and develop a statement that expresses your opinion on the subject. On a fresh piece of paper, write a paragraph that starts with that statement and continues by giving two or three reasons for your opinion.

Make sure all your sentences contain subjects and verbs.

INCOMPLETE VERBS

A sentence fragment may lack some part of the verb, usually a form of *to be* or *to have*.

> At the moment, we dreaming of a visit to Peru.
> The idea of travel been on our minds recently.

Review the forms of *to be* and *to have* used as auxiliaries in the chart below.

forms of to be	*forms of* to have
am, is, are	have, has
was, were	had
be, being, been	

APPLICATION 1.   Correct each fragment below by completing the verb with a form of *to be* or *to have*.

Example: They *have* been reading a lot of mystery stories recently.

1. The boys thinking about starting their own business.

2. My hip broken in the accident.

3. Those goats making a mess of the Stimsons' lawn.

4. The oil pan leaking all the time.

5. Your little mistake forgotten in all the excitement.

6. Some of the seeds sprouting inside the log.

7. Probably she given him a second chance.

8. Some people taken more than their share.

9. Since the end of school, the children begun to enjoy life.

10. Ted spending a lot of extra time at the lumber yard.

DISCONNECTED PREPOSITIONAL PHRASES

A prepositional phrase all by itself is a sentence fragment.

> After the long, frightening ordeal in the blizzard.

A prepositional phrase must be part of the same sentence as the word it modifies:

> We were tired ⟨after the long, frightening ordeal⟩ in the blizzard.

To refresh your memory of prepositional phrases, see Chapter 4, pp. 57–59.

APPLICATION 2.   Fix each fragment below by making the prepositional phrase act as a modifier within a complete sentence.

> *Example:*   By resorting to card tricks. *Their last babysitter quieted them down by resorting to card tricks.*

1. In my neighbor's driveway. _____

_____

2. With a purple hat and a frantic face. _____

_____

3. Before my first class in the old building. _____

_____

4. Past the library and the cafeteria. _____

_____

5. After leaving out the most important part. _____

_____

APPLICATION 3.   Combine each group of ideas below into one complete sentence. Put each prepositional phrase as close as possible to the word you want it to modify.

> *Example:*   I returned the phone to the desk. In disbelief. After our long conversation. *After our long conversation, I returned the phone to the desk in disbelief.*

1. The graduates joked and sang loudly. After the long, formal dinner. In their dignified academic robes. _____

_____

2. Lourdes followed the action. With passionate interest. Just like the coach's mother. _____

_____

3. Blake leaped. Toward the bright orange mat. On the red tiled floor. With fierce determination. _____

_____

4. After all the crazy arguments. We always find ourselves joking. In the end. About who washes the dishes. _____

_____

5. Matt drove all night. Without stopping to eat. Through Ohio. And on to Chicago. On top of the world. Since his conversation. With Gina. _____

_____

_____

DISCONNECTED VERBAL PHRASES

A verbal phrase all by itself is a sentence fragment.

> Speaking of Halloween with Aunt Josie.

A verbal phrase must be embedded in a complete sentence; it then plays a non-verb role.

> ⟨Speaking of Halloween with Aunt Josie⟩, I suddenly remembered the extra cookies in the cabinet.

To refresh your memory of verbal phrases, see Chapter 5, pp. 72–73.

APPLICATION 4.   Fix each fragment below by giving the verbal phrase a role to play in a complete sentence.

Example: Thoroughly disgusted by the workers' behavior. *Thoroughly disgusted by the workers' behavior, we decided to complain to their supervisor.*

1. Being left behind. _____

2. Tanned all over by the wind and the sun. _____

3. To make the best of a bad situation. _____

4. Taking a vacation in February with five friends. _____

5. To work extra hard for a reward. _____

APPLICATION 5.   Combine each group of ideas below into one complete sentence.

Example: We cheered when the auctioneer's helpers brought in Kim's huge sculpture. Groaning and sweating with exertion. Covered with burlap. *We cheered when the auctioneer's helpers, groaning and sweating with exertion, brought in Kim's huge sculpture covered with burlap.*

1. We watched poor Francis. Trying not to laugh at him. Staring in innocent amazement at the escalator. _____

2. The gate was draped with rugs. Faded and tattered by the weather. Drying after the storm. _____

3. Talking about nuclear war. Makes me realize how little I know. In a class full of eighth graders. _____

4. We waited restlessly for the feature. Bored and irritated by the previews. Stuffing ourselves with popcorn. _____

_____

5. Sharon finally started. Trying wholeheartedly. To let go of the past. Relieved of her anxiety over Emmet. _____

_____

DISCONNECTED DEPENDENT CLAUSES

A dependent clause standing alone is a sentence fragment.

Because they were bored and restless.

A dependent word makes its clause unable to stand alone as a sentence and defines a role for that clause to play within a complete sentence.

They auditioned for the circus ⟨because they were bored and restless⟩.

To refresh your memory of dependent clauses, see Chapter 5, pp. 67–70.

APPLICATION 6.   Fix each fragment below by giving the dependent clause a role to play in a complete sentence.

Example: That Helen had described so carefully. *We were unable to find the house that Helen had described so carefully.*

1. Which only encouraged the troublemakers. _____

_____

2. Even though you probably disagree. _____

_____

3. Ever since the trial began this morning. _____

_____

4. Whoever broke my basketball hoop. _____

_____

5. That someone will be arriving before long. _____

_____

APPLICATION 7.   Combine each group of ideas into a single complete sentence.

Example: That no one could get to the station on time. As soon as they realized. They decided to take a later bus. *As soon as they realized that no one could get to the station on time, they decided to take a later bus.*

1. Because Clyde was so wound up. No one wanted to argue. When he insisted on that restaurant. _____

_____

2. Although I kept putting in dimes. Some of your clothes are still wet. Whenever the dryer stopped. _____

_____

3. This party is for you. Because it's your birthday. And for whoever else wants to come. _____

_____

4. I'll run back to get you. Before the bus leaves. So that you can work until the last minute. _____

_____

5. If he doesn't call today. I'm completely convinced. That she'll give up on the whole plan. Before he leaves for work. _____

_____

Dependent clauses beginning with *who, whom, whose, which,* or *that* are particularly likely to appear as sentence fragments.

My brother's house is on Alp Street. Which is getting new sewers next week.

A clause of this type, like any other dependent clause, must be connected to an independent clause. An independent clause is a clause that can stand by itself as a complete sentence.

My brother's house is on Alp Street, which is getting new sewers next week.

APPLICATION 8.   Combine each group of ideas into a single complete sentence. Put each dependent clause as close as possible to the word it modifies.

Example: This is the injured dog. That was saved by the vet. Whom your aunt recommended. *This is the injured dog that was saved by the vet whom your aunt recommended.*

1. The people will introduce you to Pablo's boss. Who work in the shipping department. Who has lots of friends. _____

    _____

2. I was up until 2:00 A.M. watching the game. That Red had taped for me on his VCR. Which explains my crabby mood today. _____

    _____

3. I found the shoes in your closet. That you lost. Which looks like an abandoned shed. _____

    _____

4. She told me an amazing story. That even your dad will believe. Who doesn't fool easily. _____

    _____

5. Those dazzling young dancers may be the reason for the show's success. Whose silver tunics are covered with feathers. _____

    _____

TIP FOR FINDING FRAGMENTS: Remember that a fragment is any group of words that is not connected to an independent subject + verb combination. Therefore, to check for fragments, look for subject + verb combinations. A subject + verb combination is independent as long as it is not introduced by a dependent word.

REVIEW AND PRACTICE

A.

A sentence with an incomplete verb is a fragment.

Insert appropriate forms of *to be* or *to have* wherever they are needed in the following sentences.

1. Lonnie coming home from school soon.

2. Trevor's favorite singer featured on the radio last night.

3. I seen enough of your silly behavior now.

4. She knits all day while you are traveling.

5. Finally the teachers begun their meeting.

A prepositional phrase that stands alone is a sentence fragment.

Combine each numbered set of ideas into one complete sentence. Put each prepositional phrase as close as possible to the word it modifies.

6. The lions roar. From their dark cages. In the early hours of morning. _____

    _____

7. They crave a special food. In the spring. With the taste and smell of African antelope. _____

    _____

8. Their food is shipped. On airplanes and trains. In huge crates. _____

    _____

9. It reaches the zoo. In less than a week. On the other side of the world. __

    _____

10. The zoo can't afford this extravagance. Except in the spring. For the demanding lions. _____

    _____

A verbal phrase that stands alone is a fragment.

Combine each numbered set of ideas into one complete sentence. Put each verbal phrase as close as possible to the word it modifies.

11. Lost in thought. I didn't hear my son. Slamming the front door. _____

_____

12. I ignored the stew. Burning on the stove. Perfectly contented. To continue my daydream. _____

_____

_____

13. My son rushed into the kitchen. Looking like a maniac. _____

_____

_____

14. Filling up rapidly with smoke. He was yelling at the top of his lungs. To warn me about the house. _____

_____

15. My daydream fled. Swallowed up in the confusion of reality. _____

_____

A dependent clause that stands alone is a sentence fragment.

Combine each numbered set of ideas into one complete sentence.

16. When she got the divorce. That she was so nervous about. You were Vivian's best friend. _____

_____

17. Although she never asked you for help. Because you understood her shyness. You were patient with her. _____

_____

18. Until the court battle was over. Since she was embarrassed. She didn't talk to anyone. _____

_____

19. Her other friends were all mad at her. After she'd snubbed them for so
long. Even though by then she needed support more than ever. _____

_____

20. What would have become of her. I often wonder. If you hadn't been waiting and ready for her to talk at that point. _____

_____

**A dependent clause beginning with *who, whom, whose, which,* or *that* is
especially likely to appear as a fragment.**

Combine each numbered set of ideas into one complete sentence. Put each
dependent clause as close as possible to the word it modifies.

21. Those noisy people want to get out. Who are in the car. That Gerry just
bought. _____

_____

22. They want to look for the movie star. Whose face is on the ad for the hotel.
That was recently built in this run-down town. _____

_____

23. They have been traveling together for three weeks. Which is a long time.

_____

24. But Gerry isn't happy about stopping. Who has to get to the West Coast
by Sunday. _____

_____

25. On Monday, he'll sign up for the Army program. That will train him in
radio communications. Which he has always wanted to study. _____

_____

B.

Rewrite the following paragraph, correcting the fragments. You may drop dependent words to make clauses independent, remove periods and capital letters to connect phrases or clauses, complete a verb, or make any other necessary changes.

The team started the season with skill and style. Determined to prove to all the noisy critics. That the new school could make the playoffs. Even in the big, tougher league. But in the past few weeks, something going wrong. The trainer is worried. Because the players gaining so much weight on their tours. Eating all those steaks and drinking too much beer. Whatever they crave. Like snacks, ice cream, or junk food. Losing their self-discipline. The coach getting pretty angry, too. Especially after that great pep talk of his that should have inspired the team. He really disgusted.by their attitudes. When they were so sluggish. Which was hard to believe. That they could have fallen so far so fast.

_____

_____

_____

_____

_____

_____

_____

_____

_____

_____

_____

_____

Return to your writing

Read aloud the opinion paragraph you wrote at the beginning of this chapter. Look and listen for sentence fragments, and correct any that you find. Then make any other changes you think might help a reader understand your ideas.

Read a classmate's paragraph, looking for fragments. Suggest ways of correcting them.

Complete your work on sentence fragments by taking the Mastery Test on p. 339.

Chapter 9

Run-on Sentences

A run-on sentence contains two or more indepenent clauses with no connectors between them. If independent clauses are not separated into distinct sentences by a period, then they must be compounded by a conjunction or by a semicolon. Eliminating run-on sentences from your writing will help you make your thoughts easy for your reader to interpret.

Chapter 9 helps you to

- recognize run-on sentences.
- choose among four ways of correcting run-on sentences.
- avoid writing the three main types of run-on sentences.

You may want to start your work on run-ons by taking the Pretest on p. 317.

Writing

Think of things you know how to do; for instance, how to fix something, how to make something, how to play something. Pick one thing that you can do well and imagine what you would say to teach someone else to do it. Jot down all the steps in the process, including details and examples. Read over your notes and organize them into a paragraph that explains the process. Fit in the details and examples that would help a reader follow the explanation, and then rewrite your paragraph on a fresh piece of paper.

Look over your paragraph, making sure that independent clauses are either separated by periods or connected by conjunctions.

SPOTTING RUN-ON SENTENCES

When independent clauses meet in a sentence, they must be correctly compounded, or else they create a run-on sentence.

> This is not such an elegant playground,/still, the kids love it.

In the sentence above, a slash marks the spot where two independent clauses collide within the sentence. A comma does not prevent the collision; a run-on sentence with a comma between the two independent clauses is still a run-on sentence (this is sometimes called a *comma splice*).

Before you can recognize and correct run-on sentences, you need to be sure of the differences between independent and dependent clauses. Review Chapter 5, pp. 65–66.

Whenever you find more than one clause in a sentence, check to see whether some are embedded and whether any independent clauses collide. Start by circling any dependent words you see. Then underline subject + verb combinations, using broken lines for those that are introduced by dependent words.

> Those <u>swings</u> <u>are</u> the ones (that) <u>Dina</u> always <u>chooses</u>,/they <u>are</u> just her size.

The slash marks the point where a new independent clause begins without a conjunction.

APPLICATION 1.   Mark each sentence below:
Circle dependent words.
Put straight lines under the subjects and verbs of independent clauses. Put broken lines under the subjects and verbs of dependent clauses.
Draw a slash at the point where independent clauses collide.

Example: (Because) the <u>weather</u> <u>turned</u> so cool, <u>we</u> <u>changed</u> our plans,/<u>we</u> <u>will go</u> to the beach tomorrow.

1. The papers were all jumbled up, therefore, we couldn't find the report when we needed it.

2. Although the patients thrive there, the hospital isn't perfect, it seems awfully far from the center of town.

3. My boss has an idea that we should consider it might solve our problems.

4. The application is due tomorrow, could you type it up today, please?

5. These phone bills are puzzling me I refuse to pay them until you explain them.

6. Since Coleman came along, the bouncers have left us alone, they respect the reputation that he earned last fall.

7. It's dangerous to walk there alone you shouldn't go without me.

8. The icicles were melting, the tin bucket caught them.

9. Some household cleansers should not be mixed for example ammonia and bleach give off a poison gas when they're combined.

10. Look for hummingbirds around that tree, they've been nesting.

CORRECTING RUN-ON SENTENCES

The first way to correct a run-on sentence is to separate the independent clauses into distinct sentences.

playground. Still,

This is not such an elegant ~~playground, still,~~ the kids love it.

To correct a run-on sentence by this method, you need a period to mark the end of one sentence and a capital letter to mark the beginning of the next one.

APPLICATION 2.   Correct each of the following run-on sentences by crossing out the words at the point of collision and separating the sentences using a period and a capital letter.

plans. We

Example: Because the weather turned so cool, we changed our ~~plans, we~~ will

go to the beach tomorrow.

1. The papers were all jumbled up, therefore, we couldn't find the report when we needed it.

2. Although the patients thrive there, the hospital isn't perfect, it seems awfully far from the center of town.

3. My boss has an idea that we should consider it might solve our problems.

4. The application is due tomorrow, could you type it up today, please?

5. These phone bills are puzzling me I refuse to pay them until you explain them.

6. Since Coleman came along, the bouncers have left us alone, they respect the reputation that he earned last fall.

7. It's dangerous to walk there alone you shouldn't go without me.

8. The icicles were melting, the tin bucket caught them.

9. Some household cleansers should not be mixed for example ammonia and bleach give off a poison gas when they're combined.

10. Look for hummingbirds around that tree, they've been nesting.

A second method of correcting run-on sentences is to compound the independent clauses with a comma and a conjunction or with a semicolon.

, but
That dog is the one that helped me he still scares me.
^

When you compound independent clauses, put a comma in front of the conjunction. Remember that a comma by itself is not enough. Review these conjunctions:

and	so
but	or
yet	nor
for	

You may compound two clauses with a semicolon (;) in those rare cases where the clauses are so closely related that you don't need another word to show their relationship.

;
By 7:30, it was too late the show had already begun.
^

APPLICATION 3.   Correct each run-on sentence below by adding a comma and a conjunction. Use *and* only when no other conjunction will work. Instead of a conjunction, you may use a semicolon once or twice.

Example: I didn't finish yesterday's assignment ⌃ I have to do it before I start

tonight's work.

(insertion above caret: , and*)*

1. Glenda had better hurry she's sure to be late.

2. Make sure you have the pan ready to catch the oil then you can loosen the bolt.

3. Christmas toys are usually broken by the end of the day plan some other activities for your kids.

4. The papers were all jumbled up therefore, we couldn't find the report when we needed it.

5. Tino loves gourmet foods hot dogs are also fine with him.

6. This suntan lotion will make you the most popular person on the beach try some before it's too late.

7. Little bubbles of air form when you stretch your joints that's what you hear popping when you crack your knuckles.

8. Pollution control is important the ozone layer that blankets the earth is fragile.

9. The heaviest land bird in North America is the wild turkey there are heavier species in Australia.

19. The wind is filled with pollen in the spring take your allergy pills.

A third method of correcting run-on sentences is to take away the independence of one of the clauses by adding a dependent word.

> *unless*
> I won't pay these bills ^ you explain them to me right now.

When you put a dependent word in front of one clause, you deprive it of its independence and allow it to become embedded in the other clause (see Chapter 5, p. 74). The dependent words *who, whom, whose, which,* and *that* are special. When one of these introduces a clause, it replaces a word in the process:

> *which*
> This is Myrella's winning lottery ticket ^ she bought ~~it~~ at Corsetti's Market.

APPLICATION 4.   Correct each run-on sentence below by adding the dependent word shown in parentheses.

> *before*
> *Example:*   I think you met Alan ^ we borrowed his car on Tuesday. (before)

1. Type the application today, please it is due tomorrow. (since)

2. Those brittle leaves won't feel good under your sleeping bag they flatten out. (when)

3. Outside my window I caught sight of Mr. Battle's butterfly, it was emerging from its chrysalis. (which)

4. I might spray my plants with eggshell water it makes their roots grow faster than their leaves. (because)

5. The nearest star is Proxima Centuri it is 4.25 light-years away. (although)

6. It's dangerous to walk there alone, don't go without me. (because)

7. Franklin D. Roosevelt was a wartime president he was elected to four terms of office. (who)

8. Some difficult constitutional questions have arisen as a result of the surrogate mother custody suit it is being appealed in federal courts. (that)

9. She'll do well on her own she calls me every week. (unless)

10. The class is canceled the professor is finally arriving. (even though)

A final method of correcting run-on sentences is to reduce one independent clause to a verbal or verbal phrase.

> *The melting icicles*
> *Verbal*: ~~The icicles were melting they~~ dripped into the bucket below.
>
> *Moving slowly to the south side of the house, the sun*
> *Verbal phrase*: ~~The sun was moving slowly to the south side of the house it~~

thawed the roof gutters.

When you reduce a clause to a verbal or a verbal phrase, you can embed it in the remaining independent clause (see Chapter 5, pp. 75–76). This method doesn't work with all run-on sentences, but when it does, it packs the combined ideas efficiently into a small number of words.

APPLICATION 5.   Correct each run-on sentence below by changing the word or words in italics to a verbal or a verbal phrase. You will have to rewrite each sentence because you will be rearranging some of the words.

Example: Those firecrackers *are frightening* I don't think they should be part of the children's Fourth of July program. *I don't think those frightening firecrackers should be part of the children's Fourth of July program.*

Verbals

1. These phone bills *are puzzling* I won't pay them until you explain them.

   _____

   _____

2. Be careful of those snowmobiles they *are racing*. _____

   _____

3. You'll love this old recording it *has been taped*. _____

   _____

4. Mazie served us a platter of biscuits they *had been steamed*. _____

   _____

5. I don't want to ride on this trolley it's *crowded*. _____

_____

Verbal phrases

6. The toads *are sitting on the shoulders of the road in the rain* they don't fear the cars. _____

_____

7. I need to replace the blue sock it *was lost in the washing machine.* _____

_____

8. Marvin Hagler and Sugar Ray Leonard *were taking enormous risks* they faced each other for the ultimate fight of their careers. _____

_____

9. It's fascinating to watch the CIA it's *changing its strategy in Central America.*

_____

_____

10. The Berlin Wall *was erected overnight in August of 1961* it shows the human dimension of international policy. _____

_____

SUMMARY OF SOLUTIONS

When you discover a run-on sentence, you can correct it in one of four ways.

Run-on sentence: This cup is cracked, I don't want it.

Method 1 — Make two distinct sentences:

This cup is cracked. I don't want it.

Method 2 — Compound the independent clauses:

This cup is cracked, so I don't want it.

Method 3 — Embed one of the clauses using a dependent word:

If this cup is cracked, I don't want it.

Method 4 — Embed one of the clauses by reducing a verb to a verbal:

I don't want this cracked cup.

APPLICATION 6.   Correct the run-on sentences below by using each method.

Run-on sentence: That woman is snoring give her a nudge.

Method 1. _____

Method 2. _____

Method 3. _____

Method 4. _____

Run-on sentence: We were inspired by the news feature, we became organ donors.

Method 1. _____

Method 2. _____

Method 3. _____

Method 4. _____

AVOIDING RUN-ON SENTENCES

Be careful when one independent clause gives a command.

> When the command is based on the idea in the other clause, the close relationship between the ideas in the two clauses may make you feel that one is just a continuation of the other.
>
> *trap. Don't*
> A command can cause a punctuation ~~trap don't~~ fall into it.

APPLICATION 7.   Correct each run-on sentence below by using a period and a capital letter to create two distinct sentences.

mind. There
Example: Try to keep an open ~~mind there~~ are two sides to every argument.

1. This suntan lotion will make you the most popular man on the beach, try it before it's too late.

2. Christmas toys are usually broken by the end of the day plan some other activities for your kids.

3. Don't cook fancy meals for us there's not enough time for that.

4. Cigarettes gave me a nasty cough, avoid them if you're smart.

5. My children usually get home on time, don't count on it though.

6. Give me a chance to show you around there's plenty to do in this town.

7. Their apartment is on the fourth floor, take the elevator at the end of the hall.

8. Check the door I think the mail just came.

9. Almost everyone is a sucker for flattery don't get caught.

10. Talk with Sima soon, she thinks you're still in love with her.

Be careful when an independent clause begins with one of these pronouns: *I, you, he, she, it, we, they, this* or *that*.

These pronouns may make you feel that a new independent clause is a continuation of the previous one.

A pronoun refers to something that you've just ~~said that's~~ *said. That's* how a pronoun

creates a feeling of unity between sentences.

APPLICATION 8.   Correct each run-on sentence below by using a period and a capital letter to create two distinct sentences.

Example: We took good care of the bicycles that we rode up the ~~mountain,~~ *mountain.*
~~they~~ *They* were our only way of getting home.

1. The strongest light isn't bright enough that's why I wanted a lantern.

2. Your dentist won in the cash sweepstakes, he's retiring next week.

3. The strange moth hovered outside my window it was drying its wings.

4. Cheryl's car made it all the way to Montgomery, this proves my point about tune-ups.

5. Glenda had better hurry up she's sure to be late.

6. Those brittle leaves won't feel good under your sleeping bag they will flatten out immediately.

7. This watch is too much for me to handle, it's got an hourly chime and two video games built in.

8. Marcus is on a campaign against computers he's afraid of them.

9. Last year I tried surfing, it wasn't my sport, to put it mildly.

10. You should talk to my mother, she has lived here for thirty years.

Be careful when an independent clause begins with or includes a transitional expression.

Transitional expressions (also known as *adverbial conjunctions*) are neither dependent words nor conjunctions. They are simply expressions that show relationships between independent clauses.

These words link ideas ~~logically~~ ~~however~~, *logically. However,* they don't join clauses grammatically.

Here are some common transitional expressions:

Showing time and sequence	*Showing other relationships*
also	accordingly
besides	consequently
eventually	however
finally	likewise
first	nevertheless
furthermore	otherwise
later	similarly
meanwhile	still
moreover	therefore
next	thus
now	for example
then	for instance

Transitional expressions offer some of the occasions when semicolons are useful.

Transitional expressions show the relationship between two ideas; therefore, a semicolon is all you need to connect the clauses.

Notice that when a transitional expression begins a clause, it is followed by a comma.

APPLICATION 9.   Correct each run-on sentence below by adding a semicolon before the transitional expression and a comma after it.

Example: A college degree does not always make it easy to get a good job ⌃; for

example ⌃, my sister is still working at the supermarket.

1. You begin shucking the corn meanwhile Dan and I will get to work in the kitchen.

2. Tania said that she'd love a ride to the concert besides I know you wanted to ask her about yesterday's class.

3. The managers have been in the conference room all morning with the door shut eventually they will come out with answers to our questions.

4. The new phone system was supposed to help our calls go through more quickly however it does not seem to be working very well today.

5. I noticed little green shoots poking up in the garden nevertheless I don't think that spring has arrived to stay.

For more on transitional expressions, see p. 135 and p. 294.

APPLICATION 10.   Correct each run-on sentence below by using a period and a capital letter to create two distinct sentences.

Example: Gina has a great summer ~~job besides,~~ *job. Besides,* she can continue working ⌃

part-time after school opens.

1. You must first get the pan ready to catch the oil, next, you can loosen the bolt.

2. Students sort themselves by race, sex, and age in the cafeteria, for instance, look at the soda machine corner.

3. The washing machine kept chugging noisily the whole episode finally became a joke.

4. The groundhogs raided the lettuce patch however, the cat protected the blueberries.

5. Somebody must have told Zeke about the workshop, otherwise, he would never have gotten so excited.

REVIEW AND PRACTICE

A.

To see if a sentence is a run-on, check for two or more independent clauses with no conjunction between them. A comma is not a conjunction.

In each sentence below, put a slash at the point where one independent clause runs into another.

1. The three friends were laughing they threw wads of newspaper at each other until they wore themselves out.

2. The mess in the kitchen was forgotten, finally Jamaal decided to tackle it with a broom that he found in the hallway.

3. Meanwhile, the sun was rising, it gradually lit up the gray windows.

To correct a run-on sentence, you can separate the independent clauses into distinct sentences using a period and a capital letter.

Correct each of the following run-on sentences. Make each one into two distinct sentences.

4. The three friends were laughing they threw wads of newspaper at each other until they wore themselves out.

5. The mess in the kitchen was forgotten, finally Jamaal decided to tackle it with a broom he found in the hallway.

6. Meanwhile, the sun was rising, it gradually lit up the gray windows.

To correct a run-on sentence, you can compound the independent clauses using a conjunction or a semicolon.

Rewrite two of the following run-on sentences by compounding the independent clauses with a comma and a conjunction. Rewrite one of the run-ons by using a semicolon to compound the independent clauses.

7. The three friends were laughing they threw wads of newspaper at each other until they wore themselves out.

8. The mess in the kitchen was forgotten, finally Jamaal decided to tackle it with a broom he found in the hallway.

9. Meanwhile, the sun was rising, it gradually lit up the gray windows.

To correct a run-on sentence, you can embed one clause in the other, using a dependent word.

Rewrite each run-on sentence below as a sentence with an embedded dependent clause.

10. The three friends were laughing they threw wads of newspaper at each other until they wore themselves out.

11. The mess in the kitchen was forgotten, finally Jamaal decided to tackle it with a broom he found in the hallway.

12. Meanwhile, the sun was rising, it gradually lit up the gray windows.

To correct a run-on sentence, you can reduce one verb to a verbal and embed the verbal or verbal phrase.

Rewrite each run-on sentence below as a sentence with an embedded verbal or verbal phrase.

13. The three friends were laughing they threw wads of newspaper at each other until they wore themselves out.

14. The mess in the kitchen was forgotten, finally Jamaal decided to tackle it with a broom he found in the hallway.

15. Meanwhile, the sun was rising, it gradually lit up the gray windows.

You may be tempted to run two independent clauses together when one of them makes a command.

Correct each of the following run-on sentences by the method indicated.

16. Pickles and cheese make good garnishes for hot dogs, just try them. (Separate with a period and a capital letter.) _____

_____

17. You'd better get your motorcycle fixed you'll end up hitchhiking. (Combine with a conjunction.) _____

_____

18. Some candidates have behaved outrageously look out for bribes. (Deprive one clause of its independence by adding a dependent word.) _____

_____

19. Save the old wood for landfill it is rotting. (Reduce the second clause to a verbal and rewrite the sentence.) _____

_____

20. It's late and I'm in a hurry get your own lunch. (Combine with a semi-colon.) _____

_____

You may be tempted to run two independent clauses together when the second clause begins with a pronoun.

Correct each of the following run-on sentences by the method indicated.

21. Harmonicas are my favorite instruments they remind me of organ grinders and popcorn. (Separate with a period and a capital letter.) _____

_____

22. You're entitled to your opinion I wish you'd explain it to me. (Combine with a conjunction.) _____

_____

23. Bubblebath is a frivolous extravagance I buy it every week. (Deprive one clause of its independence by adding a dependent word.) _____

_____

24. I got tired of listening to that man in my carpool he was bragging. (Reduce the second clause to a verbal and rewrite the sentence.) _____

_____

25. Beatrice felt around in her pocket she was sobbing. (Deprive one clause of its independence by adding a dependent word.) _____

_____

You may be tempted to run two independent clauses together when the second clause contains a transitional modifier.

Correct each of the following run-on sentences by the method indicated.

26. Some of the animals have regained their strength, for example, the birds are returning. (Separate with a period and a capital letter.) _____

_____

27. The flowers fell from her hand, however, she didn't notice. (Combine with a semicolon.) _____

_____

28. Freddie says he'll climb Pike's Peak, then his brother will have to stop teasing him. (Combine with a conjunction.) _____

_____

29. The pitches swerved wildly, therefore, the umpire objected. (Separate with a period and a capital letter.) _____

_____

30. The wealthy executives gathered around the clown he was delighted. (Reduce the second clause to a verbal and rewrite the sentence.) _____

_____

B.

Rewrite the following paragraph, correcting the run-on sentences. You may separate independent clauses with a period and a capital letter, connect independent clauses with a conjunction or a semicolon, embed a clause using a dependent word, or change a clause to an embedded verbal or verbal phrase. Use as many different methods as you like.

The two runners started out evenly then the tall one pulled ahead the shorter one lagged behind she appeared discouraged already. The wind was harsh, after all this was October in Montana. The spectators began to disperse, suddenly the shorter runner put on speed she also lengthened her stride she was moving surprisingly fast, however, there were still twenty yards between her and the leader. The sun began to set the runners leaned into the turn in the road they seemed to shrink into the purple light, it was fading finally they disappeared over the crest of the hill.

_____

_____

_____

_____

_____

_____

_____

_____

_____

_____

_____

_____

Return to your writing

Read aloud the paragraph you wrote at the beginning of this chapter describing how to do something. Correct any run-on sentences that you find. Make any other changes you'd like in the paragraph.

Read a classmate's paragraph, looking for run-on sentences. Suggest ways of correcting them.

Complete your work on run-on sentences by taking the Mastery Test on p. 341.

Chapter 10
Final -*ed*

Both the simple past and the past participle form of regular verbs end in -*ed*. When you speak, you might be in the habit of dropping this ending. In writing, however, you must use standard English verb forms. If you omit a final -*ed* when writing a simple past or past participle form of a regular verb, you make it hard for a reader to follow your thought.

Chapter 10 will help you to

- recognize and use -*ed* endings in the simple past tense and in past participles.
- avoid incorrect uses of final -*ed*.

You may want to start your work on final -*ed* by taking the Pretest on p. 319.

Writing

Think about doing something for the first time. List the memorable first times in your life: for example, your first day of school, your first special religious occasion, your first failure, your first moment of triumph, your first job interview, your first day on the job, your first apartment, your first child, your first long trip, the first funeral you attended, your first experience with injustice. Now pick just one event to write about. Imagine the situation in detail and jot down some notes about this event. Organize your notes into a paragraph, then copy your paragraph onto a fresh piece of paper.

Read your paragraph aloud. Circle every word that ends in *-ed*.

RECOGNIZING FINAL -*ed*

Sometimes final -*ed* is hard to hear in speech.

> As the acrobats waited for their turns on the ladder, they looked* dashing in their spangled* tunics.

In speech, the sound of each of the starred -*ed* endings gets swallowed up in the beginning sound of the next word.

APPLICATION 1. The following paragraphs are the introduction and conclusion of a student's essay. Read them through, circling each word that ends in -*ed*. Then read the paragraphs aloud, listening for the -*ed* endings.

Have you ever walked across a dark, lonely, deserted street or parking lot and for one reason or another been scared because you thought you were going to be mugged or battered? If you've answered "yes" to this question, don't feel ashamed because you're in the great majority. I asked myself this same question about seven years ago and bravely decided to do something about the problem. I wanted to be able to control fear before it controlled me. I learned to control my fear and become more self-confident through the martial arts. . . .

I have now earned my orange belt in Kenpo and my green belt in Shorin-Ryu. Looking back over the past seven years, I realize that I have learned much more than I had first wanted to. The philosophies of the martial arts can be used for much more than self-defense. To sum it all up, let me recall the words of my master, Eddie Parker: "I come to you with only karate, empty hands. I have no weapons, but should I be forced to defend myself, my principles, or my honor, then here are my weapons: karate, my empty hands."

— Andrew DiSilvestro

If you have to make a special effort to pronounce the -*ed* endings in your speech, you're not alone. Many of us, speaking at a normal pace, slur some -*ed* endings, so we can't expect to rely completely on our ears to tell us where to put -*ed* endings in our writing.

In standard English, *regular verbs* end with *-ed* in four situations:

1. A regular verb in the simple past tense ends with *-ed*.

   I will borrow your shirt because you **borrowed** my hat.

2. A regular verb in a perfect tense consists of some form of the auxiliary *to have* (*has, have,* or *had*) and the past participle of the main verb, which ends with *-ed*.

   I **had borrowed** a belt before the concert, but now someone **has borrowed** it from me.

3. A regular verb in the passive voice consists of some form of the auxiliary *to be* (such as *is, are, were*) and the past participle of the main verb, which ends with *-ed*.

   I think that it **was borrowed** by the announcer.

4. The past participle can be used as a verbal that modifies another word. If the participle is a form of *regular verb*, it will end in *-ed*.

   Leaving **borrowed** clothes in the costume room was a bad idea.

APPLICATION 2.   Go back to the two paragraphs in Application 1. Look closely at the words you've circled. Above each circled word, mark 1, 2, 3, or 4 to indicate the type of *-ed* ending:

1 = simple past tense   3 = passive voice
2 = perfect tense   4 = modifying participle

Check the Answer Key at the back of the book before you go any further. Discuss any questions you have with your teacher until you feel sure that you can identify each of the *-ed* endings.

Your work on *-ed* endings in the rest of this chapter will be easier if you review the relevant verb and verbal patterns. Take a few minutes to review Chapter 2, pages 26–28, and Chapter 5, pages 70–72.

USING THE FINAL *-ed* IN THE SIMPLE PAST TENSE

The simple past tense expresses past action through a one-word verb. Although irregular verbs have unpredictable spellings for their simple past forms, every regular verb in the simple past tense ends in *-ed*.

> Einstein **dreaded** the development of the atomic bomb, although he **recognized** that his work made it inevitable.

APPLICATION 3.   Rewrite each of the following sentences, changing the verbs to the simple past tense. Some of the verbs are irregular, but most are regular.

> *Example:*   The waiter approaches the table and suddenly starts to sing.
> *The waiter approached the table and suddenly started to sing.*

1. When the singing waiter finishes "Happy Birthday," the large woman pushes her chair back from the table. _____

2. Angrily she whispers to her husband something about waiting in the car.

3. He glances in surprise at her face and notices her red cheeks. _____

4. As she stalks out, he observes that her usual carefree walk seems stiff.

5. He tries to understand what is wrong. _____

6. Normally she thrives on being the center of attention. _____

7. Then it dawns on him that she hates surprises. _____

8. Blushing, he apologizes to the waiter and goes to face the music in the car.

   _____

   _____

9. The other people in the restaurant politely turn away and pretend not to

   notice. _____

   _____

10. But as the door closes behind him, everyone begins to comment on the

    little scene. _____

    _____

Now read your new sentences aloud, listening for the *-ed* endings.

APPLICATION 4.   The paragraph below is from the same essay on karate as the paragraphs you read earlier, but here the verbs have been changed to the present tense. Cross out each present tense verb and replace it with the simple past form to restore the paragraph to its original time framework.

The incident that ~~convinces~~ *convinced* me to learn martial arts happens when I am in the navy. Walking back to my ship with two friends one night, I notice some guys ahead of us who start making some stupid, drunken remarks. I realize immediately that these people are fairly intoxicated, and I try to ignore their antics. But one of my buddies is pretty drunk himself, and he decides not to let his friends be badgered by anyone. So he responds with his own nasty comments. This continues as we approach our ship. Now the gentlemen ahead of us stop and wait for us to reach them. They begin to zero in on my drunken buddy, who just becomes more agitated. My sober friend and I are trying to talk our drunken friend out of a confrontation when suddenly, out of the blue, I feel myself taking a couple of steps backward. I have been sucker-punched for no reason! Of course, this annoys me and I tackle my opponent. I'm not a good fighter, so I just want to hold him back from hitting me again. The fight is broken up by the quarterdeck personnel.

Now read the new version of the paragraph aloud, emphasizing the -*ed* endings.

USING THE FINAL -*ed* IN THE PERFECT TENSES

The perfect tenses combine a form of the auxiliary *to have* with the past participle of a main verb. When the main verb is regular, the past participle ends in -*ed*.

If Einstein **had lived** longer, he **might have worked** for a test ban treaty.

APPLICATION 5.   Rewrite the following sentences, putting each verb in the present perfect tense. You will be using either *has* or *have* as an auxiliary. Some of the verbs are irregular, but most are regular.

Example: I see few performers who appeal to a wider audience than that musician. *I have seen few performers who have appealed to a wider audience than that musician.*

1. I listen to some great conversations when I wait in ticket lines. _____
   _____

2. People confess all sorts of things to absolute strangers. _____
   _____

3. Today one woman describes the diet she uses for increasing her spiritual awareness. _____
   _____

4. A middle-aged man explains why he always leaves his wives after three years of marriage. _____
   _____

5. A tall teenager brags about how she succeeds in the lottery every week.
   _____
   _____

6. Each time, someone responds. _____

7. I don't believe all of these stories, but I enjoy them. _____

_____

8. I jot down some of these conversations. _____

_____

9. I try to imagine a novel including all these characters and their stories.

_____

_____

10. Taking notes for my novel entertains me during long waits that bore even

my most patient friends. _____

_____

USING FINAL -ed WITH VERBS IN THE PASSIVE VOICE

In the passive voice, a form of the auxiliary *to be* is used with the past
participle of a main verb. If the main verb is regular, it will end in *-ed* in
the passive voice.

> Soon the yard will **be cleared** and Sophie will be happy to see how care-
> fully the trees **were pruned**.

Remember that the passive voice indicates a sentence structure in which the
subject isn't performing the action of the sentence (see Chapter 2, p. 28). Notice
in the sentence above that the time of the verb is marked by the auxiliary, not
by the main verb. The main verb is always in its past participle form, no matter
what time the verb is expressing.

APPLICATION 6.   Change each of the following sentences from the active to the passive
voice. Make sure that each new verb in the passive voice expresses the same
time as the verb in the original sentence.

Example: The new treasurer budgets the funds for the class trip.

The funds for the class trip _are budgeted_ by the new treasurer.

1. In the chemistry lab, the assistants measure the powders. In the chemistry

lab, the powders _____ by the assistants.

2. Then for each group of students, the professor assigns a task. Then for each group of students, a task _____ by the professor.

3. Students in pairs will complete the experiments. The experiments _____ by students in pairs.

4. They will record their results in lab logs. Their results _____ _____ in the lab logs.

5. The students have finished last month's big projects. Last month's big projects _____ by the students.

6. The assistants stored those powerful acids immediately. Those powerful acids _____ by the assistants immediately.

7. Everyone rinsed out test tubes carefully after that. Test tubes _____ _____ carefully by everyone after that.

8. In a matter of seconds, one drop of that acid can damage a thick leather boot. In a matter of seconds, a thick leather boot _____ _____ by one drop of acid.

9. The lab assistants passed a new rule. A new rule _____ _____ by the lab assistants.

10. The whole department now requires everyone to use safety goggles in the lab. Everyone's use of safety goggles _____ by the whole department.

USING THE FINAL -ed IN PAST PARTICIPLES THAT ACT AS MODIFIERS

When a past participle appears by itself, without any auxiliary, it becomes a verbal that acts as a modifier. The past participle of a regular verb ends in -ed.

Agitated by the music, the crowd waved hundreds of **painted** flags.

Most modifying participles are closely related to verbs in the passive voice. Look at the verb in the sentence below:

The crowd **was silenced** by the words of the nun.

Although *was silenced* is the complete verb string, notice that *silenced* actually describes the subject. You could drop the auxiliary *was* and embed *silenced*, making it work as a modifying verbal:

Silenced by the nun's words, the crowd drew closer. The nun spoke quietly to the **silenced** crowd.

APPLICATION 7.   Review the sentences you wrote in the passive voice for Application 6. Several of those passive verbs have been turned into modifying verbals listed below. Write a new sentence using each phrase.

Example: the budgeted funds *Happily, the budgeted funds were recovered before the end of the school year.*

1. the measured powders _____

    _____

2. the assigned task _____

    _____

3. the completed experiments _____

    _____

4. last month's finished projects _____

    _____

5. a damaged leather boot _____

    _____

APPLICATION 8.   The first sentence in each pair below contains a clause in the passive voice. The second sentence in each pair leaves a blank for a modifying past participle that comes from the passive voice verb. Insert the appropriate past participle in the blank.

Example: Nuclear warheads *that have been disarmed* remain a powerful symbol of the threat of global war. *Disarmed nuclear warheads* remain a powerful symbol of the threat of global war.

1. The tree, *which was brightly decorated*, amazed the pedestrians. The brightly _____ tree amazed the pedestrians.

2. They had never seen a tree *that was so brilliantly finished.* They had never seen such a brilliantly _____ tree.

3. The mayor, *who was pleased,* smiled at the crowd. The _____ mayor smiled at the crowd.

4. He studied their faces, *which were delighted and dazzled.* He studied their _____ faces.

5. Then he threw away his speech *that had been prepared.* Then he threw away his _____ speech.

AVOIDING INCORRECT *-ed* ENDINGS

Do not add *-ed* to any verb form that immediately follows the word *to*.

With -ed	Without -ed
Gordon climbed the ladder.	Gordon hurried **to climb** the ladder.
He looked in the window.	He tried **to look** in the window.

In the sentences on the left above, *climbed* and *looked* are verbs. In the sentences on the right, *to climb* and *to look* are infinitives and therefore have no *-ed* endings.

APPLICATION 9.   On each line below, complete a sentence that uses the infinitive of the italicized verb.

Example: I *entered* my essay in the statewide competition. I decided <u>*to enter my*</u> <u>*essay in the statewide competition.*</u>

1. Smoke *filled* the room. Smoke started _____.

2. Gordon *called* to the baby. Gordon began _____.

3. Finding her, he *shouted* for joy. Finding her, he needed _____ _____.

4. Olga *offered* her congratulations. Olga wanted _____ _____.

5. She *acted* relaxed and casual. She tried _____ _____.

Do not add *-ed* to the first verb that follows any auxiliary other than *to be* and *to have*.

With -ed	*Without -ed*
We sprayed for cockroaches today.	We should spray for cockroaches today.
We slowed down the invasion.	We might slow down the invasion.

In the sentences on the left, *sprayed* and *slowed* are single-word verbs. In the sentences on the right, *spray* and *slow* are main verbs following an auxiliary other than *to be* or *to have*. Here is a list of the auxiliaries that must be followed by a base form:

> will, shall
> can, could
> would, should
> may, might, must
> do, does, did

APPLICATION 10.   On each line below, complete a sentence that contains a two-word verb string by using one of the auxiliaries listed above and the base form of the italicized verb.

Example: She *arrived* in plenty of time. She ___*should arrive in plenty of time.*___

1. My children *saved* their outgrown baseball cleats. _____

   _____

2. They *collected* several years' worth. _____

   _____

3. Then they *lined* them up on a table. _____

   _____

4. They *talked* about them with their friends. _____

   _____

5. Those old shoes *helped* them to recall their glorious games. _____

   _____

APPLICATION 11.   Turn each of the following sentences into a question, and then answer the question with a negative statement. Use the auxiliary *did* in each question and answer.

Example: Charlotte joined Jeanne at the lake.

Question: *Did Charlotte join Jeanne at the lake?*

Answer: *Charlotte did not join Jeanne at the lake.*

1. Charlotte baited the hook.

   Question: _____

   Answer: _____

2. She hated that job.

   Question: _____

   Answer: _____

3. Her line sailed out over the water.

   Question: _____

   Answer: _____

4. The sinker dropped neatly beside a marker buoy.

   Question: _____

   Answer: _____

5. She settled down for a slow and satisfying afternoon.

   Question: _____

   Answer: _____

REVIEW AND PRACTICE

A.

An *-ed* ending that is hard to hear in speech may be easy to forget in writing.

Read the following sentences aloud, circling all words that end in *-ed*. Put an asterisk (*) by those in which the sound of the *-ed* is hard to hear.

1. At the forum, some people claimed that inflation could be reduced by wage and price controls.

2. The most respected researcher insisted that controls would hurt newly hired trainees.

3. Most of the panelists agreed to present their statements in the published report.

4. When the forum ended, the audience applauded for a long time.

5. Someone asked if the discussion might be continued later.

A final *-ed* marks a regular verb in the simple past tense.

Fill each blank with the simple past tense of the designated verb.

6. Our visitors _____ longer than we _____.

to stay   to expect

7. We _____ up some leftovers and _____ throughout

to warm   to talk

   supper.

8. They _____ our grown-up kids.

to remember

9. We _____ having a chance to reminisce.

to enjoy

10. I even _____ them our old pictures.

to show

A final *-ed* marks the past participle of a regular verb used in a perfect tense.

Fill each blank with *has* or *have* plus the past participle of the designated verb.

11. Wanda and Paul _____ seeing each other.
        to stop

12. I _____ Wanda what _____.
        to ask   to happen

13. Each time she _____ it off.
                    to shrug

14. She _____ me like this before, too.
            to evade

15. Usually, though, I _____ her to talk.
                        to convince

A final *-ed* marks the past participle of a regular verb used in the passive voice.

Fill each blank with *is* or *are* plus the past participle of the designated verb.

16. Students in this college _____ by publicity tricks.
                                to influence

17. I   _____   at   how   easily   their   opinions
            to surprise

_____.
    to sway

18. For instance, a lot of students are voting for the new class schedule just

    because it _____ so cleverly.
                to advertise

19. But others _____ against the schedule because they
                    to prejudice

    don't like the tune of the advertising jingle.

20. The issue of propaganda power _____ to become a big
                                        to predict

    one on campus in the coming months.

A final *-ed* marks the past participle of a regular verb that works as a modifying verbal.

Modify each underlined word by adding the past participle of the designated verb.

21. We call this a _____ world, but it operates on some pretty prim-
    to civilize

    itive principles.

22. Physical force is still our most _____ form of security.
    to trust

23. A few people try to direct the future of the whole planet from behind

    _____ doors.
    to close

24. Some groups are beginning to challenge the old _____ ways of
    to accept

    doing things.

25. The _____ old slogans are being questioned.
    to tire

Don't add *-ed* to a verb form that follows the word *to*.

Cross out the incorrect *-ed* endings in the sentences below.

26. Finally Angela decided to delivered the package herself.

27. She wanted to considered the boss's reaction.

28. She started to steered the truck onto the highway.

29. She planned to explained her action with an appeal to April's sense of humor.

30. April was too amazed to laughed.

Don't add *-ed* to the first verb that follows one of these auxiliaries: *will, shall, can, could, would, should, may, might, must, do, does, did*.

Cross out the incorrect *-ed* endings in the sentences below.

31. Every time Wallace warmed up to tell a joke, Frank would nudged him to be quiet.

32. Wallace did not liked feeling that his jokes were censored.

33. But Frank believed that Wallace's wit might wrecked their chances for this job.

34. Frank could remembered at least two occasions when Wallace got carried away.

35. This interview should not ended the same way.

B.

Remember the student essay on karate whose opening and closing paragraphs you worked with at the beginning of this chapter. The writer of this essay used the simple past tense to establish the time of the events, and -ed endings appeared on past participles wherever they were needed. The two paragraphs below are from the same essay, but their -ed endings have been removed. Put them back where they belong.

As I thought about that fight the following day, I realize two things. First, I didn't enjoy being punch. Second, I didn't know how to defend myself. Fortunately, one of my supervisors was highly skill in karate, and after I explain what had happen, he suggest that I should learn karate. I eagerly agree and we began exercising then and there. Every day he demonstrate and I practice the assign techniques. After I learn the basics, we discontinue our class.

About two and a half years later I was discharged from the navy. Upon returning to my hometown, I decide to pursue the martial arts beyond the basics. I enroll at the local Kenpo karate school and began learning the Kenpo style and its philosophy. It became very clear to me that there was more to the martial arts than just self-defense. I learn how to meditate, how to be more alert, and how to control pain through breathing techniques of the *Khi* (inner force).

Return to your writing

Read aloud the paragraph you wrote at the beginning of this chapter. Listen for *-ed* endings. Check to see that they are all in the right places. If not, correct them. Make any other changes you feel might be helpful to a reader.

Read a classmate's paragraph, looking especially for misplaced or missing *-ed* endings. Suggest corrections.

Complete your work on final *-ed* by taking the Mastery Test on p. 343.

Chapter 11

Final *-s*

Final *-s* causes confusion because it has several different meanings in standard English. The *-s* on the end of a verb usually marks a singular form, whereas *-s* on the end of a noun usually marks a plural form. To complicate matters further, the spelling of some words (such as *loss* and *gas*) includes an *-s* ending that carries no grammatical information at all. Understanding the uses of final *-s* will help you to write clearly.

Chapter 11 helps you distinguish among three *-s* endings and use them correctly:

- natural *-s* (built into the spellings of some words);
- plural *-s* on nouns;
- third person singular present tense *-s* on verbs.

- You may want to start your work on final *-s* by taking the Pretest on p. 321.

Writing

Think of someone you know very well. How can you tell when that person is sad, tired, pleased, angry, touched, proud, and so on? Pick one emotion and picture how the person shows that emotion through actions and gestures. Does he wave his hands in the air? Does she talk very slowly? Does he move his eyes in a certain way? Does she rush from one place to another? Jot down the clues that you notice when you realize the person is feeling the emotion you've picked. Then arrange your ideas into a paragraph and write it on a fresh sheet of paper. Start your paragraph with this sentence:

I can always tell when _____ is feeling _____ because . . .

Read your paragraph aloud. Circle every word that ends in -*s*.

RECOGNIZING FINAL -s

Many speakers do not pronounce final -s.

Read this sentence aloud:

The earth rotates on its axis 93 million miles away from the sun.

In some speech communities, the words *rotates* and *miles* will sound like *rotate* and *mile*. However, standard English requires that these -s endings should be heard in speech and seen in writing.

APPLICATION 1.   The following essay was written by a student. Read it, circling each word that ends in -s. Then read it aloud, listening for the -s endings.

Making money these days is a real challenge. First you have to race with inflation. Every time you start to catch up, something happens to set you back. The price of food seems to go up whenever you go to the store, and your food bills just get bigger every week. Then there are the gas and oil bills. They're all right in the summer, but when winter comes along, you either freeze or go broke. On top of all that comes paying the rent, which is just like burning money. The way things look now, we won't ever see prices going down — only up.

Another challenge is finding a good job that pays well. It seems you have to have either a college education or some kind of trade before you can apply, and that still does not mean you'll get hired. There are so many people who are looking for work and so few jobs available that the competition gets fierce. Lots of times you just have to settle for a job that will get you by until you find something better. As long as unemployment stays this high, even those jobs are hard to find.

The only way things are going to change is for the government to get out of debt. Interest rates can't go down until the government gets the deficit under control. And as long as interest rates are high, companies can't afford to borrow the money they need to stay in business. When companies cut back on business or fold, more people get laid off, and jobs become even scarcer for everyone. Making enough money to live on will just get harder and harder until something changes. I hope that happens soon.

— John Carey

If the -s endings sound strange, then your speaking dialect may be one that doesn't use the added -s. Start listening carefully to your own speech and to that of other people, tuning in to the sound of final -s. Every day as you read textbooks, newspaper or magazine articles, or a novel, pick out several paragraphs to read aloud, listening to the -s endings as you pronounce them. Train your ear to hear them in conversations and your eye to notice them as you read. Meanwhile, study the rules of standard English to understand where to put the final -s in your writing.

In standard English, -s appears on words in three situations.

1. Some words simply wouldn't be complete without the final -s. This is the **natural -s**.

kiss   conscious
bus   his

2. An -s (sometimes -es) is added to most nouns to signal a quantity of more than one. This is the **plural -s**.

one noun ⟶ two nouns
one home ⟶ several homes
an idea ⟶ many ideas
this quality ⟶ these qualities

(Chapter 14 explains how -y often changes to -i before the -es ending and when to use -es instead of -s in other situations.)

3. An -s (sometimes -es) appears on verbs in the present tenses with singular subjects other than *I* or *you*. This is the **present tense -s**. This -s is added to the end of single-word verbs, or absorbed into the word *is, has,* or *does* in verb strings.

I drink tea but she drinks rum.
You lose whenever your horse los**es**.
We're doing a terrific job while Mark i**s** doing nothing at all.
All of our visits have been pleasant, but this ha**s** been the best.

APPLICATION 2.   Go back to the essay in Application 1. Look closely at the words you've circled. Above each circled word, mark 1, 2, or 3 to indicate the type of -*s* ending:

     1 = natural -*s*

     2 = plural -*s*

     3 = present tense -*s*

Check the Answer Key at the back of the book before you go any further. Discuss your questions with your teacher until you're sure that you can identify each of the -*s* endings.

The natural -*s* won't give you much trouble. You probably use its sound in your speech and therefore represent its sound in your writing. But the plural -*s* and the present tense -*s* often cause problems. The following pages examine these added -*s* endings more closely.

USING FINAL -*s* ON PLURAL NOUNS

Final -*s* signals the plural form of most nouns.

Most nouns need an added final -*s* (sometimes -*es*) when they label more than one person, place, or thing.

     this captain ⟶ these captains
     a mansion ⟶ several mansions
     an insult ⟶ a few insults

Natural -*s* nouns have to end in -*s* even when they don't represent a plural quantity, so these nouns add -*es* when they become plural.

     one loss ⟶ three losses
     a glass ⟶ several glasses
     that lens ⟶ those lenses

But a few nouns don't need -*s* to represent a plural quantity. They form their plurals in some other way. These are **irregular plurals**.

     a child ⟶ many children
     one man ⟶ ten men
     this woman ⟶ these women
     that person ⟶ those people

TIP: Except for the natural -*s* nouns, singular nouns do not end in -*s*. Except for the irregular plurals, plural nouns end in -*s*.

APPLICATION 3.   Rewrite the sentences below, changing each italicized singular noun to a plural noun.

Example: Please bring your *journal* to the meeting this afternoon. <u>*Please bring*</u> <u>*your journals to the meeting this afternoon.*</u>

1. Chris wanted to develop a *skill* after he graduated from high school. Chris wanted to develop some _____

   _____

2. He applied to a computer *school*. He applied to three _____

   _____

3. Belinda was an old *friend* who studied programming. Belinda and Simon were two old _____

4. They convinced him he'd find a *job* when he finished. They convinced him he'd find many _____

5. So he went to an *interview* and talked to the *person* in the admissions office. So he went to a few _____

   _____

6. One *woman* told him what the first *class* would probably be like. A couple of _____

7. Suddenly he realized that he'd go crazy sitting in a *chair* all day long watching shadows move around on some *screen*. Suddenly he realized _____

   _____

8. Then he met an electronic *technician* who told him about the *pleasure* of working on the insides of a big *computer*. Just then he met three electronic

   _____

9. Chris changed his *plan* immediately. Chris changed _____

   _____

10. He has been taking an electronics *course* for a *year* now, and he has already signed one repair *contract*. He has been taking several _____ for

    three _____ now, and he has already signed two _____

    _____

APPLICATION 4.   In the following paragraph, cross out every singular noun and write its plural form above it. You may have to cross out the word *a* at times or change a singular pronoun to a plural one (*he* to *they; his* to *their*) in order to complete the plural pattern.

        engines
At last the ~~engine~~ stopped idling. The pilot couldn't see around the hangar, but his control panel reassured him. The seat behind the cockpit held a plump commuter sipping contentedly from a glass. This man clearly thought he deserved his comfort. His face reflected the expectations that his journey would be as mild and sweet as the drink in his hand. As the wing of the plane rounded the bend by the searchlight, the pilot looked up from the panel and gasped. Toward him, as if emerging from a mirror, taxied an identical airliner, piloted by an identically gasping captain.

A prepositional phrase beginning with *of* often requires a plural noun, even when the word modified by the phrase is clearly singular.

        One ⟨of my shoes⟩ is covered with mud.
        I'll wipe it with the last ⟨of your rags⟩.

APPLICATION 5.   In the following sentences, fill each blank with the plural form of the noun below the line.

   1. Either of the _____ is likely to work this time.
                 machine

   2. Even the most dedicated of the _____ is eager for a break.
                                 student

   3. The last one of my potato _____ has been eaten.
                          chip

   4. The only one of the _____ without a smudge is this one.
                         menu

   5. We expect that one of the _____ will fit.
                          bolt

APPLICATION 6. In each of these sentences, a singular noun is italicized. Rewrite each sentence, putting that noun in a phrase beginning with the preposition *of*. You will have to add an *-s* to make the noun plural in its new prepositional phrase.

Example: I was sitting on the porch and admiring the oldest dogwood *tree*.

I was sitting on the porch and admiring the oldest of the dogwood trees.

1. One *blossom* fell from the tree. _____

2. Suddenly the wind increased and bent one *clothesline* down. _____

_____

3. I watched anxiously for the last *kid* to come in for shelter. _____

_____

4. I couldn't see either *girl* through the heavy rain that had started. _____

_____

5. That was one *storm* we'll never forget. _____

_____

USING FINAL -s FOR PRESENT TENSE VERBS

With singular subjects other than *you* or *I*, verbs in the simple present tense add *-s*.

Some liquids **boil** at low temperatures, but water **boils** at 212 degees Farenheit.

Except for *to be*, all English verbs use their base forms to express the simple present tense (see Chapter 2, p. 25). But when the subject of the verb is **singular** (only one), and is neither *you* nor *I*, the verb takes an added *-s*. Here's how it works with the verb *to think*:

Singular	*Plural*
I think	we think
you think	you think
she thinks, he thinks, it thinks	they think
⟨*any other singular subject*⟩ thinks	⟨*any other plural subject*⟩ think

APPLICATION 7.   Fill each blank with the simple present tense form of the designated verb.

to watch

1. I _____ for the changes.

2. You _____ for them, too.

3. My brother _____ from his own angle.

4. He _____ for new evidence.

5. We all _____ in great suspense.

to hope

6. You _____ for a clue.

7. I _____ you'll find one.

8. The moody woman around the corner _____ for a clue.

9. She _____ for one every day, and so does her sister.

10. They _____ to solve the mystery.

APPLICATION 8.   Fill each blank with the simple present tense form of the verb given below the line. Put only one word in each blank.

The old house ____*sits*____ in the field, surrounded by trees. The roof
                to sit

_____ and the door _____ on its hinges. Occasionally
  to droop   to sag

a whine _____ from the chimney. Then, abruptly, silence
        to rise

_____ over me like a soft blanket. I _____ as I
  to fall   to tremble

_____ the house. But it _____ me and it _____
  to face   to fascinate   to draw

me forward.

The present tense *-s* is built into the words *is, has,* and *does*.

Here are the present tense forms of *to be, to have,* and *to do*.

PRESENT TENSE FORMS

	Singular	*Plural*
TO BE	I am	we are
	you are	you are
	he is, she is, it is	they are
	⟨any other singular subject⟩ is	⟨any other plural subject⟩ are

	Singular	*Plural*
TO HAVE	I have	we have
	you have	you have
	she has, he has, it has	they have
	⟨any other singular subject⟩ has	⟨any other plural subject⟩ have

	Singular	*Plural*
TO DO	I do	we do
	you do	you do
	he does, she does, it does	they do
	⟨any other singular subject⟩ does	⟨any other plural subject⟩ do

---

You can see from the charts that the words *is, has,* and *does* are used only with singular subjects other than *I* and *you*.

APPLICATION 9.   In each blank, insert the correct form of *to be* in the simple present tense.

If I _____*am*_____ your uncle, then you _____ my long-lost nephew. Finally we _____ together after all those years of upheaval in our homeland. In front of all these people, I _____ too shy to say

much. Some of them _____ relatives, too, but you _____
the only one I want to laugh and cry with. Let's tell that photographer that he
_____ a nuisance. The lady beside him _____ a gentle soul.
She'll get him out of here for us. It _____ amazing to me that my
dream _____ a reality at last.

APPLICATION 10.   In each blank, insert the correct form of *to have* in the simple present
tense.

You _____*have*_____ no idea how tired I am of that bus driver's attitude. I
_____ three children who horse around now and then on the bus.
After school they _____ so much pent-up energy that I think they
_____ every right to be a little high-spirited. But their bus _____
a real sourpuss for a driver. She _____ a long list of rules that she
refers to whenever she _____ any excuse, and she barks them out at
the kids. She _____n't got any kids of her own. I'll bet you a week's
groceries on that.

APPLICATION 11.   In each blank, insert the correct form of *to do*
in the simple present tense.

When you _____*do*_____ time in jail, the other prisoners sometimes
_____ a job on your self-image. It's a good plan to watch what the
most experienced prisoner _____ when people are baiting him.
_____ not try to copy what he _____ exactly; just try to
figure out why he acts the way he _____. That always _____
a lot to put you on top of the situation.

**When present tense forms of *to be*, *to have*, and *to do* act as auxiliaries in
verb strings, they follow the same pattern.**

> I **am drying** my hair. ⟶ The sun **is drying** my hair.
> The breezes **have dried** my hair. ⟶ The breeze **has dried** my hair.
> You **don't dry** my hair. ⟶ Your towel **doesn't dry** my hair.

Remember that only singular subjects other than *I* and *you* take the present tense -*s*.

The present progressive tense combines the present participle form of a verb with a present tense form of *to be*.

> The Asian Student Union **is planning** a marathon open only to bilingual or multilingual students who **are living** in this state.

APPLICATION 12.   Fill each blank with the present progressive tense of the verb given. Use *am, is,* or *are* plus the present participle form of the main verb.

to sing

1. You _____ on the porch.
2. I _____ in spite of myself.
3. The caged bird _____ along with you.
4. The wind _____ as splendidly as that bird.
5. We _____ to celebrate the coming of the rain.

to dance

6. I _____ until midnight.
7. A cranky old chaperone _____ with me.
8. The picture of him _____ hilariously through my mind.
9. It _____ in my imagination.
10. You and the gang _____ there, too.

APPLICATION 13.   Fill each blank with the present progressive tense of the verb given below the line. Put a two-word verb in each blank.

The old house _____*is sitting*_____ in the field, surrounded by
                          to sit

trees. The roof _____ and the door
                          to droop

_____ on its hinges. Occasionally a whine
        to sag

_____ from the chimney. Then, abruptly, si-
        to rise

lence _____ over me like a soft blanket. I
            to fall

_____ as I _____ the house. But it
     to tremble   to face

_____ me and it _____ me forward.
     to fascinate   to draw

The present perfect tense combines the past participle of a main verb with a
present tense form of *to have*.

> Finally the printer **has completed** the poster and the sponsors **have signed**
> for the bill.

APPLICATION 14.   Fill each blank with the present perfect tense of the verb given. Use *has*
or *have* plus the past participle form of the main verb.

to work

1. You _____ on that suit for a long time.

2. The two new tailors _____ on it from time to time,
   too.

3. In the same period of time, I _____ on three dresses.

4. Maybe my sewing machine _____ better than yours
   this week.

5. Oiling it every day _____ all its kinks out.

to begin

6. I _____ my daily exercises, right here on the bus.

7. Someone in the back seat _____ to laugh.

8. The people sitting in front of me _____ to turn
   around.

9. The bus driver _____ his speech about staying seated.

10. You _____ to be embarrassed about sitting next to me.

APPLICATION 15.   Fill each blank with the present perfect tense of the verb given below the line. Put a two-word verb in each blank.

The old house _____*has sat*_____ in the field, surrounded by

to sit

trees.   The   roof   _____   and   the   door

to droop

_____ on its hinges. Occasionally a whine

to sag

_____ from the chimney. Then, abruptly, si-

to rise

lence _____ over me like a soft blanket. I

to fall

_____ as I _____ the house. But it

to tremble   to face

_____ me and it _____ me forward.

to fascinate   to draw

When statements containing present tense single-word verbs are turned into questions or negative statements, the verb becomes a verb string combining the base form of the main verb and a simple present tense form of *to do*.

What **does** Ralph **think** of the abstract design at the top? Some of the students **don't understand** its purpose.

APPLICATION 16.   Turn the first five sentences into negative statements, and the last five into questions. Use the simple present tense of each verb. Include *do* or *does* in each sentence.

Change to negative statements

1. I watch for the changes. I _____ for the changes.

2. My brother watches from his own angle. My brother _____ from his own angle.

3. He hopes to discover new evidence. He _____ to discover new evidence.

4. You hope for a clue. You _____ for a clue.

5. The moody woman around the corner hopes for a clue. The moody woman around the corner _____.

Change to questions

6. She hopes for one every day. _____ for one every
   day?

7. The caged bird sings along with you. _____ along
   with you?

8. You sing along with it. _____ along with it?

9. They dance in the rain. _____ in the rain?

10. That cranky old gentleman dances all night. _____ all
    night?

An added -*s* on a noun means plural. An added -*s* on a verb means singular.
Added -*s* therefore has two entirely different purposes. Learn to tell them
apart.

REVIEW AND PRACTICE

A.

Some words have a final -s built right into their spelling. Others add final -s only in specific situations.

In the following sentences, circle all words that end in -s. Put an asterisk (*) next to the ones to which the -s is added.

1. This shopping mall shows a lot of class.

2. Very few of the stores make a fuss when you return items that don't fit your kids.

3. Don't miss the big sales that the mall sponsors during the two weeks before Thanksgiving.

4. My favorite dress shop faces the fountain near the escalators.

5. Across from the doughnut counters, Santa Claus sets up his throne each year.

An -s is added to most nouns to make them plural.

Fill each blank with the plural form of the noun given below the line.

6. I'd be happy with two _____ to the movie.

ticket

7. Still, I'd be even happier if you gave me ten _____ instead.

dollar

8. I promise not to spend it on practical _____ like

thing
   _____.

egg

9. Birthday _____ should not disappear into the family budget.

gift

10. I know you want me to use your _____ for special

present
    _____.

treat

An *-s* is added to a verb in the simple present tense with any singular subject other than *I* and *you*.

Fill each blank with the one-word verb that expresses the simple present tense of the verb named below the line.

11. Whenever your sister _____ to Jordan, he _____.
    to speak   to blush

12. I _____ what that _____.
    to know   to mean

13. She certainly _____ how he _____, too.
    to guess   to feel

14. It _____ her more than she _____.
    to please   to admit

15. The two of them _____ charmingly embarrassed when they

    _____ together.
    to sit

When the verb begins with a present tense form of the auxiliary *to be*, the final *-s* is part of the word *is*.

Fill each blank with the two-word verb string that expresses the present progressive tense of the verb named below each line.

16. The show _____, and the head usher
    to end

    _____ his arms toward the balcony.
    to wave

17. He _____ to get the audience's attention.
    to try

18. The people _____ for an encore.
    to scream

19. The singer on stage _____ back for another bow, and
    to come

    very few fans _____ the usher.
    to notice

20. The usher _____ wildly up and down in the aisle.
    to jump

When the verb begins with a present tense form of the auxiliary *to have*, the final -s is part of the word *has*.

Fill each blank with the two-word verb string that expresses the present perfect tense of the verb named below the line.

21. In spite of her refusal to be polite on the phone, Lorinda _____
    <u>to receive</u>

    _____ five phone calls tonight.

22. Some of the calls _____ important ones.
    <u>to be</u>

23. Her boyfriend _____ her that her sullen behavior
    <u>to warn</u>

    _____ on long enough.
    <u>to go</u>

24. She _____ a few of her friends already.
    <u>to offend</u>

25. Lorinda _____ me with a good idea for dealing with
    <u>to inspire</u>

    high-pressure telephone salespeople.

When the verb begins with a present tense form of the auxiliary *to do*, the -s is part of the word *does*.

Turn each sentence into a question and then into a negative statement.

Roz earns money by washing windows.

26. Question: _____

27. Negative: _____

Above the third floor, she wears one of those safety harnesses.

28. Question: _____

29. Negative: _____

The views from there delight her.

30. Question: _____

31. Negative: _____

The ships on the river look like toys.

32. Question: _____

33. Negative: _____

She spies into the offices of some hot-shot executives.

34. Question: _____

35. Negative: _____

B.

When Barry McLean, a student, finished writing this paragraph, all the *-s* and *-es* endings were where they belonged. Now all the *-s* and *-es* endings for plural nouns have been removed. Put them back.

When I was two-year-old, there was a certain tree my two brother would climb. Sometimes I went with them, not to climb but to watch. I sat right under these branch and looked up, watching them climb. They would go one by one and jump from limb to limb. They would climb all the way to the top of the tree and yell how many mile they could see. Some of those day they could even see New Haven.

That same student's next paragraph was written in the past tense. Change the past tense verbs to present tense verbs.

Anyway, this day as they were going up, they saw a dead branch. One of my brothers decided to pull it down. Well, when the branch broke, it was coming straight for me. I didn't get out of the way fast enough, and the branch came to rest on my head. When my brothers saw this, they came out of the tree faster than squirrels. My brother Skip picked me up and ran home to show my mom. She took me to the clinic and I had twenty stitches put on the cut.

Return to your writing

Read aloud the description you wrote at the beginning of this chapter. Listen for -*s* endings and check to see that they are all in the right places. If not, correct them. Then make any other changes you think might be helpful to a reader.

Read a classmate's paragraph, looking especially for the correct use of final -*s*.

Finish your work on final -*s* by taking the Mastery Test on p. 345.

Chapter 12

Subject-Verb Agreement

The fundamental rule of subject-verb agreement is that verbs must *agree with*, or match, their subjects. This means that singular subjects must go with singular verbs and plural subjects must go with plural verbs. Chapter 11 shows how the addition of final *-s* changes both nouns and verbs. Be sure you understand the effect of *-s* endings before you start this chapter.

Chapter 12 gives you practice with

- making subjects and verbs agree in the present tenses and in situations requiring a choice between *was* and *were*.
- identifying subjects that are hard to find.
- choosing between singular and plural verbs when it is difficult to tell whether the subject is singular or plural.

You may want to start your work on subject-verb agreement by taking the Pretest on p. 323.

Writing

Think of a category of things or people: foods, dreams, jobs, schools, movies, sports, teachers, families, bosses, children, subway riders, rich people, and so on. Pick a category that interests you. On a piece of scrap paper, list all the things or people that belong to that category. Now sort them into two, three, or four groups. What characteristics define each group? What do members of each group have in common? Arrange your thoughts into a paragraph that follows this pattern:

> There are three kinds of _____ in the world. First there are the ones who [describe them]. Second come the people who [describe them]. And finally there are the ones who [describe them].

Discuss each group, giving examples and explaining the differences among the groups. Then copy the finished paragraph onto a fresh piece of paper.

Look over what you've written. Underline all verbs twice and all subjects once.

SUBJECT-VERB AGREEMENT IN THE PRESENT TENSES

In the present tenses, verbs change in form to agree with their subjects.

> The cars move to the side of the road as the hot-air balloon moves slowly toward the median strip. The balloonist is calling out greetings while the police are calling to him through their megaphones. He has floated hundreds of miles under this patchwork canopy and the winds have always floated him to his landing sites.

To agree with singular subjects other than *I* and *you*, simple present tense verbs take an added *-s*, and verbs in the present progressive and perfect tenses include a final *-s* in their auxiliaries (see pp. 170–176). Remember that the English language uses final *-s* in two different ways:

> *-s* added to a noun means plural.
>
> *-s* added to a verb means singular.

Subject-verb agreement, then, implies that there is room for only one added *-s* in any subject-verb combination.

APPLICATION 1.   Rewrite each sentence below, changing the subject as indicated and making the verb agree. Don't change the tense.

From Plural to Singular

Example: Believe it or not, these old grandfather clocks keep perfect time. Believe it or not, *this old grandfather clock keeps perfect time.*

1. Today those gigantic pancakes remind me of home. Today that _____

    _____

2. My daughters are wolfing them down. My _____

    _____

3. My friends are always asking me to explain how I make those fluffy ones at home. My _____

    _____

4. But the crucial ingredients have remained a family secret. But the crucial

    _____

5. Even my cousins do not know how to make those heavenly little clouds.

Even _____

From Singular to Plural

Example: Bronson's sister is usually fairly quiet. Bronson's three *sisters are usu-*
ally fairly quiet.

6. Now Bronson's brother has given up playing the drums. Now Bronson's

two _____

7. The neighbor has prayed for such luck all winter. The _____

_____

8. But now, in the spring, the open window is imposing loud radio music on
everyone within a hundred yards of the house. But now, in the spring, the

_____

_____

9. Does the complaint about noise matter to Bronson? _____

_____

10. Apparently his brother doesn't care a bit. _____

_____

SUBJECT-VERB AGREEMENT WITH *WAS* AND *WERE*

Verbs including past tense forms of *to be* must also change to agree with
their subjects.

The <u>flowers</u> <u>were sprouting</u> indoors, but the <u>parsley</u> on the porch <u>wasn't</u>
<u>sprouting</u> yet. The <u>garden</u> <u>was fertilized</u> with manure in the fall, and the
<u>pots</u> indoors <u>were fertilized</u> chemically.

Here are the simple past tense forms of *to be*.

Singular	*Plural*
I was	we were
you were	you were
she was, he was, it was	they were
⟨*any other singular subject*⟩ was	⟨*any other plural subject*⟩ were

Whether *was* and *were* act as single-word verbs or as auxiliaries, they follow this pattern. Practice them first as single-word verbs.

APPLICATION 2.   In each blank, insert *was* or *were*.

It _____*was*_____ risky for us to let the press interview you. You _____ completely ignorant of the serious facts. Still, I _____ sure you'd give the reporters a story that _____ worth remembering. You _____ able to keep their jaws dropping the whole time. The front page _____ filled with your crazy comments. We _____ glad that you _____ in good form that day.

When *was* or *were* act as auxiliaries in verb strings, *was* goes with all singular subjects except *you*.

I was drying my hair

You were drying your hair.

The wind was drying our hair.

APPLICATION 3.   Choose between *was* and *were* to complete each of these sentences.

I _____*was*_____ thinking this morning about that picnic we had in August. On the little hill above the harbor, a cool wind _____ blowing, and the clouds _____ moving lazily across the sky. We _____ eating chicken, tomatoes, and Dutch cookies. You _____ telling funny stories, but I _____ listening with only half an ear. The boats _____ zipping around the harbor, crossing back and forth, and I _____ concentrating on watching the people on the boats. As the afternoon wore on, we _____ getting sunburned, and so we decided to leave. We _____ sure we'd be back again soon.

APPLICATION 4.   Rewrite each sentence below, changing the subject as indicated and then making the verb agree. Don't change the tense.

From plural to singular

Example: Our prize-winning pumpkins were hit by an early frost. Our one and only prize-winning *pumpkin was hit by an early frost.*

1. Some graduates were returning the last caps and gowns. A graduate _____

   _____

2. In the nearly empty library, a few students were putting away the books from the reserve shelf. In the nearly empty library, a single _____

   _____

3. Some proud relatives were laughing and congratulating someone. A proud

   _____

4. From underneath the eaves, three birds were singing. From underneath the eaves, a _____

5. The patient janitors were relieved to see the end of the day. The patient

   _____

   _____

From singular to plural

Example: Her outrageous statement was quoted in every newspaper in the state. Her numerous outrageous *statements were quoted by every newspaper in the state.*

6. Yesterday some stranger was trying to get hold of you. Yesterday several

   _____

7. For a while he was calling every half hour. For a while _____

   _____

8. Apparently your old army buddy was recommending you as a speaker for the Veterans Day celebration. Apparently your old _____

_____

9. The program organizer was hoping you'd call back tonight. The program

_____

10. Probably your commanding officer was consulted about the invitation. Probably your commanding _____

_____

THERE IS, THERE ARE, THERE WAS, AND *THERE WERE*

When a clause begins with one of these expressions, the verb should agree with the first noun or pronoun *after the verb*, as long as that noun or pronoun is not part of a modifying phrase or clause.

There is no doubt that eating habits are changing in the USA.

A decade ago, there were no labels on packages boasting, "All natural; no preservatives."

Besides, there is now, among many young people, a ritual of daily diet and exercise.

Notice that in the last example above, the first noun after the verb is *people*. But it is part of a modifying phrase, so the fact that it is plural is irrelevant. The next noun is *ritual*, and that's the one that matters. When you look after the verb and find the first noun outside a modifying phrase or clause, note whether it is singular or plural and then choose the verb to match:

Singular	*Plural*
there is	there are
there was	there were

APPLICATION 5.   Insert *is* or *are* to complete each sentence correctly.

1. There _____ only one good reason to go to St. Thomas.

2. There _____ only two good reasons to go to St. Thomas.

3. There _____ nothing I like better than pink lemonade with gin.

4. There _____ few things I like better than pink lemonade with gin.

5. Inside the mall, there _____ hundreds of shoppers milling about.

6. Inside the mall, there _____ a huge crowd milling about.

Insert *was* or *were* to complete each sentence correctly.

7. There _____ a clamshell in my shoe!

8. There _____ clamshells in my shoe!

9. There _____ always, in a situation like that one, at least one person you could count on.

10. There _____ always, in a situation like that one, a few people you could count on.

MODIFYING PHRASES OR CLAUSES BETWEEN SUBJECT AND VERB

When a prepositional phrase modifies the subject of a clause, the verb must still agree with the subject, not with any noun in the prepositional phrase.

The hole ⟨in my pants⟩ looks ugly.

The holes ⟨in my coat⟩ look ugly.

APPLICATION 6. In each sentence below, underline the one-word subject, and then insert the correct form of the verb named below the line. Use the tense indicated.

Simple present (one word in each blank)

1. The mailboxes for our building _____ hard to reach.
   to be

2. The mailbox for the apartments on the third floor _____ hard to reach.
   to be

3. Sometimes that librarian with the glasses _____ me of my
   <u>to remind</u>

   father.

4. Sometimes the librarians in the research room _____ me of my
   <u>to remind</u>

   family.

Present perfect (combine *has* or *have* with the past participle form of the main verb)

5. You'd better not go because the fire marshal under the new team of super-

   visors _____ a warning.
   <u>to issue</u>

6. You'd better not go because the fire marshals from the North End

   _____ a warning.
   <u>to issue</u>

7. Don's two partners _____ town.
   <u>to leave</u>

8. Don, along with his two partners, _____ town.
   <u>to leave</u>

9. Don, along with his two partners and their families, _____
   <u>to leave</u>

   town.

Present progressive (combine *is* or *are* with the *-ing* form of the main verb)

10. The phones for our office _____ all the time.
    <u>to ring</u>

11. The phone for the file clerks _____ all the time.
    <u>to ring</u>

12. The students around the corner _____ us about the thinness of
    <u>to tease</u>

    the walls.

13. The student in the rooms behind ours _____ us about the thin-
    <u>to tease</u>

    ness of the walls.

14. Today the final report on the negotiations _____ to the board.
    <u>to go</u>

15. Today the final reports on the negotiation with the union _____
    to go

    to the board.

When a dependent clause or verbal phrase separates a subject from its verb, the verb must still agree with the subject, not with a noun in the clause or phrase.

The <u>noise</u> ⟨that they're making with the dishes⟩ <u><u>gives</u></u> me an idea.

The <u>noises</u> ⟨that they're making with the dishes⟩ <u><u>give</u></u> me an idea.

APPLICATION 7.   In each sentence below, underline the one-word subject, and then insert the correct form of the verb named below the line. Use the tenses indicated.

Simple present (one word in each blank)

1. Our truck, which finally has new tires, _____ to be tuned up.
   to need

2. Our trucks, recently outfitted with new tires and brake shoes,

   _____ to be tuned up.
   to need

3. The upstairs tenants, constantly irritated by other people's clutter,

   _____ a lot.
   to yell

4. The other tenant, who keeps her bicycle and skis in the hallway,

   _____ a lot.
   to yell

5. A grower who plants a third crop _____ extra profits.
   to make

6. Growers planting a third crop in a single year _____ extra
   to make

   profits.

7. My uncle who lives with his daughters _____ cantaloupes.
   to love

8. My uncles who sleep with their lights on because they're afraid of ghosts

   _____ cantaloupes.
   to love

Past progressive (combine *was* or *were* with the *-ing* form of the main verb)

9. The phones that our offices used _____ all the time.
   <small>to ring</small>

10. The phone shared by our two offices _____ all the
    <small>to ring</small>

    time.

11. The student who drops by every day after classes

    _____ us about the noise.
    <small>to tease</small>

12. The students living around the corner _____ us about
    <small>to tease</small>

    the noise.

13. This morning the final reports summarizing the negotiation process

    _____ to the board.
    <small>to go</small>

14. This morning the final report that summarizes the negotiations with the

    union _____ to the board.
    <small>to go</small>

15. The shadow slowly covering the driveway and the front steps

    _____ a welcome coolness.
    <small>to bring</small>

INDEFINITE PRONOUNS AS SUBJECTS

When a singular indefinite pronoun acts as a subject, it always takes a singular verb. When a plural indefinite pronoun acts as subject, it always takes a plural verb.

Everybody dreads going to the dentist.

I've tried nine dentists, and several have been real jokers.

Anyone who cracks jokes while his hands are in my mouth is in danger of being bitten.

Here are the indefinite pronouns.

INDEFINITE PRONOUNS

Singular	*Either Singular or Plural*	*Plural*
everyone/everybody	any	both
anyone/anybody	all	many
someone/somebody	some	few
no one/nobody	most	several
each/much/one	more	
either/neither	none	

Pay particular attention to the ones that are always singular or always plural. Remember that a modifying phrase or clause between the subject and verb doesn't change the number of the subject:

Nobody is waiting for the light.

Nobody who can see past those cars is waiting for the light.

Few have even slowed down.

Few of the drivers in the line have even slowed down.

APPLICATION 8.   In each sentence below, underline the subject, and then insert the correct form of the verb named below the line. Use the tenses indicated.

Simple present (one word in each blank)

1. Around the holidays, several of my customers from the fancy part of town

   _____ me to make marzipan.
   to ask

2. Anyone who can work with tools _____ how to fix that mailbox.
   to know

3. Neither of the actors _____ much time memorizing lines.
   to spend

4. Everybody in the grandstands _____ to avoid trouble.
   to want

5. Very few of the stones that are in this bag _____ in value over
   <u>to increase</u>
   the years.

Present perfect (combine *has* or *have* with the past participle of the main verb)

6. Nobody in my classes _____ very hard this week.
   <u>to work</u>

7. Instead, many _____ in the sudden sweetness of the
   <u>to bask</u>
   weather.

8. Matt   and   Lena   are   sunbathing   every   day,   but   neither
   _____ to swim in the river yet.
   <u>to try</u>

9. The   select   few   who   talk   often   with   Matt   and   Lena
   _____ the rumor about their secret marriage.
   <u>to contradict</u>

10. Matt and Lena are stubborn people and each _____ a
    <u>to develop</u>
    strong desire to stay independent.

**A few indefinite pronouns agree with either singular or plural verbs,
depending on the rest of the sentence.**

More of that fruit is coming tomorrow.

More of those apples are coming tomorrow.

Review the chart of indefinite pronouns on page 194. The pronouns in the two
outer columns are fixed in number, no matter what words are in their modifying phrases. But each pronoun in the middle column changes number to
match the object of the first preposition that follows.

APPLICATION 9.   In each of the sentences below, underline the subject and then insert the
simple present tense form of the verb named below the line.

1. All of the bread _____ moldy.
   <u>to look</u>

2. All of the slices _____ moldy.
   <u>to look</u>

3. Some of the bottles _____ strange.
   to smell

4. Some of the milk _____ strange.
   to smell

5. None of the eggs _____ those tiny cracks.
   to show

6. None of the butter _____ any spoilage.
   to show

7. Most of this warehouse _____ a new refrigeration system.
   to need

8. Most of these rooms _____ new refrigerators.
   to need

9. Any of the cosmetics that you find in the drawer _____ to the
   to belong

   people who lived here before.

10. Any of the medicine in those drawers _____ to the people who
    to belong

    just moved out.

WHO, WHICH, AND *THAT* AS SUBJECTS

When *who, which,* or *that* acts as the subject of a clause, the verb in the
clause must agree with the word that the clause modifies.

> Here's the girl ⟨who shovels snow⟩.
>
> Here are the girls ⟨who shovel snow⟩.

Who, which, or *that* can play two parts at the same time: dependent word and
subject of a dependent clause. In such a case, the verb must agree with the
word that the clause modifies.

> The hot water faucet, ⟨which has been dripping for days,⟩ is hard to fix.
>
> None of the pipes ⟨that lead to the sink⟩ seem to have shut-off valves.

APPLICATION 10.   In each sentence below, insert the simple present tense form of the verb
named below the line.

1. The teams that _____ must pay the fee.
   to win

2. The team that _____ must pay the fee.
   <u>to win</u>

3. Anyone who _____ in overtime should be paid double.
   <u>to put</u>

4. Workers who _____ in overtime should be paid double.
   <u>to put</u>

5. The trash that _____ so fast might be from the oily pile.
   <u>to burn</u>

6. The bags that _____ so fast might be from the oily pile.
   <u>to burn</u>

7. Households that _____ less than $15,000 this year will not get
   <u>to earn</u>

   much of a tax break.

8. A person who _____ less than $15,000 this year will not get
   <u>to earn</u>

   much of a tax break.

9. Phonophobes are people who _____ afraid of noises.
   <u>to be</u>

10. A phonophobe is a person who _____ afraid of noises.
    <u>to be</u>

COMPOUND SUBJECTS

When two or more subjects are compounded with *and*, they agree with a *plural* verb.

> <u>Rain</u> <u><u>makes</u></u> arthritis flare up.
>
> <u>Rain</u> **and** <u>fog</u> <u><u>make</u></u> arthritis flare up.

APPLICATION 11.   In each of the following sentences, underline the subject or subjects and insert the simple present tense form of the verb named below the line.

1. A freckle on his elbow _____ him.
   <u>to identify</u>

2. A freckle and a small scar on his elbow _____ him.
   <u>to identify</u>

3. The tropical stick insect _____ to become thirteen inches long.
   <u>to grow</u>

4. The tropical stick insect and the Andaman Island centipede
_____ to become thirteen inches long.
   to grow

5. Probably Marisa _____ professionally by now.
                    to dance

6. Probably Marisa and Leonard _____ professionally by now.
                                to dance

7. Cleaning often _____ the whole atmosphere of the house.
                   to improve

8. Cleaning and painting often _____ the whole atmosphere of the
                                to improve
house.

9. In a special diving machine called a bathysphere, an ocean diver
_____ a depth of almost 36,000 feet.
   to reach

10. In a special diving machine called a bathysphere, an ocean diver and
equipment _____ a depth of almost 36,000 feet.
           to reach

When subjects are compounded with *or* or *nor*, the verb agrees with the subject closest to it.

Blueberries <u>taste</u> good after a spicy meal.

Either <u>blueberries</u> or <u>pineapple</u> <u>tastes</u> good after a spicy meal.

Either <u>pineapple</u> or <u>blueberries</u> <u>taste</u> good after a spicy meal.

Read the last two sentences aloud and listen to the way each verb agrees with the subject closest to it.

APPLICATION 12. In each of the following sentences, underline the subject or subjects and insert the simple present tense form of the verb named below the line.

1. Tim's watch or the alarm clocks _____ us on schedule.
                                    to keep

2. The alarm clocks or Tim's watch _____ us on schedule.
                                    to keep

3. Either Andra or the Seville boys _____ after the chickens when
   _{to look}
   we're away.

4. Either the Seville boys or Andra _____ after the chickens when
   _{to look}
   we're away.

5. Neither my kids nor Lillie _____ skating on that pond.
   _{to go}

6. Neither Lillie nor my kids _____skating on that pond.
   _{to go}

7. A cake or cookies always _____ mysteriously at my door on Mid-
   _{to appear}
   summer's Eve.

8. Cookies or a cake always _____ mysteriously at my door on Mid-
   _{to appear}
   summer's Eve.

9. Neither my father nor my friends _____ to me about money.
   _{to talk}

10. Neither my friends nor my father _____ to me about money.
    _{to talk}

Watch out for the difference between compound subjects joined by *and* and
compound subjects joined by *or* or *nor.*

Rain **and** fog make arthritis flare up.
Rain **or** fog makes arthritis flare up.

APPLICATION 13.   In the following sentences, underline the subjects and then insert the
simple present tense form of the verb named below the line.

1. Toan and his brother _____ on Fridays.
   _{to work}

2. Either Toan or his brother _____ on Fridays.
   _{to work}

3. Either the motion of the boat or the sunshine _____ me dizzy.
   _{to make}

4. The motion of the boat and the sunshine _____ me dizzy.
   _{to make}

5. Neither the stars nor the moon _____ through the clouds
   _{to break}
   tonight.

REVIEW AND PRACTICE

A.

A singular subject takes a singular verb, and a plural subject takes a plural verb. Subject-verb agreement allows only one -s to be added to any subject-verb combination.

In the sentences below, make singular subjects plural and make plural subjects singular. Change each verb to agree with its new subject.

1. The tomato seedling grows well in this corner.

2. The stem has doubled in thickness.

3. The pepper plants are progressing more slowly.

4. The delicate melon vines do not thrive in a drafty place.

5. My southern windows offer the perfect environment for sprouts.

When a verb includes a past tense form of *to be, was* goes with all singular subjects except *you; were* goes with *you* and all plural subjects.

For each blank, choose between *was* or *were*.

6. All last year, Dinnell _____ saving money for a car.

7. The Martoral sisters _____ offering to sell him theirs.

8. Their car _____ just sitting on the street where it _____ not doing anyone any good.

9. I, for one, _____ happy for him to get a chance at it.

10. The neighborhood kids _____ pleased, too, because Dinnell _____ always such a pushover about giving them rides around town.

When choosing between *there is* and *there are* (or between *there was* and *there were*), look after the verb for the agreement clue.

For each blank, choose between *is* and *are.*

11. There _____ some advantages to working the night shift.

12. When I get off work in the winter, there _____ still an hour more of darkness.

13. In the air there _____ a fresh smell, and the streets are still.

14. Just as the sun rises, there _____ often a glow in the sky that transforms dingy buildings into colored palaces.

15. Because there _____ so few people on the streets at that hour, I can stand and stare without feeling foolish.

For 16–40 below, complete each sentence with the **simple present tense form** of the verb named below the blank space.

When a modifying phrase or clause separates the subject from its verb, the verb must agree with the subject and not with any noun in the modifying phrase or clause.

16. A woman who takes most of her classes during the same hours as I do

   _____ to box.
      to love

17. The person pictured in all the newspapers for winning the Golden Gloves

   _____ her.
      to teach

18. Her parents, worrying about her safety and probably disapproving of the

   sport as a whole, _____ to convince her to quit.
            to hope

19. However, her friends in the athletic crowd _____ her.
            to encourage

20. In fact, the director of counseling and student affairs, who has worked

   with her for two years, _____ that boxing has been good for her.
         to claim

Singular indefinite pronoun subjects require singular verbs. Plural indefinite pronoun subjects require plural verbs.

21. Anybody who ever saw Derek at work ＿＿＿＿＿＿＿＿ that he can be
    to know

    trusted.

22. And yet several of the people in the head office ＿＿＿＿＿＿＿＿ that he's
    to report

    dealing in drugs.

23. I can't understand why so few of the people on his crew ＿＿＿＿＿＿＿＿
    to seem

    to realize that he needs their help.

24. Everybody who has worked with him over the past few years

    ＿＿＿＿＿＿＿＿ how he used to stick out his neck to help others.
    to remember

25. At this point, neither of his supervisors ＿＿＿＿＿＿＿＿ to file a report.
    to want

A few indefinite pronoun subjects agree with either singular or plural verbs, depending on the modifying phrases that follow them.

26. All of that ice in the cooler ＿＿＿＿＿＿＿＿ that you are ready for a great
    to show

    party.

27. Some of your guests ＿＿＿＿＿＿＿＿to have brought fancy casseroles, too.
    to appear

28. You have a great reputation as a party giver, but surely some of the credit

    ＿＿＿＿＿＿＿＿ to your gourmet-cook guests.
    to belong

29. Arranged on the side table, all of those platters ＿＿＿＿＿＿＿＿ a grand
    to promise

    feast.

30. But most of the newcomers ＿＿＿＿＿＿＿＿ too shy to dig in.
    to feel

When *who, which,* or *that* acts as the subject of the clause it introduces, the verb must agree with the word that the clause modifies.

31. The experiences that _____ in people's memories are often the
    <u>to stick</u>

    surprising ones.

32. A big, special event that _____ according to expectations may
    <u>to happen</u>

    fade from long-term memory.

33. But a small, ordinary event that _____ a person by surprise may
    <u>to take</u>

    be remembered vividly for years.

34. Scholars who _____ artificial intelligence believe that surprise is
    <u>to study</u>

    an important factor in the storage of information.

35. Computer programs, which _____ fundamentally unable to re-
    <u>to be</u>

    spond to surprise, are revealing critical limitations in this area.

When *and* compounds subjects, the verb must be plural. When *or* compounds subjects, the verb should agree with the subject closest to it.

36. The sound of the sewing machine and the smell of biscuits

    _____ Lydia home every vacation.
    <u>to welcome</u>

37. Either her sisters or her mother _____ out to meet her.
    <u>to rush</u>

38. In the back shed, Lydia's father and the boys _____ away on
    <u>to hammer</u>

    their customers' furniture orders.

39. Often either the women's eagerness or the men's casualness

    _____ Lydia.
    <u>to irritate</u>

40. But this time, she and her new friend _____ the warmth of the
    <u>to appreciate</u>

    family after their long trip.

B.

Correct the subject-verb agreement errors in the following paragraphs.

Everyone who go to horror movies have some reason for spending good money on a bad experience. And nobody denies that those two hours in the theater feels, in fact, perfectly ghastly. Most of the people who comes out looking dazed and paranoid eagerly agrees that the movie were really awful and that they can't wait for the next one. Why do they do this to themselves?

Some of the people comes just for the physical sensation of fear, a sensation that a wild ride at an amusement park also provide. But these rushes of excitement responds to nothing but illusions of danger. Everybody know that neither the movie's monsters nor the peril of the amusement park ride are real. In either case, a customer buys five bucks' worth of fear and confront it heroically in complete security.

Most of the viewers gives other reasons for loving these movies. Many simply like the fantasy of them. The characters and plot of one movie isn't much different from the characters and plot of another one, so the horror stay within predictable limits, even when its subject is completely unreal. In addition, the simplicity of the stories are appealing. Neither the good guys nor the monster ever forget what's good or what's bad, so there is no gray area in the viewer's value judgments. And finally, horror movies are relaxing. After all, a monster or a demon are easier to cope with than the arms race or job insecurity, and all that screaming and shaking over horror movies help to relieve other tensions, too. So even though such movies may force people to check under their beds and bolt all their windows for a few days, while they was sitting in the theater, their minds were resting in some deeper way. So why has people always laughed at me when I've told them I wish that life could be as safe, simple, and restful as a good horror movie?

Return to your writing

Read the paragraph you wrote at the beginning of this chapter. Check each verb to see that it agrees with its subject, and correct any errors you find. Make any other changes you think a reader would appreciate.

Read a classmate's paragraph for subject-verb agreement. Suggest corrections.

Complete your work on subject-verb agreement by taking the Mastery Test on page 347.

Chapter 13

Pronouns

Pronouns are words that take the place of nouns. By avoiding repetition of words, pronouns make language more efficient, but at the same time they can introduce new problems. Using pronouns correctly in your writing will help you to express your thoughts in a way that is clear to your readers.

Chapter 13 alerts you to potential trouble spots and helps you to

- recognize which word each pronoun refers to.
- understand how some pronouns change form when their role in a sentence changes.
- make pronouns agree with the words they refer to.

You may want to start your work on pronouns by taking the Pretest on p. 327.

Writing

Try to picture a perfect world. What kind of food, clothing, shelter, and medical care would people have? What would families, schools, and homes be like? How would people handle birth, mating, old age, and death? What would people do for work or leisure? Jot notes about your image of a perfect society. Then organize your ideas into a paragraph. Use the words *everybody* and *nobody* at least twice each.

Look over your paragraph. If you have used any of these words, circle them:

she, her	it, its
he, him, his	they, them, their

RECOGNIZING PRONOUNS

Pronouns offer short substitutes for nouns or for groups of words.

Talk to the dance teacher. ~~The dance teacher~~ *He* will know what to do. ~~The person listening to me~~ *You* will learn a lot from ~~the dance teacher.~~ *him* ~~All people~~ *Everybody* will agree with ~~the person talking.~~ *me*

A COLLECTION OF PRONOUNS

Personal Pronouns
These refer to specific people or things.

	Subject Forms		Object Forms		Possessive Forms	
	Singular	*Plural*	*Singular*	*Plural*	*Singular*	*Plural*
1ST PERSON	I	we	me	us	my/mine	our/ours
2ND PERSON	you	you	you	you	your/yours	your/yours
3RD PERSON	he	they	him	them	his	their/theirs
	she	they	her	them	her/hers	their/theirs
	it	they	it	them	its	their/theirs

Indefinite Pronouns
These are less specific than personal pronouns.

Singular	*Singular or Plural*	*Plural*
everyone/everybody	all	both
anyone/anybody	some	many
someone/somebody	none	few
no one/nobody	more	several
each/much/one	most	
either/neither	any	

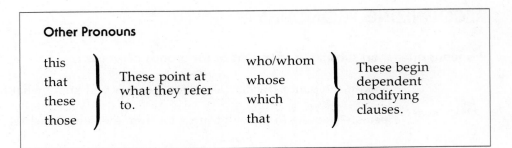

Other Pronouns

this
that   } These point at
these   what they refer
those   to.

who/whom
whose   } These begin
which   dependent
that   modifying
                clauses.

APPLICATION 1.   Circle the pronouns in the paragraph below.

Dave brought (me) a chart clipped from (his) evening newspaper. It showed the responses of American executives to the question "How many hours should there be in an average workday?" The majority of the executives interviewed favored the status quo; 57 percent of them voted for the eight-hour day. However, Dave was excited because 10 percent favored a seven-hour day. That was enough to get him started on a fantasy about how fifty years from now everyone will consider an eight-hour day a violation of human rights. But when I asked him to add up the numbers further down the chart, he stopped gloating. A significant portion of the executives — 11 percent of them, in fact — thought everyone should buckle down to nine- and ten-hour workdays. Dave and I decided not to pay attention to the vote of anyone who could show such ignorance of human nature, and we used the clipping to light our barbecue.

FINDING A PRONOUN'S ANTECEDENT

An antecedent is the word or group of words that comes before a personal pronoun and establishes the pronoun's meaning.

There's gravy on the table. Please clean (it) up.

whole } Mario and his friends are washing the dishes while (they) plan the bowl-
idea } ing tournament.

(That's) almost too good to be true.

Without the antecedents (the words the arrows point to), the circled pronouns would have no meaning. The word *antecedent* means "going before," so most personal pronouns point back to their antecedents. In the third example, the antecedent is the whole previous sentence.

APPLICATION 2.   The personal pronouns are italicized in the paragraph below. Draw an arrow from each pronoun to its antecedent.

The new tractor had a big scratch on (*its*) side. Mr. Larsen said *he* thought the Bradley boys had been driving *it,* but *they* denied that *they* had been anywhere near *it. Their* mother, of course, angrily defended *her* boys. Mr. Larsen eventually gave up *his* accusation, but not until the argument had run *its* usual boring course.

APPLICATION 3.   In the following paragraph, the italicized personal pronouns have no antecedents. Provide them by replacing some of the pronouns with nouns. Then go back and draw an arrow from each remaining pronoun to its new antecedent.

The immigrants
Example: ~~They~~ waited for two weeks with *their* fingers crossed.

It finally arrived in the mail. *He* opened it while *they* looked on eagerly.

She was over in the corner, unable to watch, but *they* kept leaning over *his* shoulder, nagging *him* to hurry up and get *it* out. *She* hadn't wanted *it* to come this way, not with all *her* hopes resting on *it*. *Her* hands shook as she watched *him* take *it* out.

Some pronouns don't need antecedents.

> **I** wonder what to do about the rising pork prices.
>
> **Everyone** is asking what **you** think about the situation.

The pronouns above don't need antecedents because their meanings are clear without reference to words that go before them. The first person pronouns (*I*, *me*, *we*, *us*) always mean the speaker(s) or writer(s). The second person pronoun (*you*) always means the listener(s) or reader(s). Many of the indefinite pronouns explain their own meanings.

APPLICATION 4.   Return to Application 1. Draw an arrow from each pronoun to its antecedent. The antecedent for one pronoun is a whole thought; underline that thought before drawing the arrow. If a pronoun doesn't need an antecedent, write NA over it. Your first sentence will look like this:

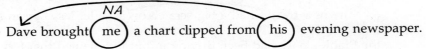

Dave brought (me) a chart clipped from (his) evening newspaper.

CHOOSING BETWEEN SUBJECT AND OBJECT FORMS OF PERSONAL PRONOUNS

A personal pronoun changes form when its role in a sentence changes.

> Don't make faces at **me** now because **I** am trying to be serious.

In this sentence, the first person singular pronoun appears in two forms because it must play two different roles: object of a preposition (at *me*) and subject (*I* am trying). The chart on p. 209 separates personal pronouns into subject and object forms. Use that chart as you do the exercises below.

Use the subject form for pronouns playing the role of subject in any clause.

> **She** will graduate tomorrow.
> My brother and **I** are going to the ceremony.
> **She** hopes that **we** will stay for the reception.

The second example above shows that the rule holds even with compound subjects. The third example shows that the rule holds for dependent as well as independent clauses.

APPLICATION 5.   Fill each blank below with a personal pronoun that can take the place of the word or phrase below the line.

Example: _____*He*_____ enjoyed every exhibit at the county fair.
                          my son

1. Yesterday _____ took my seven-year-old sister to the arcade.
                  1st person singular

2. _____ thought it was some kind of paradise.
      my sister

3. It was amazing to see how _____ could beat me at Space
                                      my sister
   Invaders.

4. _____ wouldn't believe how fast those little hands could move.
      2nd person

5. My friends gathered around, and _____ just watched and
                                          1st person plural
   cheered for half an hour.

6. Then _____ took my sister home for supper.
            1st person singular

7. My parents worry about her fascination with video games, but

   _____ can't help being sort of proud, too.
      my parents

8. My father admits that even _____ can't top my sister's hand-eye
                                  my father
   coordination.

9. Our brother wants to break her record, so _____ must practice
                                                    our brother
   at the arcade in his free time.

10. _____ just laugh at him, though, because my sister is clearly un-
    1st person singular

beatable.

APPLICATION 6.   Now rewrite each sentence in Application 5. Make the pronoun part of a compound subject by adding the words in parentheses.

Example: (___*He*___ and his friends): *He and his friends enjoyed every*
   exhibit at the county fair.

1. (Felix and _____): _____

   _____

2. (Her friend and _____): _____

   _____

3. (_____ and Brenda): _____

   _____

4. (Your girlfriend and _____): _____

   _____

5. (the arcade owner and _____): _____

   _____

6. (Emmie and _____): _____

   _____

7. (_____ and Brenda's family): _____

   _____

8. (_____ and Mr. Cherry): _____

   _____

9. (_____ and his tough-looking buddies): _____

   _____

10. (My parents and _____): _____

   _____

In formal speech and writing, when a form of *to be* acts as a single-word verb or a main verb, any pronoun that acts as its completer will be in the subject form:

> The Boltons weren't the ones who visited last year, even though you seem to think it was *they.*
>
> "Hello, is this Mr. Bolton?" "Yes, this is *he.*"

If these sentences sound strange to you, it's because informal English is loosening up on this use of the subject form. In formal writing, however, these pronoun forms are correct.

Use the object form (*me, you, him, her, it, us, them*) for pronouns playing any role other than subject in a sentence.

> The teacher led **me** to believe that the test would be postponed.
>
> Brad says the conversation gave Tony and **him** the same idea.

The second example above shows that the rule holds even with compound structures.

APPLICATION 7.   Fill each blank below with a personal pronoun that can take the place of the word or phrase below the line.

Example: Are you sure that this is the best vacation for _____*her*_____?
                                                                    Maria

1. Benny has invited Jim to move in with _____.
                                              Benny

2. It was always clear to _____ that Benny's place was too big for
                              2nd person

    just a couple.

3. But Benny had promised his wife that the two extra rooms could be for

    _____ to use for crafts projects.
        his wife

4. Benny and Edy are both hobby-lovers, and I admire _____.
                                                          Benny and Edy

5. Then, yesterday, Benny told _____ that Jim was moving in.
                                   1st person singular

6. I doubt that Edy knows about the plan yet, because when Mom talked with

   _____ this morning, the conversation was all about the same old
        Edy

   stuff.

7. And when I ran into _____ during lunch, nobody was talking
                        Edy and Mom

   about the big news.

8. So it's probably best for _____ to lie low until the storm passes.
                              1st person plural

9. Eventually, Edy will get used to the idea of having Jim around and will

   make _____ part of the family.
            Jim

10. But I don't want to be around when Benny first tells _____ about
                                                            Edy

    the plan.

APPLICATION 8.   Now rewrite each sentence in Application 7. Make the pronoun part of a compound structure by adding the words in parentheses.

   Example: (_her_____ and her mother): _Are you sure that this is the best va-_

   _cation for her and her mother?_____

   1. (_____ and his wife): _____

   _____

   2. (your neighbors and _____): _____

   _____

   3. (_____ and my mom): _____

   _____

   4. (_____ and their industriousness): _____

   _____

   5. (Ted and _____): _____

   _____

   6. (_____ and Cindy): _____

   _____

7. (_____ and their friends): _____

   _____

8. (the other neighbors and _____): _____

   _____

9. (his cats and _____): _____

   _____

10. (my mom and _____): _____

   _____

To decide which pronoun form to use, ask yourself, "Is this pronoun the subject of a clause?" If so, use the subject form. If not, use the object form.

Remember that when you compound a pronoun with any other word, you should not change the pronoun's form.

> Probably the Knicks game tonight will make **me** happy.
> Probably the Knicks game tonight will make **Frieda and me** happy.

APPLICATION 9.   In the sentences below, circle the correct pronoun in each pair.

Example: ((He) / Him) and ((I)/ me) have been arguing about this matter for months.

1. (I / Me) want to talk with Bill.

2. Callie and (I / me) want to talk with Bill.

3. (We / Us) haven't seen (he / him) in several days.

4. Nobody has seen Floyd and (he / him) in several days.

5. Someone needs to give (they / them) an important message.

6. Someone needs to give the security guards and (they / them) an important message.

7. The superintendent told (I / me) that (he / him) would be closing the building for a week in February.

8. The superintendent told the maintenance crew and (I / me) that the inspector and (he / him) would be closing the building for a week in February.

9. It ought to be up to (they / them) to contact the security guards.

10. It ought to be up to the landlord and (they / them) to contact the security guards.

MAKING PRONOUNS AND ANTECEDENTS AGREE

A personal pronoun must agree with its antecedent.

> The **people** on the boat will need **their** jackets.
> The **guide** doesn't seem to want **his** coat, though.

In the first sentence above, the pronoun, *their,* is plural because its antecedent, *people,* is plural. In the second sentence, *his* is singular because its antecedent, *guide,* is singular. When the pronoun and antecedent match in this way, we say they *agree.*

APPLICATION 10.   In the sentences below, the plural pronouns refer to singular antecedents. Draw an arrow from each pronoun to its antecedent and then change the pronoun to agree.

Example: That firm has kept every promise ~~they~~ *it* made to the local environmental protection group.

1. The working woman may not be any more independent than *their* neighbors who stay at home with the kids.

2. The administration keeps forgetting what *they* promised last fall.

3. The human race is rushing to destroy *themselves* in this struggle for nuclear superiority.

4. No boy ever had to leave that camp because *their* parents couldn't afford the fee.

5. The average childless woman has more resources today than *they* had ten years ago.

Pronoun-antecedent agreement is difficult when a singular antecedent offers no gender clues.

> One of your **roommates** left **her/his**(?) lights on.
> Can a small **child** explain what **she/he**(?) wants?
> Give this free sample to the first **customer** who comes in and ask **him/her**(?) to taste it.

There are three possible solutions to the problem.

1. Use both the masculine and the feminine pronoun forms, with the word *or* between them. This invites the reader to share the uncertainty about the gender of the antecedent.

> Give this free sample to the first customer who comes in and ask **him or her** to taste it.

This solution sometimes creates a clumsy sentence.

2. Make your own decision about the sex of the person the pronoun refers to and choose a pronoun to match. (The old rule was to use the masculine forms whenever the sentence didn't give you any gender clues, but we are moving away from that now.) There is no simple answer about which form to choose.

> Give this free sample to the first customer who comes in and ask **her** to taste it.
>
> *or*
>
> Give this free sample to the first customer who comes in and ask **him** to taste it.

This solution forces you to guess about the sex of the person the pronoun refers to.

3. Change the antecedent to a plural form so that you can use a plural pronoun to match it.

> Give this free sample to the first customers who come in and ask **them** to taste it.

This solution doesn't always work, because it forces you to change the meaning of the original sentence slightly.

Because each solution has its drawbacks, there is no single one you can use all the time. You need to become familiar with all three solutions, and choose among them in your writing.

APPLICATION 11.   In the sentences below, use Solution 1 to make the pronouns agree with their singular antecedents. Draw an arrow from each pronoun to its antecedent. Then cross out the plural pronoun and write in both the feminine and the masculine form, with the word *or* between them.

Example: A new employee cannot afford to be careless about ~~their~~ *his or her* appearance.

1. Your first step is to greet the customer in a friendly manner and ask them for any coupons or bottle returns.

2. Many parents interrupt the child's vocalization by embracing them.

3. The average student at this college cares too much about their grades.

4. There are laws supporting the rights of a minor even though they may be handicapped.

5. A person can take up to fifty milligrams of methadone, and the dosage won't have any effect on them.

APPLICATION 12.   In the sentences below, use Solution 2 to make the pronouns agree with their singular antecedents. Draw an arrow from each pronoun to its antecedent. Then decide whether to use a masculine or a feminine pronoun. Cross out the plural form and insert a singular pronoun that matches the gender you have chosen.

Example: Every defendant has the right to have ~~their~~ *his* attorney advise ~~them.~~ *him*

1. It's up to each individual to decide what their primary values are.

2. In the old days, a person never questioned what they should do with their life.

3. A student will have to take the time to study and do their homework by themselves.

4. Not every young person has an open relationship with their parents.

5. If a kid teases the teacher too often, they could get in trouble.

APPLICATION 13.   In the sentences below, use Solution 3 to make the antecedents agree with the plural pronouns. Draw an arrow from each pronoun to its antecedent. Then cross out the singular antecedent, leaving the pronoun alone. Write in a plural form of the antecedent.

Example: If a person can find time to be alone, they may observe details more

       intently than when they are among friends.

1. Don't ever try to tell an adolescent how they could have handled a problem

    better; it will just hurt their feelings.

2. Why destroy one of the few places a young person can go to get the help

    they need?

3. A news announcer must be able to adjust their program when something

    special happens at the last minute.

4. No doctor can ever be sure that the pills they prescribe will be the right

    ones.

5. When the parent decided on a day-care center, they usually considered

    the cost first of all.

Pronoun-antecedent agreement is difficult when the antecedent is a singular indefinite pronoun.

    Nobody could have used **his/her**(?) charge card here.

Review the list of indefinite pronouns on p. 209. When one of these words acts as the antecedent for a personal pronoun, the gender problem immediately arises. In addition, since indefinite pronouns don't refer to anyone in particular, we may hesitate to use a singular personal pronoun to refer to one of them, because singular is too specific. A plural pronoun looks particularly attractive when the antecedent is *everyone* or *everybody*. These words imply a large number of people, and yet these words (as well as any nouns preceded by the word *every*) are always singular. Any personal pronoun that refers to one of these words must be in the singular form:

Everybody in my classes can look up **his** or **her** grade on the test.

Standard English may be slowly changing on this issue, but the rule still stands, and you should respect it in college or public writing.

APPLICATION 14.   Correct the sentences below by using Solution 1. Draw an arrow from each personal pronoun to its antecedent. Then cross out each personal pronoun and correct it to agree with its antecedent.

1. The student who was absent should take the responsibility for asking somebody what they did the previous day.

2. When anybody is hospitalized, they may go into debt for the rest of their life.

3. Nobody in the jail cell could understand why they had been arrested.

4. All the women in the group are mothers, and each has their own style of talking with their children.

5. I didn't agree with anyone on the panel who claimed that they should make the final decision.

APPLICATION 15.   Correct the sentences below by using Solution 3. Draw an arrow from each personal pronoun to its antecedent. Then cross out the antecedent and correct it to agree with the pronoun.

1. Everybody saw that mean-looking man on their television screens.

2. I wouldn't blame anybody for refusing to do an exercise that might hurt them.

3. Everybody's freedom should be their most prized possession.

4. Those parties were a drag because everyone sat around laughing at their own jokes.

5. I like someone with their own way of looking at the future.

REVIEW AND PRACTICE

A.

A pronoun is a substitute for a noun or for a group of words.

In the sentences below, cross out repetitive words and replace them with appropriate pronouns.

1. The cable TV station started broadcasting today, and the cable TV station devoted a whole hour to local events.

2. One report was about a woman and the woman's struggle to keep the woman's home.

3. The state is trying to force owners of property near the woods to sell the owners' land to make room for the new highway.

4. The woman in the report is a Native American, and the woman in the report claims the land is the woman's by an ancient treaty.

5. Taking the issue to court will be expensive, but taking the issue to court may be inevitable.

A pronoun refers to its antecedent. Some pronouns don't need antecedents.

In the sentences below, circle each pronoun and draw an arrow from the pronoun to its antecedent. If the pronoun doesn't need an antecedent, write NA above it.

6. People returning to school after many years often find that they learn faster than they used to.

7. However, going to college at the age of forty has its disadvantages.

8. Molly was amazed at how old her classmates made her feel.

9. The other students seemed so sure of their strengths.

10. Nobody realized that Molly was depending on me so heavily.

The subject forms of personal pronouns are for subjects. The object forms are for pronouns performing all other sentence functions, except (in formal situations) completers for forms of *to be*.

In the following sentences, circle the correct pronoun.

11. While Hong and (I / me) were laughing, Nadia led (we / us) into the hall-way.

12. There (she / her) and the bakers told us to close our eyes.

13. In a few minutes, we heard Nadia and (they / them) clanking pans in the kitchen, and then they called (we / us) in.

14. What (we / us) saw will give (we / us) something to talk about for years.

15. One baker and Nadia were standing in the middle of the table where (he / him) and (she / her) were building a human-sized cake castle around themselves.

A personal pronoun must agree with its antecedent. This can be difficult when the gender of the antecedent is unclear.

In each of the next three sentences, cross out the incorrect pronoun and write in a correct one.

16. Each dog trainer should sign up for the show at their nearest YMCA.

17. Everybody thought they would read about this year's show in the paper.

18. But neither of the reporters was able to get their editor to publish the event.

In each of these last sentences, cross out the singular antecedent and write in a plural one.

19. A winner from last year's show can usually expect that they will be invited early.

20. However, nobody in the club seemed to want Margie to come to their show this year.

B.

Correct the pronoun errors in the following paragraphs. If you change an antecedent that is acting as a subject, you might have to change its verb as well.

A person's vision is adapted to their environment. The Pygmies provide one good example. They live in forests where trees limit his field of view to about fifty yards, but within that space, he must make shrewd observations. A person in that situation can develop a very accurate sense of the relationships among objects near to them. However, when a Pygmy is taken to a hill in another part of Africa where they can suddenly see for miles, they look out at elephants on the plain ten miles away and act as if the elephants are nearby and only about the size of lizards. He doesn't perceive the distance and the distortions of perspective. The inversion-glasses experiment provides another example of how anybody's vision shapes itself to their needs. In this experiment, volunteers were asked to wear special glasses that showed them everything upside-down. Nobody was allowed to take off their glasses for a week. Everybody went around for a few days tripping over their own feet and having a terrible time, but then they began to see things right side up again without ever taking off their glasses. Then the researchers removed the glasses. Suddenly each volunteer saw everything upside-down again, and it took several days for their vision to return to normal.

When my friends and me learned about that, we began to think it might be fun to participate in a vision experiment. My professor told Willie and me that we should go over to the psychology department at the university and see if any researchers could use us. In fact, when him and me got there, somebody was looking for volunteers, but it didn't sound appealing to him and I. The researcher wanted the other volunteers and us to sit in a chair and guess what word was being held up on a card behind us. If we all guessed wrong, we would get a little electric shock. If someone guessed right, him and the rest of us would be rewarded with a little rocking motion in our chairs. Willie and me decided that although human vision may be very adaptable, he and me didn't have eyes in the backs of our heads. I wondered who volunteers for experiments like that. You have to admire people like they and others who are willing to suffer a little for the sake of science.

Return to your writing

Review your paragraph about the perfect society. Check to see that the personal pronouns fit the roles they play in their sentences and that they agree with their antecedents. Correct any pronoun errors. Read the paragraph aloud and make any other changes you think might be helpful to a reader.

Read a classmate's work, looking especially for pronoun errors. Suggest corrections.

Complete your work on pronouns by taking the Mastery Test on p. 351.

Chapter 14

Spelling

In many cases, groups of words are spelled in similar ways. The rules that explain such spellings are reliable and worth learning. In other cases, though, there seem to be no helpful rules at all. Therefore, the best way to master the spelling of many words is to start marking up your copy of a good dictionary. When you have to look up a word, circle it so that you can find it easily in case you have to look it up again. Meanwhile, in the spelling chart on pages 247–250 of this chapter, record the words you're practicing so that you need to look up fewer and fewer words as time goes on.

Chapter 14 presents

- three rules about changes in words before added endings.
- advice about creating the possessive form of nouns.
- help in using words that sound alike.
- a spelling chart and a strategy for mastering difficult words.

You may want to start your work on spelling by taking the Pretest on p. 331.

Writing

Think of something that many people own: for example, a television, a bathing suit, a refrigerator. Make notes describing the one you own. Then make notes describing the ones that two or three other people own. Write at least two sentences describing each one, identifying the owners as you go. For instance:

> There's always something to eat in my refrigerator. Whenever I'm hungry I can find an egg or two, some leftovers, maybe even some ice cream. Bridgette's refrigerator is a lot bigger and fancier than mine, but . . .

Organize your sentences to form a paragraph and write the finished version on a fresh piece of paper. Look over your paragraph. Circle any words that contain added endings such as *-s, -es, -'s, -s', -ed, -er, -ing.*

CHANGES BEFORE AN ADDED ENDING

For some words, double the final letter before adding an ending that begins with a vowel.

Finally it **occurred** to me that the taps and thuds of the water **lapping** the shore were making a **bigger** impression on our guest than we expected when we first opened the window.

Double the consonant before adding an ending that begins with a vowel when the last syllable of the word is accented and that syllable ends in a single vowel followed by a single consonant. In the sentence above,

occur is accented on its last syllable, and its last two letters are a single vowel, *u,* and a single consonant, *r.* Therefore, the *r* is doubled before the *-ed.*

lap contains only one syllable, and it is therefore accented. The last two letters are a single vowel followed by a single consonant. Therefore, the last consonant is doubled before the added ending.

big is the same as *lap.*

expect is accented on its last syllable, but its last two letters are two consonants in a row. Therefore, the last consonant isn't doubled before the *-ed.*

open is accented on its first syllable, so the last consonant isn't doubled.

tap, thud are each adding an ending (*-s*) that does not begin with a vowel, so the last consonant is not doubled.

APPLICATION 1.   Correctly add the given ending to each word below.

1. red + est _____

2. quiet + er _____

3. omit + ed _____

4. nap + ing _____

5. benefit + ing _____

APPLICATION 2.   Change the tense of the verb in each sentence below as indicated. Some consonants will double and some won't.

*To present progressive (use **are** + the **-ing** form of the main verb)*

Example: The salesclerks ~~get~~ *are getting* tired of standing on their feet all day.

1. Lou's kids run a lawn-mowing business these days.

2. They get extra gas from the can in our shed sometimes.

3. They begin to bother me.

4. After all, those gallons cost me a pretty penny.

5. We plan to talk about it tomorrow.

*To simple past (these are regular verbs, which will end in **-ed**)*

Example: My cousins ~~want~~ *wanted* me to apply for summer work splitting logs.

6. Some people stop smoking because of the concern expressed by their families.

7. Others wait for more urgent motivations.

8. The people in my office nag me every day to stop.

9. I develop a pretty bad cough every spring.

10. Therefore, every summer I submit to their pressure for a few weeks.

For some nouns and verbs, add -e before a final -s. (See Chapter 11 for more about final -s.)

Now that Carol **goes** to seventh grade, she insists on packing her **lunches** in bags instead of **boxes**, even though the **tomatoes** in the **sandwiches** are more likely to get squashed. She claims that the other students all carry radios to school, too, but I don't believe that.

Add -e along with a final -s when a word's natural ending is -s, -x, -sh, or -ch. Usually, but not always, this -es goes on a word ending in -o with a consonant right before it. In the sentences above,

lunch, sandwich both end in *-ch,* so they add *-es.*
box ends in *-x,* so it adds *-es.*
insist, bag, claim, kid each end in consonants that aren't on the list, so they simply add *-s.*
go, tomato both end in a consonant + *-o,* so they add *-es.*
radio ends in a vowel + *-o,* so it adds only *-s.*

APPLICATION 3. Make each word plural.

   1. wish _____

   2. echo _____

   3. stereo _____

   4. kiss _____

   5. church _____

APPLICATION 4.   Change each sentence below as indicated. Some *-s* endings will include the *-e* and some won't.

To simple present tense

                  insists   *matches*
Example: He ~~insisted~~ that the old wallpaper ~~matched~~ his carpet better than

       the new paint.

   1. Leona always watched movies on her homemade VCR.

   2. She munched popcorn noisily, but at home nobody complained.

   3. She taught the dog to pick up what she spilled.

   4. When the signal went bad, she always fixed the VCR with a screwdriver.

   5. She never missed more than five minutes because of breakdowns.

Change the italicized singular nouns to plurals

                  reasons   *patches*
Example: For what ~~reason~~ did your dad mention the ~~patch~~ on my jeans?

   6. When he was a kid, Jim hung on the *wall* by his bed *a poster* of his

       baseball *hero.*

7. Ten years later, as a minor league slugger, he was used to the fast *pitch* himself.

8. His *friend* began begging him for *a pass* to the home *game.*

9. His *success* allowed him to quit his job selling ski *wax* to sports stores.

10. The *flash* of the newspaper *camera* greeted him the day he made it up to the major league.

For some words that end in -*y*, change the -*y* to -*i* before adding an ending.

> After their **weariness** wore off, the talent show participants **partied** all night. They weren't **worried** about studying for the test on the short **stories**, because the exam period had been delayed.

Change the -*y* to -*i* before any added ending except -*ing* when the last letter of the word is -*y* with a consonant before it. After any -*y* to -*i* change, final -*s* changes to -*es*. In the sentences above,

> **weary** ends in a consonant + -*y*, so the -*y* changes to -*i* before the -*ness*.
> **party, worry** both end in a consonant + -*y*, so the -*y* changes to -*i* before the -*ed*.
> **story** ends in a consonant + -*y*, so the -*y* changes to -*i*. (Notice that the final -*s* becomes -*es* here.)
> **study** ends in a consonant + -*y*, but it is adding -*ing*, so the -*y* doesn't change.
> **delay** ends in a vowel + -*y*, so the -*y* doesn't change.

APPLICATION 5.   Correctly add the given ending to each word below.

1. funny + est _____

2. imply + ed _____

3. fry + ing _____

4. magnify + s _____

5. inventory + s _____

APPLICATION 6.   Change the tense of the verb in each sentence as indicated. Sometimes the -*y* will change to *i* and sometimes it won't.

*To simple past (all verbs in these sentences will end in **-ed**)*

Example: We ~~bury~~ all our weather-beaten flags.
            buried

1. Terry and Don hurry to the dock.

2. Their friends steady the launches while the kids play with the ropes.

3. Finally the boats carry them and their gear toward the mainland.

4. The twins cry, one on each parent's arm, but the others enjoy the trip.

5. These old motorboats ferry people back and forth to the island every year.

*To simple present (all verbs in these sentences will end in **-s** or **-es**)*

Example: He ~~is relying~~ on your discretion.
            relies

6. The new skyscraper is amplifying the sound of traffic on the corner.

7. The medical association has been saying that in several cities, routine mid-day noise is destroying people's hearing.

8. Here the noise is staying at about 65 decibels at noon.

9. At over 80 decibels, it will qualify as a serious health hazard.

10. The City Alliance is paying close attention to a new law that will justify corrective action.

POSSESSIVE NOUNS

An apostrophe + -s ('s) marks the possessive form of any noun that has not already added a final -s to make a plural.

A possessive form of a noun is used to show ownership.

> The **children's** room is large enough for all three of their beds and the **dog's** cushion, too. (The room belongs to the children, and the cushion belongs to the dog.)

> The **manager's** strategy was to figure out the **company's** plan. (The strategy belongs to the manager, and the plan belongs to the company.)

Notice that the 's goes with the owner (in the examples above, *children, dog, manager,* and *company*). The possessive form, with -s, is followed by the thing owned (in the examples above, *room, cushion, strategy,* and *plan*).

APPLICATION 7.   Rewrite each phrase using the possessive form of the noun in italics.

Example: The notebook that belongs to *Hannah*   Hannah's notebook

1. the sound of the *wind* _____
2. the face of your *friend* _____
3. the votes of the *women* _____
4. the wings of the *geese* _____
5. the smell of the *sea* _____
6. the faith of that *child* _____
7. the energy of those *children* _____
8. the seats of the *car* _____
9. the radio that belongs to *Grady* _____
10. the money of the *city* _____

APPLICATION 8.   Revise each sentence below to include the possessive form of the noun in italics.

That flowering shrub's fragrance
Example: ~~The fragrance of that flowering shrub~~ lasts both day and night.

1. The hopes of the *coach* rested on that rookie.

2. The outcome may match the predictions of the *media*.

3. It may turn out to be a victory that belongs to the whole *team*.

4. This tournament is like the dreams that my *children* have.

5. The pride of our *family* is wrapped up in it, too.

An apostrophe (') alone marks the possessive form of any plural noun ending in -s.

> On the night shift, we fill several **hours'** time in front of the TV letting all those detective **shows'** suspense keep us awake.

In the sentence above, the possessive forms replace phrases that would include *of* + a plural noun: the time of several *hours*, the suspense of those detective *shows*. Since *hours* and *shows* have already added *-s* to become plural, they add only apostrophes now.

APPLICATION 9.   Rewrite each phrase to use the possessive form of the italicized noun, which has already received an added *-s*.

Example: The manual of the lab *instructors* *the lab instructors' manual*

1. the sounds of the *leaves* _____

2. the faces of your *friends* _____

3. the talents of those two *sisters* _____

4. the wings of the *robins* _____

5. the smell of the *gases* _____

6. the faith of those *mothers* _____

7. the energy of those *kids* _____

8. the seats of the *buses* _____

9. the radio of his *roommates* _____

10. the money of the *cities* _____

APPLICATION 10.   Revise each sentence below to include the possessive form of the noun in italics.

Example: ~~The fragrance of those flowering shrubs~~ *Those flowering shrubs' fragrance* lasts both day and night.

1. The hopes of the *coaches* rested on that rookie.

2. The outcome may match the predictions of the *reporters*.

3. It may turn out to be a victory that belongs to the short *guys*.

4. This tournament is like the dreams that my *kids* have.

5. The pride of our *relatives* is wrapped up in it, too.

Most *-s* endings do not include apostrophes.

Amanda's son **claims** that she's watched all the midnight **shows** for two **years**. He **thinks** that's probably a record, even among those crazy **friends** of **yours**.

An apostrophe with a final *-s* marks either a possessive noun or a contracted verb. Do not use apostrophes with any other *-s* endings.

Amanda's is a possessive noun, so it includes an apostrophe.
claims, thinks are third person singular present tense verbs, so they need no apostrophe.
she's is a contraction of *she* and *has,* so it includes an apostrophe.
years, friends, shows are plural nouns, so they need no apostrophe.
That's is a contraction of *that* and *is,* so it includes an apostrophe.
yours is a possessive pronoun, not a possessive noun, so it needs no apostrophe.

APPLICATION 11.   Replace the italicized words in the sentences below to make the changes indicated.

Change to simple present tense

1. While the supervisor *talked*, Bertha always *smoked* at the other side of the room.

2. She never *had* a pack of her own, so she always *borrowed* cigarettes from me.

3. That *was* fine with me, because she always *helped* me when my drill press *broke* down.

Change to plural forms

4. During coffee *break*, the *supervisor* always sat with your *brother*.

5. They would talk about their *adventure* in their *homeland*.

6. When they moved here, they brought along their good *spirit*, even though they had to leave their *family* behind.

Replace with possessive pronouns

7. Ruth finally gave up that plan of *Ruth's* to move to Indiana.

8. She would have had to ask Tayo to sell *Tayo's* car.

9. I used to love riding in *that car's* wide back seat.

10. For years, that car has been a trademark of *Ruth's and Tayo's*.

WORDS THAT SOUND ALIKE

Then indicates a time relationship between two thoughts or introduces the result of an action in an *if . . . then . . .* statement.

Let's buy some ice cream and **then** eat it down by the river.
If we had a few fireworks, **then** we could really celebrate.

Than shows a comparison.

That would be a lot better **than** fighting the crowds for a seat in the stadium.

On a separate paper, write two or three sentences using each word.

APPLICATION 12.   Insert *then* or *than* to complete each sentence correctly.

1. The mystery surrounding the yoga demonstration last night is almost more _____ I can stand.

2. First the yogi tied his arms under his legs, _____ he squirmed into a box, and _____ his assistant immersed the box in water for twenty minutes.

3. I thought that was even more amazing _____ the walking-on-coals stunt.

4. If I don't figure out the illusion behind that man's powers, _____ I may just have to admit he's for real.

5. Amy was teasing when she suggested that I could train myself to hold my breath like that, and _____ I could become a famous yogi, too.

Two spells out the numeral *2*.

Noah must have looked hard to find **two** fleas.

Too means *excessively* (more than enough) or *also*.

It's **too** bad he succeeded.
I wish he'd left the ticks behind, **too.**

To introduces either an infinitive (the name of a verb) or
a prepositional phrase.

> I need **to check** my dog carefully every morning after I've taken him **to the field** for his run.

On a separate paper, write two or three sentences using each word.

APPLICATION 13.   Insert *two, too,* or *to* to complete each sentence correctly.

1. When Auilda went _____ the hospital, she insisted on taking along _____ bags full of games _____ play with the nurses.

2. I tried _____ convince her she had a few _____ many games, but the more I talked, the more games she decided _____ take.

3. She even counted all the playing cards in her old deck _____ be sure she had all fifty-_____.

4. The day after the operation, I went _____ see her, bringing _____ giant roses because I was sure she'd be _____ tired _____ enjoy food or conversation.

5. I found her sitting up in a chair, laughing because her card tricks had worn out _____ nurses already; and by the end of my visit, I was exhausted, _____.

No states the opposite of *yes* or represents the quantity *zero.*

> **No,** I'm afraid that pie has **no** lemon flavor at all.

To know is a verb meaning *to recognize* or *to understand.*

> I think I **know** why it came out that way.

Now identifies the present moment.

> We could still add some juice to the topping, even **now**.

> On a separate paper, write two or three sentences using each word.

APPLICATION 14.   Insert *no, know,* or *now* to complete each sentence correctly.

1. _____ that the computer revolution has arrived, everyone wonders how we used to get along without computers.

2. Most businesses have become dependent on computers for data filing, and _____ bank would consider giving out money to a patron without checking computerized records first.

3. Word processors are _____ relieving secretaries of many routine tasks, and some computer programs can check a document for spelling so that neither the writer nor the typist has to _____ how to spell the difficult words.

4. But spelling programs can't eliminate confusion among words that sound alike, such as *to* and *two,* because _____ computer can _____ enough to choose which meaning of the word is right for the whole sentence.

5. Computers, despite their awesome power, have _____ judgment.

Whether introduces a dependent clause about an uncertainty.

> The builders don't know **whether** they can finish the house by June.

Weather is a noun referring to the condition of the outdoor air.

> They can't work on the roof in stormy **weather**.

> On a separate paper, write two or three sentences using each word.

APPLICATION 15.   Insert *whether* or *weather* to complete each sentence correctly.

1. If the _____ stays sunny, Hank will be happy enough on a bike.

2. But he doesn't know _____ there will be a good place to lock it at the school.

3. Besides, it might rain, and he's not sure _____ his papers will get wet in his backpack.

4. _____ or not he takes the bike, he'd better hurry up.

5. According to the _____ report, he doesn't need to worry.

Passed **is the simple past tense form as well as the past participle form of** *to pass.*

Parents' attitudes aren't always **passed** on to their children.

Past **indicates a time before the present. It can also act as a preposition similar to** *beyond.*

However, parents often see their own **past** thoughts and feelings being acted out again as their children move **past** each milestone of growth toward adulthood.

On a separate paper, write two or three sentences using each word.

APPLICATION 16.   Insert *passed* or *past* to complete each sentence correctly.

1. Thousands of years ago, settlers from Central Asia struggled across the Aleutian Islands, pushed _____ the tundra, and wandered into the temperate forests and fields of our continent.

2. Some stayed in what is now Canada, and others _____ on in their route southward.

3. Those who found their way _____ the Rockies discovered wide plains filled with game.

4. Many centuries _____ before immigrants from Europe began to arrive.

5. Their _____ lives and motivating dreams were very different from those of the earlier settlers.

Were is the simple past plural form of *to be.*

> The 1960 Winter Olympics **were** held in Squaw Valley, California.

We're is the contracted form of *we are.*

> **We're** hoping to visit there.

Where introduces a question or a dependent clause about a place.

> **Where** is the nearest bus station? I wonder **where** we can find out.

On a separate paper, write two or three sentences using each word.

APPLICATION 17.   Insert *were, we're,* or *where* to complete each sentence correctly.

1. Exams _____ all finished yesterday.

2. Now _____ able to sit in the yard and do nothing.

3. So _____ do you think you're going?

4. _____ you on your way downtown?

5. _____ going into the station _____ we can get warm.

Their is the possessive form of *they.*

> I love **their** optimism.

They're is the contracted form of *they are.*

> Roman and Sue think **they're** going to be able to fix the car.

There often indicates a place away from *here*. At other times, *there* is used in expressions such as *there is* and *there are*.

> **There** are very few things that teach people their limits more quickly than struggling with a car engine. I'm going to stop at Sue's house on the way home and see what's happening over **there**.

On a separate paper, write two or three sentences using each word.

APPLICATION 18.   Insert *their, they're,* or *there* to complete each sentence correctly.

_____ once were two women who'd wear

_____ necklaces wrapped round _____ hair.

With _____ chains on their heads

_____ supposed to have said,

"_____ less weight on our poor necks up _____."

Your is the possessive form of *you* (note that it has no apostrophe).

> We're going to **your** house.

You're is the contracted form of *you are* (note the apostrophe).

> **You're** going to make dinner for all of us.

On a separate paper, write two or three sentences using each word.

APPLICATION 19.   Insert *your* or *you're* to complete each sentence correctly.

1. Imagine this: _____ walking across the bridge minding _____ own business when suddenly a truck pulls up beside you.

2. The driver jumps out, and before _____ eyes attaches some hook to a bridge cable, shakes _____ hand, and then leaps off the edge while _____ just standing there, rooted to _____ spot.

3. _____ too amazed to scream and also too frightened to look over the edge, so you close _____ eyes and pray _____ only dreaming.

4. After three long seconds, _____ curiosity overcomes _____ fear, and you rush to the edge just in time to see this madman one hundred feet below, bounding back toward you like a yo-yo, and then hurdling the rail to land beside you.

5. He winks at _____ questions, unfastens his huge elastic strap from the bridge cable, and drives off in his truck, whose engine had been idling loudly in _____ ears the whole time.

Its is the possessive form of *it* (note that it has no apostrophe).

What I like best about my room is **its** view.

It's is the contracted form of *it is* or *it has* (note the apostrophe).

The room is tiny, but **it's** full of the western light.

On a separate paper, write two or three sentences using each word.

APPLICATION 20.   Insert *its* or *it's* to complete each sentence correctly.

1. _____ the apostrophe's job to mark possessives as well as contractions.

2. But each personal pronoun has _____ own possessive form and doesn't need any apostrophe.

3. So if there's an apostrophe in any personal pronoun, _____ sure to mark a contraction.

4. *Their, your,* and *its* are the tricky personal pronouns, and *whose* causes _____ share of spelling problems, too.

5. _____ a good idea to check these words in every paper you write.

Whose is the possessive form of *who* (note that it has no apostrophe).

Manfred is a telephone operator **whose** dream is to get an armadillo for a pet.

Who's is the contracted form of *who is* or *who has* (note the apostrophe).

> He's the one **who's** been reading all those stories about ancient heroes and heroines who were turned into animals.

On a separate paper, write two or three sentences using each word.

APPLICATION 21.   Insert *whose* or *who's* to complete each sentence correctly.

1. Hendy keeps mentioning the week of slapstick specials to his mother, _____ not about to let him spend every afternoon in front of the TV.

2. She's one of those mothers _____ prejudiced against TV and discourages Hendy's friendships with people _____ primary subject of conversation is the afternoon soaps.

3. But Abbott and Costello, _____ films are legitimate classics, might break through her defenses.

4. After all, _____ going to stand between a son and his education in the classics?

5. Besides, Hendy's mother is a baseball fan _____ favorite quotation comes from that Abbott and Costello patter that starts out, "_____ on first?"

SPELLING CHART

Each person has different spelling problems. Concentrate on your own.

> Collect your spelling errors on the chart below. In the last column, add a comment that helps you think about why this word causes you trouble and how you can remember its correct spelling. Here are some possible comments: "added ending" (see pp. 231–235), "possessive form" (pp. 236–239), "sound-alike word" (such as those presented on pp. 240–247), form of word (such as *excellent* when you mean *excellence*), irregular verb (see list on pp. 30–32), missing ending or syllable. These comments will help you understand your spelling problems so that you can learn from them.

Phrase that includes the word as you misspelled it	Correct spelling	Comment

Phrase that includes the word as you misspelled it	Correct spelling	Comment

Phrase that includes the word as you misspelled it	Correct spelling	Comment

Using the spelling chart will allow you to organize and learn from your spelling problems. You can strengthen your mastery of spelling further if you keep a spelling notebook. At the top of each page of your notebook, write the correct spelling of each word you have had trouble with. Every day, pick one new word and on its page write four different sentences that use the word correctly. Return to this page occasionally on later days, writing new sentences each time until you are sure that the correct spelling has become a habit. Then cross out the word on your chart.

Organize, learn from, and master your spelling problems by using your chart, your dictionary, and your spelling notebook regularly.

REVIEW AND PRACTICE

A.

On an accented last syllable, a final consonant preceded by a single vowel
will be doubled before any added ending that begins with a vowel.

Fill each blank with the correct combination of the word and the ending given
below the line.

1. While the horse was _____ toward the field, a bird

                   trot + ing

   _____ past its head.

swoop + ed

2. From the _____ of its ears, it was clear that it was

          flat + ness

   _____ an impulse to rear.

control + ing

3. Then suddenly it _____ _____ with giant and beautiful

                start + ed   **run + ing**

   strides.

Final -s usually becomes final -es after an -o preceded by a consonant,
and always after -s, -sh, -ch, or -x.

Fill each blank below with the word given below the line plus final -s.

4. The science _____ are wandering through the tall

               student

   _____.

grass

5. They have wrapped _____ of cloth over their heads, because the

               patch

   sun _____ _____ on a day like this.

      scorch   **scalp**

6. Collecting samples for their _____, they look like a bunch of

                    stash

   _____ seeking discarded _____.

  hobo   **treasure**

When the last letter of a word is *-y* with a consonant before it, *-y* changes to *-i* before any added ending except *-ing*. After a *-y* to *-i* change, final *-s* becomes *-es*.

Fill each blank with the correct combination of the word and the ending given below the line.

7. Esther _____ too _____ on her lab partner.
              rely + s   heavy + ly

8. For instance, when the mixture in her test tube was _____ than
                                          cloudy + er

   she expected, she asked her partner to mix a new one, and then she left.

9. She should have _____, because her lab partner soon saw that
                      stay + ed

   Esther's result actually _____ something exciting.
                        imply + ed

An apostrophe + *-s* (*'s*) marks the possessive form of any noun that has not already added an *-s* to make a plural.

Fill each blank with the possessive form of the word given below the line.

10. You can always tell when _____ patience is wearing thin.
                            Josie

11. She starts by complaining about the _____ noise, and then
                                        television

   storms off and starts rearranging the _____ clothes.
                                baby

12. When she gets really worked up, she interferes with the _____
                                                children

   homework.

13. You have to watch out when she starts breathing down _____
                                              Aunt Julia

   neck.

An apostrophe by itself marks the possessive form of any noun that has already added an *-s* to create a plural.

Fill each blank with the possessive form of the word given below the line.

14. In the winter, you can tell trees apart by their _____ patterns.
                                                branches

15. Our three _____ trees are worth preserving because of the shade
      parks

    they provide for the _____ summer activities.
      kids

16. The last two _____ park maintenance budgets have begun to
      years

    show some changes.

17. This has been in response to eloquent speeches from the _____
      parents

    spokesperson.

An apostrophe with a final -s marks either a possessive noun or a contracted verb. No other -s endings include apostrophes.

Cross out any unnecessary apostrophes in the sentences below.

18. It's a relief that Manny seem's to be recovering his strength.

19. He's got a pretty tough pair of legs', and his lung's are as strong as ever.

20. The nurse's advice is to let him walk whenever he want's to.

For 21–50 below, complete each sentence with the correct word from each group being reviewed.

Then expresses a time relationship or a result.
Than shows a comparison.

21. Earlene slept longer _____ usual this morning.

22. She drank some coffee at 8:00, but _____ she went back to bed.

23. If this is the way she wants to spend her vacation, _____ why should we interfere?

Two spells out the numeral 2.
Too means *excessively* or *also*.
To introduces an infinitive or a prepositional phrase.

24. Hurrying down the stairs _____ the subway, Dolores saw a man who looked like her uncle who disappeared two years ago.

25. She waved at him, but he was moving _____ fast in the other direction.

26. For the last _____ weeks, Dolores has been watching for him there every morning.

No is the opposite of *yes* or indicates the quantity *zero*.
To know is a verb meaning *to recognize* or *to understand*.
Now identifies the present moment.

27. Last winter cabbage was expensive, but _____ the price has dropped.

28. So I don't _____ why Liz still refuses to buy it.

29. Whenever she does the shopping, she seems to have _____ judgment at all.

Whether starts a dependent clause about an uncertainty.
Weather refers to the condition of the air outdoors.

30. In agricultural communities, the _____ is more than just a topic for small talk.

31. Everything depends on _____ the rains come at the right time.

32. _____ or not the _____ is good for sunbathing is irrelevant.

Passed is a form of *to pass*.
Past refers to a time before the present or introduces a prepositional phrase.

33. It's hard to believe that Dan _____ his driving test.

34. He _____ a car on a curve and went _____ a blinking yellow light without slowing down.

35. The examiners must be more lenient than they were in the _____.

Were is a form of *to be*.
We're is the contraction of *we are*.
Where introduces a question or a dependent clause about a place.

36. After two blocks, turn _____ you see the rental sign.

37. _____ in the third apartment on the left, near the stairs _____ you see all the mailboxes.

38. We _____ planning to put our name on the door, but there _____ too few spaces for all the letters in our name.

Their is the possessive form of *they*.
They're is the contracted form of *they are*.
There introduces certain expressions or indicates a location.

39. On the sidewalk _____ was a pair of glasses with the lens missing from the left side.

40. My cousins put it into _____ fish tank.

41. The fish now swim in and out of the empty side when _____ chasing each other about.

Your is the possessive form of *you*.
You're is the contracted form of *you are*.

42. When _____ picking tobacco, you get sticky all over.

43. If you work near the barns, _____ nostrils go numb from the sweet, thick smell of drying leaves.

44. By the end of the day, _____ likely to be grateful for simple things like a sink of clear water and a gust of fresh air.

Its is the possessive form of *it*.
It's is the contracted form of *it is*.

45. Walt claims that _____ fun to study maps.

46. Every week he picks out a new country and memorizes _____ geographical data.

47. He's fascinated by the way a nation shapes _____ political and economic systems to fit _____ physical environment.

Whose is the possessive form of *who*.
Who's is the contracted form of *who is*.

48. I called the official _____ handling my case.

49. She turns out to be the woman _____ son was written up in the newspaper.

50. Apparently, he's one of those people _____ able to predict future events.

B.

The following story contains several examples of each spelling error discussed in this chapter. Correct each one you find.

When Lavinia and I got too the stadium, the weather was pretty bad, so the bleachers we're much less crowdded then we expected. We sat down behind some cheerful-lookking fans who's T-shirts showed that there team was the wrong one. We joked with them a bit about the standings of our teams during the past season, and then Lavinia and I settled down to business.

"Whose pitching?" she askked.

I past my eyes over the newspaper cliping I'd brought to see weather it said who the starting players where going to be. "Their puting in a rookie." I groaned.

She stopped smiling, amazed. "Oh, know, not today! They should no better by now. A rookie at a time like this always implys a desperate strategy in the dugout. Were going to lose our chance for the pennant."

We continued with our usual commentting while the team went through its warm-up play's, and then it started to drizzle. The two people in front of us immediately hauled out gigantic umbrella's. The point on the top of the big guys umbrella hovered right by my ear were it blocked my view completely. We asked them to lower the umbrellas a little, at least. They just shruged and said, "But its raining. If you can't see, than that's you're problem."

Lavinia always trys to be patient. "You shouldn't treat your rival fans' that way," she teased, and sweetly passed them some popcorn.

But I was mad. "These bleachers are geting even nastyer than the subways," I roared. The fellow who's umbrella blocked my view of left field just smirked while the other happyly took some sandwichs out of his friends' pocket. By then, the rain was comming down hard, so we got up and headed for shelter. The whether was so bad that the officials called a rain delay in the game.

As we stood inside the door eating our steaming hot dogs and french fryed potatos, I was mader than ever about those creeps. But Lavinia was begining to giggle. She nudged me and pointed out at the drenched bleachers. "You're not going to believe this," she whispered, "but those guy's are still crouching there under they're silly umbrellas." Lavinia always breaks' through even the worst of my moods, and pretty soon I was laughing, two.

Return to your writing

Review the paragraph you wrote at the beginning of this chapter. Check to see that the endings you circled are correct. Look for errors with words that sound alike. Read the paragraph one more time and make any other changes you think it needs.

Read a classmate's paragraph, looking for spelling errors.

Finish your work on this chapter by taking the Mastery Test on p. 355.

Chapter 15

Consistency

Consistency, or harmony of parts, is critical for showing your reader how your thoughts fit together. Consistency of verb tense, pronoun point of view, and sentence pattern will allow your reader to follow the path of your ideas within sentences, through paragraphs, and on to the end of a whole essay.

Chapter 15 explains consistency and gives you practice with

- consistency of parallel sentence elements.
- consistency of verb tense within a time framework.
- consistency of pronoun point of view.

You may want to start your work on consistency by taking the Pretest on p. 335.

Writing

Think of an event or a discussion that made you change your mind about something. What was your old opinion? What is your new opinion? What were the factors that caused you to change your mind? Picture that turning point as clearly as you can. Who was there? What was going on around you? How did you feel? Jot notes answering these questions, and then arrange your ideas in a paragraph that describes how you changed your mind. Write your final version on a fresh piece of paper.

Read your paragraph aloud and underline each verb twice. Circle each pronoun.

FINDING AND USING PARALLEL ELEMENTS

Parallel elements within a sentence can be linked with a conjunction.

Sentence	*Parallel Elements*
Alone **but** not afraid, Mrs. Herschel set off for the bus terminal.	Alone afraid (two modifiers for the subject)
She intended to buy her own ticket, to carry her own bag, **and** to make her own way to Missouri.	to buy her own ticket to carry her own bag to make her own way (three infinitives used as completers)
As she turned the corner **and** waited for the light, she felt that life was beginning again for her.	turned the corner waited for the light (two simple past verbs with their completers)

We call straight lines *parallel* if they move in the same direction, so we can call sentence elements *parallel* if they show readers that certain thoughts are moving in the same direction. When you have several ideas to pack into one sentence, you can often arrange some of them in words that play the same sentence role and then link them with a conjunction. Skim through the sentence-combining sections at the ends of Chapters 2 through 6 to refresh your memory of how conjunctions can connect groups of words that play the same role in a sentence.

APPLICATION 1.   Parallel sentence elements are linked by conjunctions in the sentences below. Bracket the parallel elements and circle the conjunctions.

Example: "Now we are engaged in a great civil war, testing whether ⟨that nation⟩, ⟨or⟩ ⟨any nation⟩ ⟨so conceived⟩ ⟨and⟩ ⟨so dedicated⟩, can long endure. (from Lincoln's Gettysburg Address)

1. Quickly but quietly, Sung gathered together his equipment.

2. Finally it was his turn to climb the telephone pole, to find the broken wire, and to fix it.

3. Although he loved wiring and trusted his new skill, he suddenly doubted that he would be able to succeed.

4. He held his breath until he found himself climbing the pole steadily and shifting his weight perfectly.

5. Nobody watching him from below would have guessed that Sung had ever been afraid of heights or that courage was his biggest challenge on this job.

Using parallel elements makes a sentence easier to understand.

> Those experiences have helped me to develop a strict sense of discipline that I've applied to my work habits, and I gained a clear sense of right and wrong in moral questions.

> Those experiences have helped me to develop a strict sense of discipline in my work habits and a clear sense of right and wrong in moral questions.

Which of the two sentences above is easier to follow? Look for the parallel elements in the second one.

APPLICATION 2.   In each group of sentences below, adjust some words to create two or more parallel elements that play the same sentence role. Then combine the ideas into one sentence by compounding those elements.

Example: Soon James realized that he must ask for help. Otherwise, he must fail. *Soon James realized that he must ask for help or fail.*

1. Some people fear failure. They also have a fear of success. _____
   _____

2. I like to watch the news at night. Listening to the radio at night is something I like, too. _____
   _____

3. You can get to the caves by taking a special train. It's also possible to hike there. _____
   _____

4. We want you to check in with us when you finish the training program. After you get your first job, check in with us, too. _____
   _____

5. Ruth says that the statistics prove her point. We should get the paper to publish them, she says. _____

_____

APPLICATION 3.   Lack of parallelism makes the following sentences hard to follow. In each sentence, change the wording to create two or more elements that play the same sentence role. Rewrite the sentence, compounding those elements.

Example: Developing your ideas logically, give examples, and to use clear transitions between thoughts are three elements of good writing.

Developing your ideas logically, giving examples, and using clear transitions between thoughts are three elements of good writing.

1. The three places where people learn are in the home, playing, and at work.

_____

2. You should try to gather as much knowledge as you can, because knowledge will help you with problems and cope with life. _____

_____

3. The gold charm would cost you $8 and $3.50 in silver. _____

_____

4. The techniques for getting good grades are to study course material thoroughly, testing your understanding, confidence, and to relax. _____

_____

_____

5. I meet people at work because I'm involved in answering phone calls, fix bulletin boards, and making posters, too. _____

_____

MAKING VERB TENSES CONSISTENT

A paragraph or an essay needs a time framework based on a dominant
verb tense.

> Lorna takes promises very seriously. She never forgives anyone for
> breaking one. In addition, she considers the slightest little agreement to
> be a full-fledged promise, so people often find Lorna counting on them to
> do things they have no intention of doing. She fills her life with trumped-
> up promises and then makes a huge fuss when most of those promises fall
> through.

The dominant tense of the paragraph above is the simple present. Maintaining
a single time framework helps a reader understand the sequence of events
presented in a piece of writing. Skim through Chapter 2 to refresh your memory of the ways in which verb tenses express time.

APPLICATION 4.   Rewrite the paragraph above using the simple past as the dominant
tense. When you are finished, read your version aloud. Listen to be sure that
all the verbs are expressing past time.

Lorna took promises very seriously.

_____

_____

_____

_____

_____

_____

_____

_____

Sometimes it is necessary to use several verb tenses in a single paragraph.

> Once the astronauts were in orbit, they relaxed. They had not been able to think their own thoughts for several hours, and they needed a chance to sit back and to absorb what was happening to them. Below them the Pacific Ocean edged into view. Above them the moon looked as distant as ever. We like to cover every detail of these space ventures in the news, but most of us will never know what goes on in the minds of people who are beyond the pull of their own world's gravity. What we do know is that finally the astronauts ate their rations quietly and slept.

In the paragraph above, the verbs are in several different tenses because the writer is deliberately showing shifts of time in the events being described.

APPLICATION 5. Read aloud the example paragraph about the astronauts. Complete the following tasks:
1. Underline each verb. Be careful not to underline the verbals.
2. Study the verbs you have underlined. Write the dominant tense of the passage here: _____ Cross out all the verbs in that tense.
3. List all the remaining verbs below. Beside each one, answer the question "Why isn't this verb in the dominant tense?"

Verb	*Reason it is not used in the dominant tense*
had not been	*This took place before the time of the dominant tense — before they relaxed.*

Verb   *Reason it is not used in the dominant tense*

_____   _____

                 _____

_____   _____

                 _____

Shifting tense without a good reason distracts a reader.

> While Rosa **is arguing** about the bill, I **walked** around the table and **poured** everyone some more coffee.

After reading the sentence above, we guess that the events in the restaurant happened during the same time period, but the shift to past tense after the comma makes us wonder about that guess. The time shift is distracting. In any piece of writing, all verbs should be in the dominant tense, unless the writer wants to shift the time deliberately for a reason that will be obvious to the reader.

APPLICATION 6.   In the following sentences, the verbs show shifts in time for no good reason. Correct each sentence so that all the verbs are in the same tense as the first verb in each sentence.

Example: Mr. Whitaker locks his door as soon as the paper girl ~~left.~~ *leaves*

1. He was a cheerful person who had many friends, but then his whole personality changes when his girlfriend leaves him.

2. In this picture, the man in the front shows his age more than the man behind him did.

3. When the rest of the family woke up, we told them what happened, and everyone breaks out laughing.

4. They are always playing tennis, which is more of a gentleman's game, so they weren't spending much time with me.

5. I was out the door before she was, and my father is walking toward us

carrying a bucket.

MAKING PRONOUN POINT OF VIEW CONSISTENT

A paragraph or essay needs a dominant point of view that is reflected in the pronouns.

> In this part of the country, if we want those little Mexican tomatoes called tomatillos, we have to grow them ourselves. We can't expect to find them in the supermarkets. So instead, we order the seeds from a catalogue and plant them in flats right in our kitchen. When the weather warms up, we keep them on the balcony. In a few months they're just as juicy as the sweet little balls our mother used to put in dozens of fillings and sauces.

In the paragraph above, the events are described from a *first person plural* point of view, expressed in the pronouns *we, our,* and *us.* **Person** in grammar is a technical term separating nouns and pronouns into three groups:

first person = the speaker or writer (**I, me, we, us**)

second person = the listener or reader (**you**)

third person = everybody else (**he, him, she, her, it, they, Mr. Max, love, a peanut**)

Writing with a first person point of view emphasizes the writer's involvement in the events presented. Using the second person brings the reader into focus. Using the third person creates a more distant view of the event.

APPLICATION 7.   Rewrite the paragraph above with a second-person point of view. You will have to change all the first person pronouns to second-person pronouns.

In this part of the country, if you want those little Mexican tomatoes called tomatillos,

you have to grow them yourselves.

_____

_____

_____

_____

_____

_____

_____

_____

_____

Shifting pronouns without a good reason distracts a reader.

> A girl who is looking for **her** first job knows **you'll** find help there.

Reading this sentence, we picture a girl, and then suddenly the word *you* makes us picture ourselves and forget the girl for a minute. That is distracting. Within a sentence or a paragraph, pronouns should be consistent with the dominant point of view unless the writer deliberately wants to shift the reader's attention to another character or object.

APPLICATION 8.   In the following sentences, the pronouns shift person for no good reason. Correct each sentence so that all the pronouns express the point of view established in the opening words of the sentence.

Example: When you are alone, ~~one~~ *you* may observe details more closely than
    when ~~one is~~ *you are* among friends.

1. When people watch silly or violent programs, they try to imitate the actors and you usually end up making a fool of yourself.

2. In learning, one must be able to slow down and consider what you've been experiencing.

3. When we think about how we spend our lives, you are often surprised at how our actions reflect your hidden values.

4. People are crazy to think one can become a radiologist without studying many hours because he or she just can't learn it all by cramming at the last minute.

5. As a species, humankind has always responded well when our survival has been challenged, and they'll do so again now.

REVIEW AND PRACTICE

A.

Parallel elements clarify the relationships among ideas.

The following paragraphs are taken from a speech given by President Eisenhower in 1953. Read the passage aloud, noting the use of parallelism to highlight the organization of ideas. Put brackets around any parallel elements and circle the conjunctions that link them.

The fruit of success in all these tasks would present the world with the greatest task, and the greatest opportunity of all. It is this: the dedication of the energies, the resources, and the imaginations of all peaceful nations to a new kind of war. This would be declared a total war, not upon any enemy but upon the brute forces of poverty and need.

The peace we seek, founded upon decent trust and cooperative effort among nations, can be fortified not by weapons of war but by wheat and by cotton, by milk and by wool, by meat and by timber and by rice. These are words that translate into every language on earth. These are needs that challenge this world in arms.

— Dwight D. Eisenhower, "The Chance for Peace"

A piece of writing needs a dominant point of view, expressed through the verb tenses.

The descriptive paragraph below starts out in the simple present tense. Then the verbs switch back and forth between the present and past tenses. Correct the verbs for consistency within a present time framework.

Barry unfolds his legs and leaves the couch. The top of the door frame dents his wrinkled hat as he stepped out onto the grass. From his shoulders, his binoculars had swung, bumping his hip with each stride. Ignoring them, he turned his bare eyes toward the tree where something rustles — a goldfinch. He stands as still as a stick for a moment, and then slowly fumbled in his pocket for a brown, dog-eared notebook in which he scratched something while the bird poses on an open branch and stared toward the sea. The smell of pine needles after a hard rain stings in the breeze that brushes unevenly from the shore.

A piece of writing needs a dominant point of view, expressed through the pronouns.

The following paragraph contains shifts among first, second, and third person pronouns. Make the point of view consistent by using second person pronouns to refer to the viewers of the film.

The story of Tarzan succeeds for you only if we're willing to accept the possibility of a human baby being raised by apes. If you can allow yourself that little flight of fancy, you'll probably enjoy the movie *Greystoke*. It takes the old Tarzan story and entices the viewer into its fantasy by presenting him or her with beautiful images and haunting sounds of the jungle. We soon stop worrying about whether any of it is realistic and you find yourself wondering how young John (Tarzan) will adjust to the human world. When John feels himself torn between his human and his animal natures, many viewers can sympathize almost as if this had actually happened in our own lives. Perhaps in some symbolic way it has.

B.

In the paragraph below, the verbs and pronouns are not consistent within the time framework and point of view established at the start. There are also two sentences where lack of parallelism is confusing. Correct these inconsistencies.

We are often fascinated by the harmless eccentrics in our hometowns. You become used to seeing someone like the local hat lady, who wore a different set of strange rags on her head every day, or the dancing man because of his feet which move all the time. One doesn't envy these people. After all, you realized that they are usually struggling just to survive. But you can't help admiring the way they coped with life on their own terms. Sometimes watching such people teaches one to see society in a new way and paying attention to some of life's unexpected possibilities.

Return to your writing

Read aloud the paragraph you wrote about changing your mind. Identify the time framework and the dominant point of view. If you find that your verbs or pronouns are inconsistent, change them. Then look for groups of sentences where you have made a series of points or given a number of examples. Check to see if you could strengthen the organization by using parallel elements, and correct any sentences where the lack of parallelism seems confusing. Make any other changes to help a reader.

Read a classmate's paragraph in the same way.

Finish your work on this chapter by taking the Mastery Test on p. 359.

PART THREE

Writing

Chapter 16

Techniques for Writing

Writing is a way of discovering ideas as well as expressing them. Therefore, few writers are able to make all their ideas and words work together perfectly on the first try. Most writers produce several *drafts*, or experimental versions, of a piece of writing before arriving at a *final draft*. As you write your drafts and move toward a final one for each of your writing projects, you will be examining your own thoughts and developing skills for expressing them. Chapter 16 offers some techniques and tools you can use along the way. You will learn to

- explore topics by freewriting and clustering.
- limit topics and use topic sentences.
- clarify points by using examples and specific language.
- highlight organization with paragraph breaks and transitional words.
- write thesis statements.

1. FREEWRITING

Freewriting is a way of discovering what you want to say. In freewriting, you set aside all the usual rules of writing for readers, and you write fast, without stopping. You don't have to capitalize letters or spell correctly. You can wander off your topic and say outrageous things. The point is simply to capture as much as you can of what passes through your mind in a short period, so you shouldn't waste time erasing and reconsidering what you have written. There is only one rule: **Keep your pencil moving all the time.** If you feel as if your mind goes blank at some point, just write your last phrase over and over until new words begin to come.

Here is an example of freewriting by a young woman who wanted to write an essay about working mothers. The passage is hard to read because the writer was not worrying about spelling, punctuation, and organization; she was simply trying to record her thoughts rapidly in their earliest stages so that she could go back and think about them later.

> If a woman is going leave her children in good hands prefferbly a grandmother or the childs father, she should go back to work. Because she will be doing the child some good if this is what she really wants. what she really wants. What I really wanted was to have the best of care for my child and feel good about whose caring for the baby, there was no reason not to go back to work. Its silly for a single career woman to get married have children then give up career, somebody should have told me that, I wish. Children look up to their parents. Imitate their actions, so I feel that if he sees his parents as being successful as both parents and careerwise they will thrive strive to live up to that standard.

EXERCISE: Get a pencil and paper. Write nonstop for five minutes on one of the following topics:
  a. eating out
  b. living alone
  c. writing.

2. CLUSTERING

Clustering helps you organize thoughts as you discover them. In clustering, you write a topic in the center of a page and then surround the topic with your thoughts about it, jotting ideas down as they come into your mind. When several thoughts are related to each other, put them together in a cluster, and when a completely new thought comes, put it on another part of the page. There are two rules: 1) **Don't try to write out each whole thought; just jot down a phrase quickly and see what comes next**; 2) **don't reject any thoughts; they are all potentially useful**. When you are finished, check to see that related thoughts are close together in clusters.

Here is a clustering sample that one student developed as he was preparing to write a paragraph about football. Notice that after he finished jotting his ideas in the ring, he crossed out two items and moved them closer to the clusters where he felt they belonged.

Fans
Loyalty
Spending money
Bets

Half-time shows
Cheerleaders
Big politicians come

Pay not as high as
other pro athletes

Ricky's athletic
scholarship

My inspiring coach, Joe Zeb
Teaching about working together
Endurance
Handling pressure
Hardship

FOOTBALL

Effect on grades
Staying in school to play ball
The JV year
My broken ankle
Winning the state
championship

Bodybuilding
Injuries
    Joe Zeb's operation
    My broken ankle

War tactics
Strategy- intellectual
Territory

Outlet for aggression
Channels drive to compete,
chase, possess

Scandals
Drugs
Bets

Violence

EXERCISE: Explore one of the following topics by clustering. Write the topic in the center of a blank piece of paper and spend five minutes collecting your thoughts around it.

    a. part-time jobs
    b. holidays
    c. television.

When you are finished, look for groups of related thoughts and adjust the clusters. Clustering helps you to scan the many things you might say about a topic. Later you can decide what you will say and what you won't.

3. LIMITING A TOPIC

Once you have looked over your ideas on a topic, you are in a position to select which ideas you would like to develop in writing. That means shifting your focus from the broad view to a narrower one. If you've been exploring a topic in freewriting, you can circle one or two sentences or phrases and put the rest aside. If you've been clustering, you can circle some clusters and ignore the others. There are three steps in limiting your topic: 1) **Look for connections among the ideas you have recorded**; 2) **let some ideas go for now**; 3) **find a phrase that shows the connection among the ones you keep**.

The clustering sample below shows how a student moved from a starting topic, *football*, to a limited one: *the role that football has played in my education.*

Fans
Loyalty
Spending money
Bets

Half-time shows
Cheerleaders
Big politicians come

Pay not as high as other pro athletes

Ricky's athletic scholarship

The role that football has played in my education

My inspiring coach, Joe Zeb
Teaching about working together
Endurance
Handling pressure
Hardship

FOOTBALL

Effect on grades
Staying in school to play ball
The JV year
~~My broken ankle~~
Winning the state championship

Bodybuilding
Injuries
  Joe Zeb's operation
  My broken ankle

War tactics
  Strategy- intellectual
  Territory

Scandals
Drugs
~~Bets~~

Outlet for aggression
Channels drive to compete, chase, possess

Violence

EXERCISE: Study your freewriting or your clustering for ideas that are connected. If there are several connections, pick the one that interests you the most. Circle the items you have chosen. Write a phrase that identifies your new limited topic.

4. WRITING TOPIC SENTENCES FOR PARAGRAPHS

A **paragraph** is a sequence of sentences that cooperate in supporting one main point. Sometimes that point is so obvious that it doesn't need to be stated, but often a paragraph begins with a **topic sentence**, which states the main point directly. Before you can decide on a topic sentence, you must decide what you want to say and what you don't want to say. In other words, you must first explore your starting topic and then select your limited topic. The next step is to make a statement about the limited topic. Keep these points in mind: 1) **A starting topic is usually broad, stimulating many ideas**; 2) **a limited topic is narrow, connecting a few selected ideas**; 3) **a topic sentence makes a statement about the limited topic**. For example, study this progression:

> *Starting topic*: Football
>
> *Limited topic*: The role that football has played in my education
>
> *Topic sentence*: If I hadn't played football, I might never have taken school seriously.

EXERCISE A: Study a limited topic you have chosen as a result of freewriting or clustering. What statement can you make about that topic? Write a topic sentence that could introduce a paragraph on that limited topic. Check to make sure that it is a complete sentence.

A topic sentence is always a complete sentence expressing an idea about the limited topic. It is not a title (*What football means to me*) or an explanation of the writer's plan (*I am going to tell you about the role football played in my education.*) The more clearly it focuses the reader's attention on the points covered by the paragraph, the better.

EXERCISE B: For each limited topic below, circle the numbers of the two items that make the best topic sentences.

Limited topic: how to train a cat

1. This paragraph is about how to train a cat.

2. Before a cat learns anything, it first teaches its owner a lesson in humility.

3. Everything you wouldn't have thought to ask about training a cat.

4. Training a cat takes physical stamina.

5. Animal training is a complicated subject.

Limited topic: changes in patients' attitudes as they settle into convalescent homes

6. Americans are learning how to grow old gracefully.

7. The outside world seems to shrink when seen through the window of a convalescent home.

8. Closing up a house and moving to a small room in a convalescent home can make even an extrovert turn inward.

9. It is important to look at the changes in patients' attitudes as they settle into convalescent homes.

10. The increasing delight in daily conversation as patients become accustomed to life in a convalescent home.

Notice that choosing a topic sentence helps to focus the topic still further. The student who was writing about the role that football played in his education could have chosen one of these topic sentences instead:

> My high school football coach transformed a sport into a powerful mental discipline.

> The lessons I learned from playing high school football prepared me for the challenges of college.

Each sentence declares a slightly different role that football played in this student's education and alerts the reader to a different focus in the paragraph. Therefore, the topic sentence acts as a tool for organizing the rest of the paragraph.

EXERCISE C: Below is a table showing the most popular television shows of the past thirty years. The table is followed by three topic sentences. Use the topic sentences to help you select and organize the facts in the table. Under each topic sentence, list three details a writer could include in a paragraph introduced by that sentence.

All-Time Top Television Programs

	Program	Date	Network		Program	Date	Network
1	M*A*S*H Special	2/28/83	CBS	9	Super Bowl XII	1/15/78	CBS
2	Dallas	11/21/80	CBS	10	Super Bowl XIII	1/21/79	NBC
3	Roots Pt. VIII	1/30/77	ABC	11	Bob Hope Christmas Show	1/15/70	NBC
4	Super Bowl XVI	1/24/82	CBS	12	Super Bowl XVIII	1/22/84	CBS
5	Super Bowl XVII	1/30/83	NBC	13	Super Bowl XIX	1/20/85	ABC
6	Super Bowl XX	1/26/86	NBC	14	Super Bowl XIV	1/20/80	CBS
7	Gone With The Wind-Pt. 1	11/7/76	NBC	15	The Day After	11/20/83	ABC
8	Gone With The Wind-Pt. 2	11/8/76	NBC	16	Roots Pt. VI	1/28/77	ABC
				16	The Fugitive	8/29/67	ABC

All-Time Top Television Programs, continued

	Program	Date	Network		Program	Date	Network
18	Super Bowl XXI	1/25/87	CBS	27	Beverly Hillbillies	1/8/64	CBS
19	Roots Pt. V	1/27/77	ABC	28	Roots Pt. IV	1/26/77	ABC
20	Ed Sullivan	2/9/64	CBS	28	Ed Sullivan	2/16/64	CBS
21	Bob Hope Christmas Show	1/14/71	NBC	30	Academy Awards	4/7/70	ABC
				31	Thorn Birds Pt. III	3/29/83	ABC
22	Roots Pt. III	1/25/77	ABC	32	Thorn Birds Pt. IV	3/30/83	ABC
23	Super Bowl XI	1/9/77	NBC	33	NFC Championship Game	1/10/82	CBS
23	Super Bowl XV	1/25/81	NBC				
25	Super Bowl VI	1/16/72	CBS	34	Beverly Hillbillies	1/15/64	CBS
26	Roots Pt. II	1/24/77	ABC	35	Super Bowl VII	1/14/73	NBC

Ranked by percent of average audience. Source: Nielsen Media Research. A. C. Nielsen estimates, July 1960–January 26, 1987, excluding unsponsored or joint network telecasts or programs under 30 minutes long. Reprinted by permission.

1. *Topic sentence*: During the past three decades, ABC has remained in contention with the other networks for broadcasting the most popular TV shows.

   Supporting details: _____

   _____

   _____

2. *Topic sentence*: Super Bowls have always been popular.

   Supporting details: _____

   _____

   _____

3. *Topic sentence*: Many shows from the sixties continue to hold places in the popularity polls.

   Supporting details: _____

   _____

   _____

Compare your selection of facts with those of a classmate to see whether you have considered all the possibilities. Be sure that neither of you has included facts that will not support the topic sentence.

5. GIVING EXAMPLES AND EXPLANATIONS

Giving examples and explanations helps your reader understand what has led you to a conclusion. Whenever you are writing, imagine a reader asking constantly, "What makes you say that?" "What do you mean?" If you heard that question in conversation, you would probably answer, "Well, for instance . . ." and then you would give an example. You need to give examples in writing too. Here are some statements that could lead readers to ask those questions:

Fruit is good for you.

People who live together fight sometimes.

Reading enriches your life.

An example can offer further information, apply a general statement to a specific problem, or tell a story. Its purpose is to tie your idea to other ideas that everyone recognizes, which proves that you know what you are talking about and encourages your readers to stay on the path of your thought.

EXERCISE A: Support each statement below with examples and explanations by adding one more item to each column.

Statement: Fruit is good for you.

Examples of good fruit	*Explanations with further information*
a. apples	a. contain roughage, which helps to clean digestive system
b. _____	b. _____

Statement: People who live together fight sometimes.

Examples of things they fight over	*Explanations with specific situations*
a. money	a. My roommate and I can't agree about how to divide the heating bill. She uses more than half our heat by sleeping with the windows open.
b. _____	b. _____

Statement: Reading enriches your life.

Examples of ways	*Explanations with stories*
a. by broadening a person's range of experience	a. Rita has never met an Indian, and until last summer, she'd never been out of Ohio. But last spring she read *Black Elk Speaks* and began to see that Black Elk's visions could help her understand her own life better. When she traveled across South Dakota last summer, she found she could guess what was around every bend as surely as she could interpret different neighborhoods in Toledo.
b. _____ _____	b. _____ _____ _____ _____ _____ _____

EXERCISE B: Add one sentence to each item below, giving one or more examples to clarify the words in italics.

1. I miss my family, but I know that when they join me here, I will be able to give them *the very best*. For example, _____
_____

2. When you move to a new city, you will have to make *many adjustments*. For instance, _____
_____

3. People shovel *all sorts of things* into their pockets without stopping to evaluate what they really need. For example, _____
_____

4. It was hard for me to get an education *because of my family's demands on my time*. For instance, _____
_____

5. Progress involves *taking risks*. For example, _____

_____

6. USING SPECIFIC LANGUAGE

General language describes large categories. **Specific language** describes individual things and actions. In the diagram below, notice how the general term *food* can be divided into more and more specific kinds of food, in this case ending up with three kinds of lettuce.

EXERCISE A: Circle the most specific word or phrase in each group.

1. hammer, hardware, tool

2. gems, diamonds, jewelry

3. washing machine, electrical appliance, household convenience

4. difficulties of the first year in college, problems in college, overscheduling the first year of college

5. buying a car, undertaking a major financial commitment, accepting a burden of independent life

Writing has to strike a balance between specific and general language. Often a topic sentence uses more general language than the sentences that support it:

> The sociable old moviehouse may be a thing of the past. The **jokes in the ticket line** and **the smell of popcorn** are no longer able to lure people away from the comforts of the VCR. . . .

Specific details that refer to the five senses (like *the smell of popcorn*) convey ideas vividly. The five senses are sight, hearing, smell, taste, and touch (including motion), and they form the basis for most of our thoughts about the world. If you refer to senses in your writing, you help readers to form an appropriate base on which to build their understanding of the ideas you are discussing. That makes your job of communicating and persuading much easier. Compare these two sentences:

> The dean is in a bad mood today.

> The dean is mumbling as he brushes past us in the hall and doesn't even nod when we greet him.

The second sentence contains sound, sight, and motion details, and allows readers to come to their own conclusions about the dean's mood.

EXERCISE B: Rewrite each sentence, replacing the words in italics with details from the five senses.

1. Charlie *was tired.* _____

_____

2. Gabriella *is the most beautiful child in the family.* _____

_____

3. Our motorcycle *was speeding down the road.* _____

_____

4. The air in the subways *is stale.* _____

_____

5. Lois walked *clumsily.* _____

_____

EXERCISE C: Imagine a person doing something outdoors. Picture the weather. In three sentences, describe the person in action. Do not mention the sky, the air, or the temperature, but make your reader feel what the weather is like through its effect on the person you are describing. Use details from the senses.

Read your paragraph to a classmate. Ask the classmate to describe the weather in your paragraph. Did your details give an accurate impression?

7. MAKING PARAGRAPH BREAKS

In an essay, each paragraph contains a group of sentences that discuss one limited topic. **Paragraph breaks** show readers where new limited topics begin. A writer indents a few spaces at the left margin of the page when introducing a new point in an essay or a new stage of a discussion. The patch of white space gives readers a chance to stop and think about the last limited topic before starting on the next one.

EXERCISE: When a student wrote this essay, she separated it into four paragraphs. Decide where you think the breaks should be. Underline the first words of each new paragraph.

Some people think that children are interested only in material things, and that adults invent symbols to make life complicated, but I think that symbols start in childhood. For example, I remember learning about one symbol before I could even read. A door was one of my first symbols. I was four years old when I faced that door, the door of a kindergarten in a small elementary school in Patillas, Puerto Rico. The door was big, and it was painted a bone-white color. When I saw it, I felt defenseless because I knew that beyond it, someone would take away my freedom to do the things I wanted. Besides, I was scared because the other children were bigger than I was, and the teacher wasn't my mother. I started to cry. Then my mother lost her patience and began to yell at me. At the same time, the teacher pulled me toward the door. I just saw the room on the other side and I could not see any light, any fun. I cried because I wanted to go with my mother, and I couldn't understand why she was leaving me by this door. I felt miserable and angry as she walked away. However, everything changed when I decided to go through that door. The teacher closed it in back of me, and I had to stay. First I was quiet and watched. Then I began to understand about routines. For instance, there was a time for everything: a time to play, a time to eat, a time to sleep, and the time that I liked most, a time to go home. I tried to survive. Soon I began to make friends and to behave the way the other children did. Meanwhile, I learned to make arrangements with myself to adapt to an environment full of new rules and methods. I learned to color figures, to complete puzzles, and to walk instead of run. Finally, I walked in and out of that door freely every day. Now, looking back, I can see that the door that made me afraid and confused yesterday opened the way to my present life. In addition it opened the way to other doors, more complicated, surrounded with decisions, and leading to events that have been sometimes good and sometimes bad. There are others waiting for me, and they all offer me different choices. In fact, though, they all look a little bit like that big white door I first decided to go through when I was very small.

— Luz Raquel Cruz

Form a group with three or four other students and discuss the paragraph breaks and your reasons for them. See whether your whole group can agree on where the breaks should fall. Explain your conclusions to the rest of the class before looking up the original paragraph breaks in the Answer Key.

8. USING TRANSITIONAL EXPRESSIONS

Transitional expressions, such as *therefore, however,* and *in addition,* show readers how one idea relates to another. Consider these two sentences:

> The river was gradually changing its course. The cliff continued to erode.

Is the river causing the erosion or not? Adding a transitional expression can help the reader to know the answer:

> The river was gradually changing its course; **therefore,** the cliff continued to erode.

Different transitional expressions imply different answers:

> The river was gradually changing its course. **In addition,** the cliff continued to erode.

> The river was gradually changing its course; **however**, the cliff continued to erode.

Study the chart of transitional expressions in the box. These expressions can be used within paragraphs to show the relationships between clauses and sentences, and they can be used within essays to show how paragraphs relate to each other.

TRANSITIONAL EXPRESSIONS

To show time and sequence:
meanwhile, eventually, soon, later, first, second, then, finally,
also, besides, furthermore, moreover, in addition, too, now,
at the same time

To compare and contrast:
likewise, similarly, in the same way
however, nevertheless, still, on the other hand, on the contrary,
even so

To show cause and effect:
therefore, as a result, accordingly, consequently, thus, hence,
otherwise

To offer examples and conclusions:
for instance, for example, after all, in fact, of course,
in conclusion, in other words, on the whole, in short

EXERCISE A: Circle the transitional expressions in Luz Raquel Cruz's essay on pp. 292–293.

EXERCISE B: Show the relationships between ideas in the paragraph below by adding transitional expressions in the blanks.

For some people, high school and college are a waste of time. _____, a friend of mine was an A student throughout high school. _____, he was accepted into college without any trouble. He studied hard for four years. _____, he received a degree and entered the job market. _____, he was unable to get a job in his field of study, even though he applied everywhere. _____, he was forced to apply for a job that required none of the skills he had obtained in school. _____, I have become convinced that high school and college are not always the best preparation for the real world.

9. WRITING THESIS STATEMENTS FOR ESSAYS

An **essay** is a group of paragraphs that all support a main point, or **thesis**. Often the reader will understand the ideas in the paragraphs best if the essay's main point is stated directly somewhere in the first paragraph. A **thesis statement** does for an essay what a topic sentence does for a paragraph: it helps the reader to understand the main point. A thesis statement can tell the reader how a large idea will be broken down into smaller ones, set the scene for a story, or take a stand on a controversial issue. It always expresses a firm statement in a complete sentence. For example, the thesis statement for Raquel Cruz's essay on doors is *A door was one of my first symbols.*

EXERCISE A: Identify the thesis statement for each of the following essays.

1. John Carey's essay on making money, p. 165: _____

2. The essay on the therapeutic effects of laughter, p. 299: _____

A thesis statement often uses more general language than the topic sentences of the paragraphs supporting the thesis. For example, notice the use of the general term *business and entertainment activities* in this outline for an essay:

Thesis statement: Nowadays, people stay at home for many of their business and entertainment activities.

Topic sentence #1: Mail-order catalogues eliminate the need for shopping trips.

Topic sentence #2: Giving a credit card number over the phone can bring goods and services to the door.

Topic sentence #3: A VCR and a tape deck can turn the average living room into a private theater.

EXERCISE B: Below are topic sentences for the paragraphs in two different essays. Write a thesis statement that expresses a suitable main point for each essay.

1. *Thesis statement*: _____

    _____

    Topic sentence #1: Sylvia carried good-luck charms in each of her pockets.

    Topic sentence #2: I remember one Friday the 13th when she refused to get out of bed.

    Topic sentence #3: Sylvia used to read the clouds for instructions about how she should spend each day.

2. *Thesis statement*: _____

    _____

    Topic sentence #1: Testing employees for drugs enables an employer to avoid problems with new employees and to treat the drug problems of veteran workers.

    Topic sentence #2: A company that tests employees for drug use is protecting its clients and the public.

    Topic sentence #3: Drug testing at the workplace deters drug use elsewhere.

Chapter 17

Topics for Writing

The best way to learn to write is to spend time every day with written words, reading things that you enjoy and writing about whatever interests you. Eventually you will develop your own approach to each writing opportunity and challenge, but while you are getting started, some assignments can guide you through various stages of the writing process. This chapter offers seven topics for writing. In addition, the final page of the chapter lists for easy reference the twelve paragraph-length assignments that introduce chapters in Parts One and Two.

1. AN OFFICIAL AND A PERSONAL ACCOUNT

Whenever you write, you must consider your audience (who your readers are) and your purpose (why you're writing) before you can decide *what* to say and *how* to say it.

Read this newspaper article on the therapeutic effects of laughter.

LAUGHTER: THE AGELESS PRESCRIPTION FOR GOOD HEALTH
by John M. Leighty

SAN FRANCISCO (UPI) — Laughter is an age-old elixir that modern healers should both practice and prescribe, a growing number of humor-oriented health professionals maintain.

Humor's assistance in modern medicine is no joke, says Dr. William Fry, a leading researcher into the psychology of laughter at Stanford University. He says the body gets a healthy "mini-workout," from a good guffaw.

Throughout history, philosophers and writers have noted the benefits of humor on the sick. Arnold Glasow called laughter "a tranquilizer with no side effects." Voltaire wrote, "The art of medicine consists of amusing the patient while nature cures the disease."

Philosopher Max Beerbohm noted, "Nobody ever died of laughter," while present-day scholar Norman Cousins says he was healed of a diagnosed "incurable disease" by the curative powers of hard laughing, which he dubbed an exercise akin to "internal jogging."

Fry says 20 seconds of intense laughter, even if faked, can quickly double the heart rate for three to five minutes, an accomplishment that would take three minutes of strenuous rowing exercise. Studies also show that muscles in the chest, abdomen, shoulders, neck, face and scalp get a beneficial workout and that other parts of the body are more relaxed during a laughing session.

Cousins, editor emeritus for *Saturday Review,* has attended several conferences touting the beneficial effectes of humor. He says that although diagnosed with incurable ankylosing spondylitis, a disease that would make him an invalid, he was able to laugh himself into the pink by watching Marx Brothers movies and episodes of Candid Camera.

Interest in programs that jest for the health of it has increased significantly over the past few years, says Fry, a clinical psychiatrist who has been studying humor's effects on the body since 1952.

In Los Angeles, a "humor wagon," makes weekly visits to hospitals to entertain children with cancer. Visualization and humor are employed to help cancer patients at the "Wellness Community," in Santa Monica, Calif., a program recently highlighted on CBS television's "60 Minutes." Similar clinics are sprouting in other parts of the country. . . .

The Hospital Satellite Network of Los Angeles has even created a television service specializing in humor for hospitals. Called "Patient America," the program beams classic comedies and other entertaining features to recovery rooms.

"Patient America is interested in supporting the philosophy that laughter and comedy might enhance a patient's healing process," said Dr. Ronald J. Pion, the network's vice president. "By combining these 'feel good' movies with wellness and health promotive programming, we think Patient America will augment our hospitals' total patient treatment programs."

Now imagine that you are an occupational therapy assistant in a hospital, and the article about laughter inspires you to suggest that the nursing staff might run a humor wagon like the one described in the article. Your supervisor tells you to write a proposal to be circulated among the nursing supervisors before their next meeting. Write one or two paragraphs proposing, describing, and explaining the idea.

Next imagine that you are writing a letter to a friend who is cooped up at home after an operation and whose slow recovery is worrying the family doctor. You want to suggest that your friend should watch comedies regularly. Write a letter that will convince your friend to borrow a VCR, rent some tapes, and laugh for an hour a day.

Finally, compare your two pieces of writing. How are they different?

2. A ROUND ROBIN STORY

A round robin story is a story that several people take turns developing. Writing one helps you to see how every new sentence limits what can happen next and at the same time opens up new possibilities.

Read these opening sentences:

Trudging through the foggy park, I didn't see the feet of the old woman sprawling across the bench until I stumbled over her big shoes.

Melina paced in the kitchen, waiting for the phone to ring.

Racing along the beach with a kite, Algernon felt better than he had in years.

The windows were completely dark, and the apartment was so quiet that I couldn't imagine what had woken me up.

Form a group with three or four other students. Choose someone to be time-keeper. Together, choose one of the sentences above. Each person in the group should write it at the top of a piece of paper.

Individually, write what happened next. Don't look for an ending to the story; just continue to tell it. Write for five minutes. The timekeeper will tell you when five minutes have passed. Stop immediately, even if you are in the middle of writing a word.

When the time is up, pass your paper to the person on the right. That person will continue telling your version of the story, and you must continue the version that someone has passed to you. Pick up writing right where the other person stopped. Don't end the story; just spin out the yarn for three more minutes. The timekeeper will tell you when to stop.

Pass the papers to the right again and continue the story you now have in front of you. Bring the story to a conclusion this time. When the timekeeper tells you that the last three minutes is up, finish your sentence to round out the story.

Pass the papers to the right one more time and then take turns reading aloud the different versions of the story. Each group may want to pick its favorite version and read it to the class.

3. A CHARACTER SKETCH

A character sketch uses words to create a picture of someone. When you describe a person, you base a general impression on your observation of specific details.

Think of someone you know well. Imagine that you are making a videotape of that person doing something that takes no more than five minutes. Make notes, translating into words exactly what the camera is recording in sight and sound. Include notes about motion and action, but avoid words like *excited, nice, strong, angry, shy* — these are judgments that a camera can't record. A camera captures only sight and sound. For example, here are some notes:

> Elena jumps when phone rings
> right hand, pushes hair from eyes, long manicured fingernails
> papers clatter to the floor
> two strides, she crosses room

Now decide what mood or character trait you want to show. Anxiety? Elegance? Selfishness? Without using that word, choose the sight and sound details that would help a stranger to recognize this mood or character trait. Add other details, but stick to the description of one short action. Using those observations, write a paragraph sketching the person in action and avoiding judgments.

Test your paragraph on a classmate, who should finish this sentence:

This person is (a) _____.

The classmate should use the kind of word you have been avoiding — a general judgment term such as *popular, timid,* or *thoughtful.* Did your reader get the impression you intended? Working together, write a topic sentence for the character sketch.

4. A DESCRIPTION OF A SIGNIFICANT PLACE

Memory is selective. If you can describe in detail a place from your childhood, you probably have a good reason to remember it.

Think of places you remember from your childhood: favorite spots for playing or thinking or being with someone you cared about, spots where something exciting or frightening happened, places you have dreamed about for years although you hardly remember seeing them in reality. Pick one place and describe it in detail, using specific language. Draw a picture of it in words so that the reader can see it. Then explain why the place matters to you and why you think you remember it so well.

Here is one student's description of a significant place:

A stream in one of our state parks has always been my sitting spot. I am fascinated when I see the water bubbling over and down the rocks. The water has shaped the rocks, causing deep indentations in certain places, but other parts are perfectly flat. The rocks seem to be lined up in descending order so that the water flows evenly in every direction, making white foam. The sound of the water rushing under the bridge always grabs my attention and sends chills up my spine. On the other side of the bridge is a pond full of fish. Nearby there is a place where people can go swimming or just sit on the bank and relax in the sand. Beyond that is a long bicycle path which leads behind some tall trees, and there are picnic areas along with grills and tables. I enjoy sitting on the green grass under the tall trees, just as I used to when I was a child.

— Talitha Moon

5. A DEFINITION OF AN EMOTION

Definitions are general statements that grow out of specific cases. You can use your own experience as the basis for defining an emotion.

Think of a time when you felt a strong emotion, such as fear, anger, hope, or joy. Write a paragraph describing the situation. Show exactly what was happening, and let the reader see your reactions.

Then think about how the experience you have described fits in with other ideas you have about this emotion. Write a new paragraph starting with a sentence in this form: *(name of emotion)* is _____. For example, "Relief is a feeling that comes when a great weight has been lifted from your shoulders." Go on to discuss your ideas about the emotion.

Read both paragraphs and answer the question "So what?" Develop a thesis statement about the emotion, and write an essay that follows this pattern:

Paragraph #1

Tell about the emotion. Don't use *I*. Start with this sentence: *(name of emotion)* is _____. **Describe and define** the emotion, answering some of these questions: What is it? How is it different from similar emotions? How does it make people behave? Who is likely to feel it and when? Where does it come from? Include the thesis statement expressing your main point.

Paragraph #2

Stop telling about the emotion, and **show** it through your story. Refer to yourself, using *I*. **Illustrate** the thesis statement by showing your own experience. Leave out details that bring in other emotions, and add details that show how the emotion worked in one real situation.

Paragraph #3

Tell about the emotion again. Use *I* only to give examples.
Draw a conclusion, answering some of these questions: Does this emotion have long-term effects? How does it pass? What does it leave behind? So what?

6. A CONTROVERSIAL STAND

Arguments often help to clarify issues. Taking a stand in a controversy forces you to give evidence to prove a point.

Think of some issues that people are arguing about these days. They can be national controversies, such as whether or not to declare English the only official language of the United States, or local questions, such as whether or not to allow smoking in the school cafeteria. With other students, compile a list of controversial topics. If you have time, argue about some of them.

Then pick a topic that interests you. Write an essay in which you introduce the issue, discuss the two sides of the argument, and take a firm stand on one side. In this essay, don't conclude that both sides are right; join one side and give reasons to explain why you take that stand.

Here is an outline that may help you organize your points:

Paragraph #1: Introduction of the issue — to whom it matters and why. Thesis statement of the side you are arguing for.

Paragraph #2: What the people on the other side would say — their points and their reasons for them.

Paragraph #3: Your arguments against the people on the other side — your answer to each of their points, giving facts, examples, explanations, and other evidence.

Paragraph #4: Other points that prove the thesis — your remaining ideas and reasons for supporting this position. Conclusion stating the thesis in a new way.

7. A SUMMARY

A summary is a brief account. When you summarize what someone else has written, you must condense many thoughts into a few words.

A summary should present the core of a work in as few words as possible, state the main point, and report the essential information that illustrates that point.

Here is a summary of the article on laughter printed on pp. 299–300:

An increasing number of health professionals are prescribing humor as an aid to healing. Scholars have long noted the physical benefits of laughter. ~~Norman Cousins even cured himself of a serious disease by~~

~~watching the Marx Brothers~~. Recent evidence supports the theory that laughter provides a combination of exercise and relaxation that sustains health and promotes recovery from illness. ~~A smile has been proven to strain fewer muscles than a frown~~. As a result, hospitals are establishing programs to bring humor to patients. In Santa Monica, California, a humor wagon is available to children with cancer, and in Los Angeles, a television service brings humor into recovery rooms. These humor projects are combined with other health programs for total patient therapy. ~~Laughter is good for people's spirits, and we all know that the body responds to the health of the spirit~~.

Notice that three sentences have been crossed out. The first offers one of the details that was helpful in the full article but is not necessary in the summary. The second introduces extra information that was not included in the original article. The last expresses an opinion, which is inappropriate to the task of summarizing.

Read the article that follows.

EVENTS FOR DISABLED ATHLETES OF BOTH SEXES INCREASING
AT OLYMPICS
by Ross Atkin
Staff writer of The Christian Science Monitor

CALGARY, ALBERTA — The possibility that athletes would some day ski downhill at the Olympics on one leg or over cross-country trails without the aid of vision once seemed very remote.

In today's more open-minded Olympic environment, however, it has become a reality. The disabled haven't been granted full citizenship at the Games, but they have established a beachhead at the fringes of the world's largest and most prestigious sports extravaganzas.

They first got their foot in the door at the Winter Olympics in Sarajevo four years ago, with a men's exhibition skiing event. The Los Angeles Olympics that summer had wheelchair races of 800 meters for women and 1500 meters for men.

Here their winter presence has been expanded fourfold, with men's and women's 5-kilometer cross-country races, completed earlier this week, as well as men's and women's giant slaloms scheduled for Sunday.

Where might the pressures applied by the world's increasingly ambitious disabled athletic community lead?

"A couple of ideas that are being discussed at the international Olympic level are whether to create a separate, but equal, type of event for disabled athletes, or pursue some method of integration [into the Olympics]," says Jack Benidick, program director for the US disabled ski team. "I don't think that's something that will be resolved in the real near future . . ."

All four events here have been given "exhibition" status, which places them below official and demonstration sports on the Olympic ladder. The top finishers receive medals, but not the same kind draped around the necks of the able-bodied competitors. Clearly the most distinctive feature of the exhibition medals is the Braille on one side.

The Nordic skiers are blind. Each was assisted by a sighted ski guide on the course at Canmore, site of regular Olympic cross-country events.

Although there are about 10 disabled categories, the Alpine skiing in these Games is only for the LW 2 classification (any disability, one leg). Theirs is easily identifiable as a disabled event, which may be one reason it was chosen. No artificial limbs are used, but the athletes are able to maintain their balance using special ski poles that act as outriggers or extra skis.

These athletes are delighted to have the opportunity to display their skill. Unfortunately, however, they won't get to show what they can really do. Instead of descending anything approaching the world-class layout at Mt. Allan 50 miles away, they'll tackle a relatively tame little run at Canada Olympic Park on the outskirts of town.

"It's a beginning, but we're all able to ski a much more difficult course," says Diana Golden of Lincoln, Mass., who swept all four gold medals at the 1986 world championships for the disabled and won the downhill and giant slalom golds at the 4th Winter Games for the Disabled at Innsbruck last month.

The elite disabled skiers here are accustomed to reaching speeds of 65 m.p.h. or more in downhill races. The Olympic race does not represent a true test for them, and hints at the philosophical debates within disabled sports circles.

"There are those who say the courses should cater to the abilities of the broad range of disabled skiers," Golden says. "We prefer to have . . . world-class courses, and if people aren't capable of skiing them, they better start training."

The seed of the philosophical differences often lies with those running disabled programs. One camp wants to promote athletic excellence, while the other, often populated by physical therapists, views disabled sports more as a form of recreational rehabilitation.

Those competing in Calgary, though, have achieved at a level even far beyond that of most able-bodied recreational skiers.

One indication of their proficiency is the caliber of the sighted guides who accompany them.

Craig Ward, who guides for fellow Coloradan John Novotny, is a former member of US Olympic team. He often stays ahead of John by less than 10 feet, calling out directions. (Novotny was the top US finisher here, coming in sixth as Europeans, led by gold medalists Hans Aalien of Norway and Veronika Preining of Austria, dominated both cross-country events.)

Among the Alpine competitors, Golden says she probably enters more races against able-bodied skiers than on the disabled circuit. "I finish far back in the pack racing against the top 100 girls in the East, but there are girls in that group close to my time," she says.

One disadvantage she faces is not being able to step from turn to turn. Then, too, fatigue enters the picture.

"Skiing on two legs you're shifting your weight from one ski to the other," she explains. "When you're on one ski, that leg . . . doesn't have a chance to rest and recover."

No one, of course, is suggesting ignoring these differences and holding the disabled athletes up to the standards of full-fledged Olympians. Where arguments arise is about the place of the disabled in the Olympics, where the world's unqualified best supposedly compete.

Ted Fay, Nordic director of the US disabled team, argues that the disabled belong in the same way as women, who enjoy full Olympic status without producing identical performances to those of their male counterparts.

But disabled athletes have not received uniform acceptance here. Those competing for the United States and some other countries marched in the opening ceremony, but others were not given this opportunity.

"The other American athletes wanted us there and treated us that way," says David Jamison, a slalom racer, who believes Americans are better able to push for progress. "It's easier to get up and speak . . . and demand things in the United States than it is in other countries."

Participation here of course is the greatest means of making a point, especially for an unassertive person like John Novotny.

"I'm not very militant in my crusade for disabled people and blind people in getting acceptance," he says. "For me personally the best way I can help the disabled population is through my own example. I live my life as happily as I can make it, and as successfully as I can make it. And I hope through living it that way . . . I can work toward better integration as a whole."

In terms of the Olympics, full integration of the disabled could take years, and may never happen. The torch has been lit, though, and the examples of athletes like Novotny, Golden, Jamison, and the rest are only likely to flame the fire.

Follow these steps in writing your summary:

1. When you have finished reading the article once, write a sentence that states the main point. Use your own words, but do not include any opinions of your own.

2. Now review the article, underlining the most important information that proves the main point. In the margin, write words and phrases that help you combine separate pieces of information into categories, using general language to refer to groups of specific points.

3. Write a paragraph in your own words presenting the main point and the essential information of the article. Report the ideas in the fewest words possible, and add nothing new.

4. Finally, review your paragraph, looking for more efficient ways of presenting the information you've chosen. Condense the summary further until it is under 100 words.

GUIDE FOR FINDING ANOTHER DOZEN ASSIGNMENTS.

Paragraph writing assignments introduce most chapters in Parts I and II:

> Recounting a recent incident or story (Chapter 2)
> Narrating an experience from the past (Chapter 3)
> Describing a room from direct observation (Chapter 4)
> Describing and explaining a pet peeve (Chapter 5)
> Supporting an opinion (Chapter 8)
> Describing a process (Chapter 9)
> Narrating a memorable first event (Chapter 10)
> Describing how a mood influences behavior (Chapter 11)
> Classifying things or people (Chapter 12)
> Speculating about an ideal society (Chapter 13)
> Describing several objects, implied comparisons (Chapter 14)
> Examining a turning point (Chapter 15)

PART FOUR

Tests

Chapter 18

Pretests and Mastery Tests

Part One of this book helps you to understand how sentences work, and Part Three guides you through some of the processes and possibilities of writing. Part Two concentrates on correcting errors, and since each writer makes different types of errors, some chapters may be more useful to you than others are. If you and your teacher use the Correction Key on the inside back cover, you will identify the categories of error that appear in your writing. In addition, tests may help you to discover your strengths and weaknesses. A *pretest* shows you what you need to study, and a *mastery test* shows you how much you have learned from what you've studied. This chapter contains pretests and mastery tests for the chapters in Part Two.

Checking Your Pretest Results

After taking each Pretest, check your answers in the Answer Key in the back of this book. You can use your results to guide you directly to the sections of the chapters where you need the most work. Follow these steps:

    1. On the Answer Key itself, circle the number of any wrong answer. Notice that the answers are arranged in groups.

    2. Look at the first group of answers. If you made more than one error there, follow the directions that appear to the right of that group.

    3. Examine each group of answers in the same way, studying the material suggested if you made more than one error in that group.

Chapter 8 • Sentence Fragments

Pretest

A. Some of the items below are incorrect because they are sentence fragments, and some are complete sentences. If you decide an item is incorrect, write **I** in the space beside its number. If you decide the item is correct, write **C** beside its number.

_____ 1. That noise is making it hard for me to hear.

_____ 2. Finally the appointment forgotten by both of them.

_____ 3. We been living in this town for nine years.

_____ 4. Just as you called, I thinking about you.

_____ 5. Because of all your arguing and fussing, I am confused now.

_____ 6. Sneaking around like that not making a good impression.

_____ 7. Although the hinges were missing, the door was solid.

_____ 8. With his type of personality, and in spite of his shyness.

_____ 9. The lake at the bottom of the field beyond the new bridge.

_____ 10. You'd think she would go on to college, with those good grades.

_____ 11. In his opinion, thinking of nice things to do is enough.

_____ 12. In addition to the car's unreliability and our lack of cash.

_____ 13. On the other side of town where the roads are better.

_____ 14. On the other hand, he'd look funny in a long cape.

_____ 15. To see her the way she is now amazes me.

_____ 16. Studying all the time and sometimes refusing to stop for dinner.

_____ 17. But determined to prove her point.

_____ 18. Meaning that she'll get the best grades she can.

_____ 19. However, don't criticize her for acting the way she does.

_____ 20. Making herself an afternoon snack, she often misses dinner.

_____ 21. Expecting them to tell me to come home.

_____ 22. If you can't agree with the experts on buying the missiles.

_____ 23. If they can argue, we can argue, too.

_____ 24. Because the article was so confusing, I wrote to the editor.

_____ 25. Which was quite a challenge, I can tell you.

B. The paragraph below contains several sentence fragments. Above each period is a number that corresponds to a number in the list below the paragraph. If the period marks the end of a complete sentence, write **C** beside the corresponding number in the list. If the period marks the end of a fragment, write **I** beside the corresponding number in the list.

Auilda is a dynamo.[1] I never known anyone as energetic as she is.[2] When she planning her time in the hospital, she insisting on taking along bags full of games to play with the nurses.[3] Perhaps with the volunteers and with all her visitors.[4] As usual, I tried to talk sense into her head, explaining that most people are tired in hospitals.[5] Especially after major surgery.[6] Wanting peace and quiet rather than a rousing game of Monopoly.[7] Listening to advice is not one of her strong points.[8] Smiling sweetly at me, she just went on packing the stuff.[9] Convinced that she'd have changed her tune, I went to see her the day after the operation.[10] Bringing giant roses.[11] Since I was sure she'd be too tired for food or conversation.[12] When I got there, she was sitting up in a chair, laughing because her card tricks had worn out two nurses already.[13] Whenever the intern came around, he had to play a few moves of Monopoly with her.[14] After that, I wasn't surprised when they sent her home within a week.[15] Even though the doctor had told her she'd be in the hospital for two weeks.[16] Because she was simply too energetic.[17] Which proves my point.[18] Even when she's sick, Auilda is a dynamo.[19] If you don't believe it now, I could give you a few more examples.[20]

1. _____	6. _____	11. _____	16. _____
2. _____	7. _____	12. _____	17. _____
3. _____	8. _____	13. _____	18. _____
4. _____	9. _____	14. _____	19. _____
5. _____	10. _____	15. _____	20. _____

Chapter 9 • Run-on Sentences

Pretest

A. Some of the items below are incorrect because they are run-on sentences, and some are correct sentences. If you decide an item is a run-on sentence, write **I** in the space beside its number. If you decide the item is correct, write **C** beside its number.

_____ 1. The milk is running low, please pick up some at the store.

_____ 2. When you're through digging out the car, please shovel the walk.

_____ 3. Put the kettle on, I think we could both use a cup of tea.

_____ 4. I can't read the ads every day, don't assume I'll see the job opening.

_____ 5. Give him a chance to try the ladder, I'm sure he can do it.

_____ 6. Wait a few more minutes; they said they would be here within an hour.

_____ 7. Hand me a pole because I'm ready to plant the beans now.

_____ 8. We can't wait to see you, put the date on your calendar.

_____ 9. Come with me the bus takes too long.

_____ 10. Here comes Jenny she looks as if she's on cloud nine.

_____ 11. Junk mail always makes me laugh, it's so predictable.

_____ 12. I can do my own income tax forms since I'm working for a regular wage.

_____ 13. The moon is very bright, so I don't think we need the flashlight.

_____ 14. Cooler evenings are returning, that's what's making us so frisky.

_____ 15. We've run out of paper, and that's a good reason to end this lousy report.

_____ 16. We saw layers of earth from different epochs, they were like frozen time.

_____ 17. I've just heard the news, but it can't be true.

_____ 18. The tallest woman on record was British, she was nearly eight feet tall.

_____ 19. Max cries when he's happy; meanwhile, he blushes and giggles.

_____ 20. There are about ninety elements in the earth's crust, but 98 percent of the earth's mass is made up of only eight of these elements.

_____ 21. We expected to have to wait in long lines, however we were wrong.

_____ 22. First we'll call the airport, then we'll talk about the other plans.

_____ 23. We can't see some light rays, for example, infrared rays are beyond our perception.

_____ 24. They got everything they asked for, they also won a free meal.

_____ 25. The windshield is clean, so you won't have any more trouble driving at night.

B. The paragraph below contains several run-on sentences. Above each period is a number that corresponds to a number in the list below the paragraph. If the period marks the end of a correct sentence, write **C** beside the corresponding number in the list. If the period marks the end of a run-on sentence, write **I** beside the corresponding number in the list.

Let's see if I remember Mila's story, correct me if I get anything wrong.[1] Her mother had taught her to be suspicious of strangers, so she was alert as she walked across the bridge.[2] Suddenly a truck pulled up and stopped right in front of her, so she told the driver to get lost.[3] "You're blocking my way, move your truck!" she yelled.[4] The driver didn't say a word he just jumped out smiling.[5] Before Mila's eyes, he attached a hook to a bridge cable and turned to shake her hand.[6] Then he leaped off the railing while she just stood there, she was too amazed to scream.[7] After three long seconds, curiosity overcame her fear, she rushed to the edge.[8] A hundred feet below she saw this madman bouncing back toward her like a yo-yo on a long string.[9] He reached for the railing as he rose, he hoisted himself over the side.[10] Then she began to chatter wildly at him.[11] He just winked at her questions, meanwhile he unfastened the huge elastic strap from the bridge cable.[12] The other end of the strap was attached to a harness around his chest, nevertheless he just let that trail along behind him.[13] Finally he drove off in his truck, whose engine had been idling loudly the whole time.[14] When Mila tells that story everyone gobbles it up, however I bet no one will believe it coming from me.[15]

1. _____   5. _____   9. _____   13. _____
2. _____   6. _____   10. _____   14. _____
3. _____   7. _____   11. _____   15. _____
4. _____   8. _____   12. _____

Chapter 10 • Final -ed

Pretest

A. From each set of words in parentheses, choose the correct word. In the space beside the sentence, write the letter (**a** or **b**) that corresponds to your choice.

_____ 1. When she (**a.** live / **b.** lived) in Albuquerque, Em rode in hot-air balloons.

_____ 2. They used to (**a.** watch / **b.** watched) the big exhibition every year.

_____ 3. Yesterday somebody (**a.** step / **b.** stepped) on my toe in the bus.

_____ 4. After I left, I (**a.** realize / **b.** realized) that you might misunderstand.

_____ 5. I kept trying to (**a.** explain / **b.** explained).

_____ 6. The professor simply did not (**a.** agree / **b.** agreed).

_____ 7. Before you mentioned the test, he (**a.** expect / **b.** expected) to leave at noon.

_____ 8. We didn't (**a.** want / **b.** wanted) to ask about that.

_____ 9. Finally we have (**a.** ask / **b.** asked) you the big question.

_____ 10. Mrs. Wimbush hadn't (**a.** look / **b.** looked) that good in months.

_____ 11. Many strangers have (**a.** walk / **b.** walked) through this house today.

_____ 12. I didn't know you would (**a.** invite / **b.** invited) so many people.

_____ 13. Even before he left town, Clancy had (**a.** plan / **b.** planned) his great return.

_____ 14. Reading this book has (**a.** change / **b.** changed) my mind about nursing.

_____ 15. These are the metals that are (**a.** use / **b.** used) in making jet fighters.

_____ 16. Brenda was so (**a.** petrify / **b.** petrified) by the snake that she didn't even blink an eye.

_____ 17. The trolley was surrounded so quickly that we couldn't (**a.** wave **b.** waved) goodbye.

_____ 18. When they got here, they were (**a.** welcome / **b.** welcomed) loudly.

_____ 19. We wanted to (**a.** celebrate / **b.** celebrated) in a big way.

_____ 20. Tomorrow in the little chapel they will be (**a.** marry / **b.** married).

_____ 21. I am very (**a.** please / **b.** pleased) with the way things are working out.

_____ 22. You'll just have to wear a (**a.** wrinkle / **b.** wrinkled) shirt today.

_____ 23. I could (**a.** finish / **b.** finished) the first draft of this paper before class.

_____ 24. I want to pass in a (**a.** revise / **b.** revised) copy later.

_____ 25. You should see the (**a.** carve / **b.** carved) rockers my uncle put on the chair.

B. In the paragraphs below, some of the underlined words are correct, and some are not. After each underlined word is a number. If the word it marks is correct, write **C** by the corresponding number in the list below the paragraphs. If the word is incorrect, write **I** beside the number in the list.

After Clarence strained[1] his back at the loading dock, he had to stayed[2] away from work for several weeks. He was looking forward to some peaceful days listening to a stack of borrowed[3] records. But during that time, his Aunt Verna call[4] him every day at midmorning and at suppertime. He start[5] getting very tire[6] of her worried[7] questions. Sometimes he try[8] to ignore[9] the ringing of the phone, and once he even took the phone off the hook for a day. However, he has always fretted[10] about missing important calls, and he felt he must stopped[11] that trick of self-defense.

So every day, he answered[12] Aunt Verna's questions sweetly. He reassure[13] her that his strength had improve[14] and that he was expected[15] to be back at work before long. She lecture[16] him that he should not rush[17] it, but if that's what she had really want[18], she was going about it the wrong way. You wouldn't have believed[19] how soon Clarence return[20] to work. His back was heal[21] in record time. Now he behaves like an escape[22] convict whenever the phone rings in the office. And he just shrugs when he is bossed[23] around by the shipping clerk. For him that's better than being smother[24] to death by a concern[25] and doting aunt.

1. _____	8. _____	15. _____	22. _____
2. _____	9. _____	16. _____	23. _____
3. _____	10. _____	17. _____	24. _____
4. _____	11. _____	18. _____	25. _____
5. _____	12. _____	19. _____	
6. _____	13. _____	20. _____	
7. _____	14. _____	21. _____	

Chapter 11 • Final -s

Pretest

A. From each set of words in parentheses, choose the correct word or word group. In the space beside each sentence, write the letter (**a** or **b**) that corresponds to your choice.

_____ 1. The men spent all their time playing video (**a.** game / **b.** games).

_____ 2. You have to ask if you want a (**a.** glass / **b.** glasses) of water.

_____ 3. The three (**a.** topic / **b.** topics) we have chosen are controversial.

_____ 4. These are the metals used in making jet (**a.** fighter / **b.** fighters).

_____ 5. Why do you think we should make this (**a.** exception / **b.** exceptions)?

_____ 6. I am the only one of my five (**a.** brother / **b.** brothers) to go to college.

_____ 7. Choose one of these (**a.** word / **b.** words) to complete this sentence.

_____ 8. I don't like the color of that (**a.** pillow / **b.** pillows).

_____ 9. J. J. may be the last of the great (**a.** old-timer / **b.** old-timers).

_____ 10. Give me an answer of only one (**a.** word / **b.** words).

_____ 11. Your cousin (**a.** look / **b.** looks) ridiculous in that outfit.

_____ 12. He (**a.** know / **b.** knows) better than to dress that way.

_____ 13. They (**a.** enjoy / **b.** enjoys) good music.

_____ 14. He (**a.** play / **b.** plays) piano like Ray Charles.

_____ 15. However, I (**a.** like / **b.** likes) best of all to hear him sing.

_____ 16. I think that his audiences (**a.** like / **b.** likes) that best, too.

_____ 17. That boy (**a.** are asking / **b.** is asking) for trouble.

_____ 18. He (**a.** are sending / **b.** is sending) out the wrong signals.

_____ 19. They (**a.** are confusing / **b.** is confusing) people.

_____ 20. The ice cream (**a.** have started / **b.** has started) to melt.

_____ 21. You (**a.** have done / **b.** has done) enough homework for one night.

_____ 22. Steve (**a.** have baked / **b.** has baked) a cake for your birthday.

_____ 23. They know that he (**a.** doesn't forget / **b.** don't forget) birthdays.

_____ 24. (**a.** Do / **b.** Does) they want to spend the night?

_____ 25. (**a.** Don't / **b.** Doesn't) your teacher know that you've got other courses?

B. In the paragraphs below, some of the underlined words are correct and some are not. After each underlined word is a number. If the word it marks is correct, write **C** by the corresponding number in the list below the paragraph. If the word is incorrect, write **I** beside the number in the list.

Ron has had that motorcycle[1] up for sale for about three month[2]. Every Sunday he stand[3] the big black monstrosity in front of the gate to his yard. It always look[4] freshly washed and shiny. We live[5] next door to Ron and we spends[6] our Sundays working in the yard, so we can't help noticing how hard he is[7] trying to sell that bike. What a history that new paint are[8] hiding, though. We is[9] wondering who will fall for that old trick.

Recently, Ron have[10] begun to place a huge, bright sign saying $650 beside the bike. He has[11] used some sort of shiny green paint for the numbers. But we still have[12] not seen anyone even stop to talk with Ron about the motorcycle, much less give it a test drive. We don't[13] think anyone ever will, at that price.

We knows[14] that Ron owns[15] another motorcycles[16] that he rides[17] to work, and two car[18] also. So why don't[19] he just give that old heap to Hank? Hank doesn't[20] have any vehicle of his own, and he could tinker with the old black beast to keep it in shape. If Ron get[21] six hundred dollar[22] for that bike[23], we'll be the most surprised neighbor[24] on this street[25].

1. _____	8. _____	15. _____	22. _____
2. _____	9. _____	16. _____	23. _____
3. _____	10. _____	17. _____	24. _____
4. _____	11. _____	18. _____	25. _____
5. _____	12. _____	19. _____	
6. _____	13. _____	20. _____	
7. _____	14. _____	21. _____	

Chapter 12 • Subject-Verb Agreement

Pretest

A. From each pair of verbs in parentheses, choose the one that agrees with its subject. In the space beside the sentence, write the letter (**a** or **b**) that corresponds to your choice.

_____ 1. Whenever I go into that barn, there (**a.** are / **b.** is) all those silent eyes staring at me.

_____ 2. While I'm cleaning out the stalls, there (**a.** are / **b.** is) never anyone else around.

_____ 3. I think that there (**a.** were / **b.** was) one of Toni Morrison's books on Julia's top shelf.

_____ 4. I know you're busy, but there (**a.** are / **b.** is) two men at the door asking for you.

_____ 5. Alex doesn't think that there (**a.** are / **b.** is) any insecticides that kill Japanese beetles.

_____ 6. According the municipal health department, there (**a.** were / **b.** was) no cases of AIDS reported in the city last year.

_____ 7. The whole point of those songs (**a.** were / **b.** was) to make you cry.

_____ 8. All the houses that face the pond (**a.** are / **b.** is) relying on well water.

_____ 9. That fabric is defective because the threads that go crosswise near the top (**a.** have / **b.** has) little bumps.

_____ 10. The language of the workers on the road crew (**a.** make / **b.** makes) me wonder if my kids should be playing around them.

_____ 11. The president may not like the coverage he's getting, but the Bill of Rights (**a.** prohibit / **b.** prohibits) him from censoring it.

_____ 12. The mineral that you often find in these rocks (**a.** give / **b.** gives) the cliffs a pink tint in morning or evening light.

_____ 13. One of the trainees in my class (**a.** believe / **b.** believes) that people can live after death as zombies.

_____ 14. Most of the people in her church (**a.** have / **b.** has) agreed on at least that one issue.

_____ 15. It doesn't matter to them that all of the scientific evidence (**a.** contradict / **b.** contradicts) them.

_____ 16. Burt will stop working at 3:30 even though some of the other assemblers (**a.** do / **b.** does) not stop until 4:00.

_____ 17. Not everyone in these apartments (**a.** feel / **b.** feels) that way.

_____ 18. With every day that Rene lives in town, more of his parents' motives (**a.** become / **b.** becomes) clear to him.

_____ 19. The women who (**a.** were / **b.** was) making all the phone calls for the club could have used some help.

_____ 20. In the cafeteria I met four students who (**a.** have / **b.** has) already taken that course.

_____ 21. I hope you didn't buy any more of that popcorn that (**a.** do / **b.** does) not pop.

_____ 22. Violet is eager to tell everyone about the book that (**a.** have / **b.** has) changed her life.

_____ 23. The man who (**a.** hold / **b.** holds) the world high-jump record is Vladimir Yashchenko.

_____ 24. Of all the planets in our solar system, Saturn, which (**a.** are / **b.** is) the second largest, is the least dense; in fact, it would float in any sea that was large enough to hold it.

_____ 25. Both the dolphin and the whale (**a.** sing / **b.** sings) complex melodies under water.

_____ 26. But neither the dolphin nor the whale (**a.** have / **b.** has) been included in this program about animal musicians.

_____ 27. Olive's husband, along with two of his partners, (**a.** are / **b.** is) coming over for dinner.

_____ 28. Maybe Lavar or your brothers (**a.** have / **b.** has) met the woman who signs the immigration papers.

_____ 29. Probably the professors or the department head (**a.** know / **b.** knows) the answer.

_____ 30. Both you and I (**a.** are / **b.** is) sure to receive athletic scholarships at the end of this semester.

B. In the following paragraphs, some of the underlined verbs agree with their subjects and some do not. After each underlined verb is a number. If the verb it marks is correct, write **C** in the space beside the corresponding number in the list below the passage. If the verb is incorrect, write **I** beside the number in the list.

At conferences for manufacturing executives, there is[1] a new topic for workshop sessions. It is robotics, the latest fad in automation that are[2] promising new opportunities for cutting production costs. The corporate leaders who advocate[3] investing in robotics argue that improvements in robot technology has[4] come at just the right time to rescue American industry from decline. The initial investment for a robot is[5] high, but the payback period and the breaking-in time is[6] short. Training a few new workers who does[7] not have exactly the right skills costs[8] an industry just as much. Then, once the robot is on the job, the expense of production drops[9] drastically, and the profits of the company rises[10]. Everybody on a company's board of directors are[11] sure to be grateful for that. There are[12] also the question of quality control. Some of the statistics seems[13] to support the claim that these little machines that do[14] not know the difference between a sunset and house fire can make more precise distinctions on the job than any human worker can. Finally, these advocates argue, neither fringe benefits nor the right to strike are[15] ever an issue in robot-management relations. And the repair of several broken robots wastes[16] less time and money than sick leave for a single human worker.

At the last manufacturers' conference, there was[17] several displays of robots. Some of the weird little creatures were[18] performing complex tasks programmed into their tiny metal and plastic brains. Fortunately for the factory workers of the country, there was[19] still many skeptics in the crowd. Even in this high-tech era, the average business executive and shop foreman agree[20] that human labor is still a company's best investment.

1. _____	6. _____	11. _____	16. _____
2. _____	7. _____	12. _____	17. _____
3. _____	8. _____	13. _____	18. _____
4. _____	9. _____	14. _____	19. _____
5. _____	10. _____	15. _____	20. _____

Chapter 13 • Pronouns

Pretest

A. From each set of words in parentheses, choose the correct word or word group. In the space beside each sentence, write the letter (**a** or **b**) that corresponds to your choice.

_____ 1. Nothing will ever come between (**a.** we / **b.** us) old friends now that we've learned how to laugh.

_____ 2. Elly thinks that (**a.** she / **b.** her) and Jane can make us revive our past disagreements.

_____ 3. But what could break us up after all that you and (**a.** I / **b.** me) have been through?

_____ 4. The police say that Mazie and (**a.** they / **b.** them) can find the tools that were scattered by the vandals.

_____ 5. Mazie told Jorge and (**a.** I / **b.** me) about the search that had taken place before the reporters arrived.

_____ 6. Jorge has gone off looking for some of (**a.** they / **b.** them), and he won't be back until 2 o'clock.

_____ 7. Some of these ideas about child-raising are completely new to Irene and (**a.** she / **b.** her).

_____ 8. Biff expects that his brothers and (**a.** he / **b.** him) can keep the store open while their father is gone.

_____ 9. Their father has taught his wife and (**a.** they / **b.** them) most of the accounting and management details.

_____ 10. People say that (**a.** we / **b.** us) young people are better educated than our parents are.

_____ 11. Don't be offended, but I think that you and (**a.** me / **b.** I) should probably leave separately.

_____ 12. When she is nervous about something, the little black cat prefers Paul and (**a.** her / **b.** she) to you.

_____ 13. Spectators have been gathering since noon, but few of (**a.** they / **b.** them) know what has happened.

_____ 14. People who grew up fifty years ago usually went to small schools in (**a.** his or her / **b.** their) own neighborhoods.

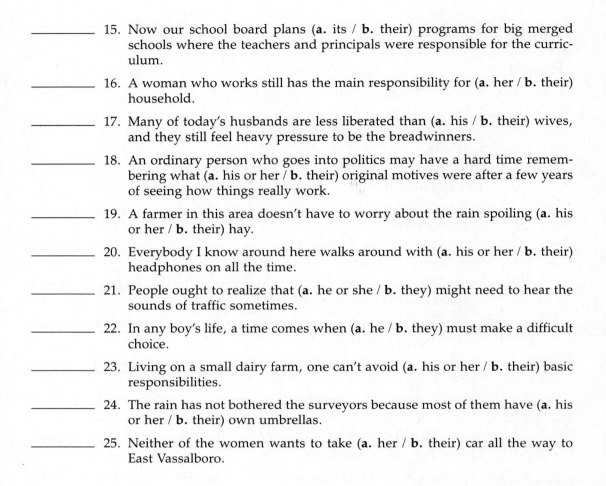

_____ 15. Now our school board plans (**a.** its / **b.** their) programs for big merged schools where the teachers and principals were responsible for the curriculum.

_____ 16. A woman who works still has the main responsibility for (**a.** her / **b.** their) household.

_____ 17. Many of today's husbands are less liberated than (**a.** his / **b.** their) wives, and they still feel heavy pressure to be the breadwinners.

_____ 18. An ordinary person who goes into politics may have a hard time remembering what (**a.** his or her / **b.** their) original motives were after a few years of seeing how things really work.

_____ 19. A farmer in this area doesn't have to worry about the rain spoiling (**a.** his or her / **b.** their) hay.

_____ 20. Everybody I know around here walks around with (**a.** his or her / **b.** their) headphones on all the time.

_____ 21. People ought to realize that (**a.** he or she / **b.** they) might need to hear the sounds of traffic sometimes.

_____ 22. In any boy's life, a time comes when (**a.** he / **b.** they) must make a difficult choice.

_____ 23. Living on a small dairy farm, one can't avoid (**a.** his or her / **b.** their) basic responsibilities.

_____ 24. The rain has not bothered the surveyors because most of them have (**a.** his or her / **b.** their) own umbrellas.

_____ 25. Neither of the women wants to take (**a.** her / **b.** their) car all the way to East Vassalboro.

B. In the paragraphs below, some of the underlined pronouns are correct, and some are not. After each underlined pronoun is a number. If the pronoun it marks is correct, write **C** by the corresponding number in the list below the passage. If the pronoun is incorrect, write **I** beside the number in the list.

People's personalities determine how they[1] will remember events. For Jerry and I[2], memory smooths over the rocky spots of our past and makes us feel as if both of us[3] have lived charmed lives. But it works differently for people who expect things to go perfectly for them[4] all the time. My parents are like that. Their friends and them[5] are always complaining about how things ought to have been. They love to talk about how life has cheated them[6]. Mom and Dad even talked that way during the big anniversary party Jerry and me[7] threw for his parents and they[8]. Dad complained that there should have been more pastries, and both him[9] and Mom moaned about the weather. For them[10], the tire marks left in the field where everybody parked were the most memorable part of the party.

I'm not like that. I'm the type that remembers the face of someone who once loaned me their[11] bike when I needed to get home fast for some emergency, but I can't remember what the emergency was all about. When people tell me their[12] recollections of various events in life, I'm always amazed at how my mind simply refuses to hold on to the unpleasant parts. Maybe my way of remembering isn't always an advantage, though. For instance, one time a good friend referred emotionally to some past disaster that she[13] had told me about the previous year, and I felt terrible that I couldn't remember the details of that experience that was very important to them[14].

When the women in my apartment sit around late at night comparing memories, we always discover new proof of the fact that everybody has her[15] own memory quirks. We find ourselves disagreeing about the facts as well as about the interpretations of events, so I have suggested that if a person wants to keep all the facts of their[16] life straight, she[17] should keep a daily journal. Even then, what the person writes in a journal at the end of a day depends on their[18] memory, which is already busy rearranging the details. Nobody can expect to control her[19] memory entirely, and the main point of the journal is simply to display the memory at its peculiar work. Since I can't control my memory, I'm glad it doles out pleasant images for me instead of the dismal kind my parents have to live with in their[20] lives.

1. _____ 6. _____ 11. _____ 16. _____
2. _____ 7. _____ 12. _____ 17. _____
3. _____ 8. _____ 13. _____ 18. _____
4. _____ 9. _____ 14. _____ 19. _____
5. _____ 10. _____ 15. _____ 20. _____

Chapter 14 • Spelling

Pretest

A. From each set of words in parentheses, choose the correct word. In the space beside the sentence, write the letter (**a, b,** or **c**) that corresponds to your choice.

_____ 1. Great Britain and Norway are (**a.** separated / **b.** separatted) by the North Sea.

_____ 2. Last year Kristin (**a.** knited / **b.** knitted) at least four sweaters.

_____ 3. There's always a controversy about (**a.** busing / **b.** bussing) children to schools.

_____ 4. Sometimes blue (**a.** go's / **b.** goes / **c.** goes') well with green.

_____ 5. Roger (**a.** talks / **b.** talkes) through his nose.

_____ 6. We aren't paying so much in (**a.** tax's / **b.** taxes / **c.** taxes') this year.

_____ 7. If you step over the line, you could be (**a.** disqualifyed / **b.** disqualified).

_____ 8. When Hoyt cleaned house, he (**a.** spraied / **b.** sprayed) the leaves of his plants with water.

_____ 9. Watch that bee when it (**a.** tries / **b.** trys) to get out of the window.

_____ 10. The cats are (**a.** laping / **b.** lapping) up the milk.

_____ 11. That film (**a.** starred / **b.** stared) Robert Redford.

_____ 12. I wish you would stop (**a.** resisting / **b.** resistting) my efforts.

_____ 13. She keeps (**a.** forgeting / **b.** forgetting) when she says she'll call.

_____ 14. When I am there, she usually (**a.** relys / **b.** relies) on me completely.

_____ 15. Linda would rather eat at Tony's because the (**a.** tomatos / **b.** tomatoes) are better there.

_____ 16. Everyone commented on that small (**a.** dog's / **b.** dogs / **c.** dogs') blue eyes.

_____ 17. All fifteen of the (**a.** unit's / **b.** units / **c.** units') were sold.

_____ 18. Little Guilda looks funny in that huge (**a.** man's / **b.** mans / **c.** mans') hat.

_____ 19. Six (**a.** island's / **b.** islands / **c.** islands') fire brigades reported for the drill.

_____ 20. Sometimes the ball (**a.** get's / **b.** gets / **c.** gets') stuck on the roof.

_____ 21. One group claims the real issue is (**a.** citizen's / **b.** citizens / **c.** citizens') rights.

_____ 22. I hear that (**a.** Nikki's / **b.** Nikkis / **c.** Nikkis') headed for Kansas.

_____ 23. My mother was an old friend of (**a.** your's / **b.** yours / **c.** yours').

_____ 24. (**a.** It's / **b.** Its) too much to expect that I will find my keys in time.

_____ 25. These (**a.** shoes' / **b.** shoes / **c.** shoe's) soles are not as sturdy as yours.

_____ 26. (**a.** That's / **b.** Thats / **c.** Thats') been making Josh very happy.

_____ 27. Don't expect the volunteers to work for more (**a.** then / **b.** than) four hours.

_____ 28. If you talk it over first, (**a.** then / **b.** than) there will be no hard feelings later.

_____ 29. Only bilingual candidates are invited (**a.** two / **b.** to / **c.** too) apply.

_____ 30. This test is (**a.** two / **b.** to / **c.** too) easy.

_____ 31. Iron and calcium are (**a.** two / **b.** to / **c.** too) of the minerals needed in human metabolism.

_____ 32. Eric didn't even (**a.** no / **b.** know / **c.** now) the girl he drove to Cleveland.

_____ 33. There's (**a.** no / **b.** know / **c.** now) alternative but to eat the ice cream sundaes.

_____ 34. Once Mark hated slow music, but (**a.** no / **b.** know / **c.** now) he's softened up.

_____ 35. Physicists used to argue over (**a.** weather / **b.** whether) light is made of energy waves or of particles.

_____ 36. In (**a.** weather / **b.** whether) like this, anything will grow.

_____ 37. That comment (**a.** passed / **b.** past) right over my head.

_____ 38. Don't worry about the client's (**a.** passed / **b.** past) offenses.

_____ 39. Whatever the girls (**a.** were / **b.** we're / **c.** where) doing, they looked contented.

_____ 40. The Persian Gulf is one of the places (**a.** were / **b.** we're / **c.** where) the economic and military interests of several nations conflict.

_____ 41. Even though it's getting dark, (**a.** were / **b.** we're / **c.** where) not ready to go home yet.

_____ 42. Are they bringing (**a.** their / **b.** they're / **c.** there) own food?

_____ 43. You can buy drinks when you get (**a.** their / **b.** they're / **c.** there).

_____ 44. The Shaws are old, but (**a.** their / **b.** they're / **c.** there) more energetic than they were five years ago.

_____ 45. Rocky says that (**a.** your / **b.** you're) going to sing tonight.

_____ 46. Don't forget (**a.** your / **b.** you're) mother when you get famous.

_____ 47. Zucchini is best stewed in (**a.** its / **b.** it's) own juice.

_____ 48. (**a.** Its / **b.** It's) a good idea to lock your car around here.

_____ 49. Do you recognize the firefighter (**a.** whose / **b.** who's) carrying the baby?

_____ 50. This is the drummer (**a.** whose / **b.** who's) band you're joining.

B. In the following paragraph, some of the underlined words are correct, and some are incorrect. After each underlined word is a number. If the word is correct, write **C** by the corresponding number in the list below the paragraph. If the word is incorrect, write **I** beside the number in the list.

Dear Mom,

Love is too[1] confusing. I feel both happyer[2] and gloomier[3] than I've ever felt. There[4] are times when Audrey give's[5] me reason to hope. Too[6] days ago, she invitted[7] me to dinner. But its[8] just when I'm filled[9] with optimism that she always sais[10] something discouraging. Yesterday, in that husky little voice of her's,[11] she told me, "Your[12] going to[13] make some woman very happy, John." I couldn't figure out whether[14] to thank her or to cry. Whose[15] this "some woman"? I have know[16] idea were[17] I stand. You we're[18] right, Mom, difficulties[19] of the heart are bad for a mans'[20] digestion. I can't eat a decent meal while I'm in the clutchs[21] of this crazy romance.

Janet and Bob have suggested that if Audreys'[22] sending mixed messages, I might be, too.[23] They think I'm hiding behind a mask, and I guess there[24] right. I'm going two[25] take their[26] advice and call Audrey now,[27] before it's[28] to[29] late. If I were as confident as I was in the past,[30] this whole thing would be easy.

Tell Dad thanks for sending me Biddy's[31] old record player. I've always liked it's[32] wavering sound's.[33] They certainly suit my mood these dayes.[34]

You're[35] son,

John

1. _____   10. _____   19. _____   28. _____

2. _____   11. _____   20. _____   29. _____

3. _____   12. _____   21. _____   30. _____

4. _____   13. _____   22. _____   31. _____

5. _____   14. _____   23. _____   32. _____

6. _____   15. _____   24. _____   33. _____

7. _____   16. _____   25. _____   34. _____

8. _____   17. _____   26. _____   35. _____

9. _____   18. _____   27. _____

Chapter 15 • Consistency

Pretest

A. Some of the sentences below include sentence elements that are not parallel. Other sentences use inconsistent pronoun points of view or inconsistent verb tenses. If you decide that a sentence shows inconsistency among its elements, write **I** in the space beside its number. If you decide all the elements of the sentence are consistent, write **C** beside its number.

_____ 1. Frankly, we enjoy listening to the radio more than to watch television.

_____ 2. Do you prefer to fly or traveling overland?

_____ 3. You will have to pay either $180 for economy-class seats or $250 for first-class passage.

_____ 4. Effective study habits often make the difference between a good grade in a course and failing.

_____ 5. If you want an athletic activity that you can engage in throughout life, you should learn to swim rather than to play football.

_____ 6. It is possible to save money by purchasing clothes that can be worn at work, dating, and in class.

_____ 7. It is not appropriate to use slang when one is writing a résumé or preparing an oral report.

_____ 8. As soon as the music dies down, everyone became aware that someone was crying.

_____ 9. He arrived so early that we fail to meet him at the station.

_____ 10. Before she resigned yesterday, Marie had given no indication that she was feeling unhappy with her job.

_____ 11. These machines usually operate reliably, but they have occasionally developed problems.

_____ 12. Because I worked hard over the weekend, I am about halfway through the project and will finish it by Wednesday.

_____ 13. We walk in, give the place a once-over, and soon settled down quietly at a booth near the door.

_____ 14. Before he could respond, I cleverly divert his attention to my second point.

_____ 15. If one has never been to an opera, you should go soon.

_____ 16. This company has no intention of wasting its time or falling behind its competitors.

_____ 17. U.S. citizens should try to learn as much as we can about the forging of their Constitution.

_____ 18. A person has no right to judge a country solely on the basis of his or her first impression of the landscape.

_____ 19. We all want good to triumph over evil in the old silent movies; that's why you cheer for the hero and hiss at the villain.

_____ 20. Many readers say Kim's writing is so vivid that they can actually see the settings she describes.

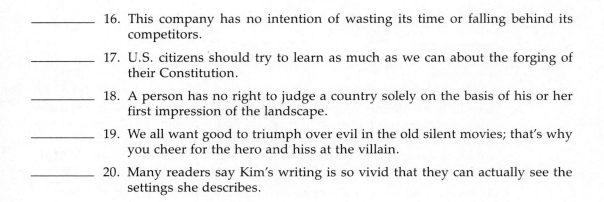

B. In the paragraphs below, some of the underlined words and phrases are correct, and some are not. After each underlined word or phrase is a number. If the word or phrase it marks is correct, write **C** by the corresponding number in the list below the paragraph. If the word or phrase is incorrect, write **I** beside the number in the list.

Students who think preparing for a final exam can be left until the last minute often learn to their sorrow that you[1] should begin studying for finals much earlier. They cram feverishly the night before the test, walk into the exam room exhausted, and actually expected[2] to get good grades. Such students need to rethink their approach before one[3] should take another final.

Of course, the best way to prepare for finals is to complete every reading assignment during the term, to take careful notes, and asking for help[4] when something is confusing. Also helpful are faithful attendance in class, frequent review of key points, and summary[5] at the end of every chapter. Other important techniques include outlining difficult topics and discussing[6] the material with classmates.

Even though students have taken all these steps, they can still do a lot to improve one's[7] final grade in the last week before the final exam. It's crucial to get plenty of sleep and to start[8] the final review early. Students who begin in plenty of time have[9] a chance to spend extra time on problem areas. They can arrange to consult their instructor on points they still didn't[10] understand. And they realize that <u>you</u>[11] can't expect to learn a whole term's worth of material in one night. Slowly but <u>for certain</u>[12], they review all the essential information in <u>your</u>[13] notes. When those students arrive for the exam, <u>they</u>[14] <u>felt</u>[15] rested and <u>prepared</u>[16]. Brilliant students or <u>they have to work hard to learn</u>[17] — it makes no difference. They <u>have studied</u>[18] effectively, and at exam time they <u>are</u>[19] ready. All students who take their time in studying for finals discover that doing so improves <u>one's</u>[20] grades significantly.

1. _____	6. _____	11. _____	16. _____
2. _____	7. _____	12. _____	17. _____
3. _____	8. _____	13. _____	18. _____
4. _____	9. _____	14. _____	19. _____
5. _____	10. _____	15. _____	20. _____

Chapter 8 • Sentence Fragments

Mastery Test

A. Some of the items below are incorrect because they are sentence fragments, and some are complete sentences. If you decide an item is a fragment, write **I** in the space beside its number. If you decide the item is a complete sentence, write **C** beside its number.

_____ 1. Watching the news once a week, she not keeping up with current events.

_____ 2. Because the wind was piercing, I was uncomfortable.

_____ 3. Since the boat was rolling, I was forced to stay on deck in the fresh air.

_____ 4. After Memorial Day, I working in the garden every evening.

_____ 5. We been working in that steel plant all our adult lives.

_____ 6. That volcano is scaring me to death.

_____ 7. After an unpleasant argument, my point understood by them.

_____ 8. In the first place, singing in the shower feels good.

_____ 9. The camel's capacity to go without water, in spite of the sandstorm.

_____ 10. Under the car with the oil dripping on his face.

_____ 11. Over my dead body he'll do that.

_____ 12. In consideration of our past, and all you have done since high school.

_____ 13. According to Mom, after supper his attitude changed completely.

_____ 14. The cottage in the meadow just beneath the snow-capped peaks.

_____ 15. Wanting desperately to warn him that she was not to be trusted.

_____ 16. When he tries to make it up to me, feeling guilty about his laziness.

_____ 17. But please don't pay him for shoveling the snow.

_____ 18. Believing that ordinary people can't change the system.

_____ 19. But inspired to write a letter to her legislator.

_____ 20. To wear the team uniform fills me with pride.

_____ 21. Plugging away and refusing to yield to political pressure.

_____ 22. Especially because sparrows are so fearless.

_____ 23. The crowd that filled the stadium to see the concert.

_____ 24. As he was about to leave the penalty box, he hiccuped.

_____ 25. Which was more than even I could handle with a straight face.

B. The paragraph below contains several sentence fragments. Above each period is a number that corresponds to a number in the list below the paragraph. If the period marks the end of a complete sentence, write **C** beside the corresponding number in the list. If the period marks the end of a fragment, write **I** beside the corresponding number in the list.

Ed definitely not a comic.[1] I've never seen anyone as blind about himself as he is.[2] When he doing his routine at the club last night, he assuming that the audience just too conventional to appreciate his humor.[3] Or under the bad influence of TV and in need of education.[4] And after all his bragging about his skill at playing to his audience.[5] It appeared that he was just too inexperienced to be in front of an audience.[6] He kept fighting their dead response instead of learning from it.[7] Trying to force them to see that his stories were truly funny.[8] Winking confidently at us in the back row, and releasing one lead balloon after another.[9] Disgusted before the show was half over, the audience turned nasty.[10] Calling for the "hook."[11] Some people just left, mocking or grumbling.[12] Because nothing could break his stubborn self-assurance, he just made light of the situation.[13] When, to top it all off, he came up with some dumb comment about "hookie monsters."[14] I looked longingly at the exit.[15] Though I believe in supporting one's friends.[16] Even when they're at their worst.[17] The poor fellow doesn't even realize that he is making a fool of himself.[18] Which is so maddening.[19] It is clear now that he will never work at that club again.[20]

1. _____	6. _____	11. _____	16. _____
2. _____	7. _____	12. _____	17. _____
3. _____	8. _____	13. _____	18. _____
4. _____	9. _____	14. _____	19. _____
5. _____	10. _____	15. _____	20. _____

Chapter 9 • Run-on Sentences

Mastery Test

A. Some of the items below are incorrect because they are run-on sentences, and some are correct sentences. If you decide an item is a run-on sentence, write **I** in the space beside its number. If you decide the item is correct, write **C** beside its number.

_____ 1. Sometimes the soccer fans would get into fistfights, meanwhile the game continued.

_____ 2. We expected to be wined and dined, however we were wrong.

_____ 3. I can't possibly help, besides, he's the one who knows about the schedule.

_____ 4. There were five all-stars on the court; still, they didn't play as a team.

_____ 5. First we'll drive to Reno, then we'll take a bus to Phoenix.

_____ 6. On the other hand, my car is in the shop again, so I need a ride.

_____ 7. Furthermore, she doesn't really want to go because she hates flying.

_____ 8. His songs are losers, for example, the one about the chipmunk was silly.

_____ 9. They won the championship also they won my respect.

_____ 10. His eye is discolored and swollen, it's been badly battered.

_____ 11. I look forward to going to work each day since my assignment changed.

_____ 12. Tempers are strained now, and that's what's making me so nervous.

_____ 13. There he sits he's as stubborn as a mule.

_____ 14. The computer is acting up again, it's driving me crazy.

_____ 15. The oldest of my children is Helen, she has a punk haircut.

_____ 16. The dog is not housebroken, and he has to stay in the cellar.

_____ 17. It has been twenty years since they were together, their eyes fill with tears.

_____ 18. The water is dripping, so please shut the faucet.

_____ 19. I can't be in two places at the same time, don't count on me to help you.

_____ 20. Please speak up, the band is awfully loud.

_____ 21. Pay him as much as you pay the company's lawyer, you know he earns it.

_____ 22. Tell her the truth, because you will not be able to hide it from her.

_____ 23. We can't fight city hall, pay the fine.

_____ 24. When you've finished reading the paper, please take out the garbage.

_____ 25. Stall him; I'll be there in five minutes with the money.

B. The story below contains several run-on sentences. Above each period is a number that corresponds to a number in the list below the paragraphs. If the period marks the end of a correct sentence, write **C** beside the corresponding number in the list. If the period marks the end of a run-on sentence, write **I** beside the corresponding number in the list.

I stood in line for the tickets, meanwhile Clarence went down the block to buy us a fast-food supper.[1] It was raining, nevertheless I held my place.[2] Finally we would see the movie whose opening we had anticipated for over a year.[3] I felt like telling the girl in front of me that I was in this movie we were about to see, however I didn't for some reason.[4] Eventually, I stopped wondering what was keeping Clarence, and recalled how our stardom began.[5]

One day while we were playing stickball, a camera truck pulled up, we were amazed.[6] A man took Clarence aside he asked if we wanted to be in a movie.[7] I stood there dumbly staring at Clarence, who shook the man's hand.[8] The man motioned to us to continue our game as he returned to the truck.[9] I couldn't hit the ball, I felt too self-conscious.[10] I heard someone yelling, "You're not watching the ball, keep your eye on the ball."[11] The next thing I heard was, "Protect those cameras in center field; that ball is dynamite!"[12]

Clarence poked me with a soggy hamburger, saying, "Everyone in the line is moving but you; quit dreaming.[13] Eat this stuff, you may never be allowed to bite into a seventy-five-cent hamburger again after the talent scouts see this movie."[14] I told him to wipe the mustard off his face as I licked my fingers (that would soon be signing autographs).[15]

1. _____	5. _____	9. _____	13. _____
2. _____	6. _____	10. _____	14. _____
3. _____	7. _____	11. _____	15. _____
4. _____	8. _____	12. _____	

Chapter 10 • Final -ed

Mastery Test

A. From each set of words in parentheses, choose the correct word. In the space beside the sentence, write the letter (**a** or **b**) that corresponds to your choice.

_____ 1. He didn't (**a.** want / **b.** wanted) to bother her with a trivial question.

_____ 2. Stupidly, we have (**a.** create / **b.** created) a big problem for ourselves.

_____ 3. Norman hadn't (**a.** work / **b.** worked) all night in years.

_____ 4. You did not (**a.** believe / **b.** believed) that the stamps had been forged.

_____ 5. He tried to (**a.** start / **b.** started) a disagreement with a silly remark.

_____ 6. Even before he left, we had (**a.** sense / **b.** sensed) his restlessness.

_____ 7. Retirement has (**a.** convince / **b.** convinced) me that leisure does not need to be dead time.

_____ 8. Yesterday they (**a.** camp / **b.** camped) in Vermont on the way to Quebec.

_____ 9. I used to (**a.** switch / **b.** switched) off the sound of the commercials.

_____ 10. In the past, we (**a.** chop / **b.** chopped) and split our firewood ourselves.

_____ 11. After the storm, we (**a.** search / **b.** searched) for driftwood on the beach.

_____ 12. I kept trying to (**a.** call / **b.** called) the Coast Guard.

_____ 13. It was not that we didn't (**a.** try / **b.** tried).

_____ 14. When your fishing rod was bent into a question mark, I (**a.** worry / **b.** worried) that it would snap.

_____ 15. You'll just have to clean up that (**a.** splatter / **b.** splattered) paint.

_____ 16. I'll (**a.** wash / **b.** washed) the floor when I'm finished with the ceiling.

_____ 17. This house has the appearance of a (**a.** feather / **b.** feathered) nest.

_____ 18. We all noticed her (**a.** wrinkle / **b.** wrinkled) hands.

_____ 19. That family does not raise (**a.** well-behave / **b.** well-behaved) children.

_____ 20. I didn't (**a.** count / **b.** counted) on them to pitch in.

_____ 21. I hid my irritation behind (**a.** force / **b.** forced) smiles.

_____ 22. He was (**a.** honor / **b.** honored) to be recognized at the tenants' meeting.

_____ 23. All the apartment houses on that block were (**a.** condemn / **b.** condemned) by the city's health department.

_____   24. Moving made my mother so mad that she couldn't (**a.** talk / **b.** talked).

_____   25. She was (**a.** advise / **b.** advised) by the neighborhood legal services office.

B. In the paragraphs below, some of the underlined words are correct, but some are not. After each underlined word is a number. If the word it marks is correct, write **C** by the corresponding number in the list below the paragraphs. If the word is incorrect, write **I** beside the number in the list.

About five years ago Bernard decided[1] to studied[2] the oboe. He was then forty-five years old and had never touch[3] an oboe in his life. In fact, he had never liked[4] any music except rock, but he became fascinated[5] by the oboe while watching a concert on TV one day. Touched[6] by the sound of the oboe, he realize[7] immediately that, as he put it, he had to learned[8] how to create[9] that sound. When he told his surprised[10] daughter, she started laughing. But he just wink[11] and called[12] his brother who work[13] at the university. A tolerant oboe teacher was engage[14] and a determine[15] Bernard began his lessons. People did not expected[16] him to get very far.

When you think of how hard it is to learn the oboe, you have to be amaze[17] that Bernard stuck with it. He practice[18] faithfully every day, and even learned[19] to make his own reeds. Last night he was invited[20] to play with a local orchestra in the next spring concert. Proud Bernard has already plan[21] for his scoffing daughter, his ex-wife, and his brother to attend[22]. He has arrange[23] for them to sit right in the front, and he has practiced[24] winking in that direction, just to keep them entertain[25] between his moments of glory.

1. _____	8. _____	15. _____	22. _____
2. _____	9. _____	16. _____	23. _____
3. _____	10. _____	17. _____	24. _____
4. _____	11. _____	18. _____	25. _____
5. _____	12. _____	19. _____	
6. _____	13. _____	20. _____	
7. _____	14. _____	21. _____	

Chapter 11 • Final -s

Mastery Test

A. From each set of words in parentheses, choose the correct word or word group. In the space beside each sentence, write the letter (**a** or **b**) that corresponds to your choice.

_____ 1. Robin (**a.** don't / **b.** doesn't) watch much junk TV.

_____ 2. (**a.** Do / **b.** Does) you want to play backgammon tonight?

_____ 3. (**a.** Don't / **b.** Doesn't) your brother read spy novels?

_____ 4. (**a.** Do / **b.** Does) they go to the theater every week?

_____ 5. They say that he (**a.** doesn't / **b.** don't) do any work after lunch.

_____ 6. Fashions (**a.** change / **b.** changes) every year.

_____ 7. Roberto (**a.** shop / **b.** shops) for clothes at least once a week.

_____ 8. I see that Barbara (**a.** think / **b.** thinks) that gossip can't touch her.

_____ 9. She (**a.** try / **b.** tries) to ignore what people say about her.

_____ 10. My parents think I'm weird because I (**a.** like / **b.** likes) to make my own decisions.

_____ 11. I hope you (**a.** are planning / **b.** is planning) to spend the holiday with us.

_____ 12. My grandmother (**a.** are leaving / **b.** is leaving) before you come.

_____ 13. He (**a.** are cooking / **b.** is cooking) the corncobs in their husks.

_____ 14. That bird (**a.** are standing / **b.** is standing) on one leg.

_____ 15. She rushes out to greet every (**a.** car / **b.** cars).

_____ 16. Walter's partner has collected dozens of (**a.** joke / **b.** jokes).

_____ 17. Somebody said Walter was on stage for fifteen (**a.** minute / **b.** minutes) last night.

_____ 18. I wouldn't buy a (**a.** ticket / **b.** tickets) for the early show if I were you.

_____ 19. Taxi (**a.** driver / **b.** drivers) often like to talk.

_____ 20. He kept recalling the advice he got from the best of the (**a.** player / **b.** players) on his minor league team.

_____ 21. Marcus couldn't stand the smell of a peanut butter (**a.** cookie / **b.** cookies).

_____ 22. The chickens (**a.** have broken / **b.** has broken) through the fence.

_____ 23. I can't believe it (**a.** have happened / **b.** has happened) again.

_____ 24. Dominick (**a.** have called / **b.** has called) the neighbors to ask for help.

_____ 25. You (**a.** have seen / **b.** has seen) this crazy chase before.

B. In the paragraph below, some of the underlined words are correct, and some are not. After each underlined word is a number. If the word it marks is correct, write **C** by the corresponding number in the list below the paragraph. If the word is incorrect, write **I** beside the number in the list.

Brandy has been breeding dog[1] for twenty year[2]. Every morning, rain or shine, he take[3] a bunch of the younger dogs[4] for a run on the hill behind the school. They almost always encounters[5] Mabel there. She is[6] recovering from her accident, and so she walk[7] on that hill every morning[8] too. Brandy don't[9] like people much, but his dogs are friendly, and one of those little springer spaniel,[10] a brown and white one named Mike, has[11] adopted Mabel. During those morning walk[12], Mike breaks[13] away from the other puppies[14] and bound[15] over to Mabel before Brandy have[16] even made it past the fence. Mabel, to put it mildly, doesn't[17] mind a bit. When she sits[18] down for a rest, Mike roll[19] over to flop one of his silky brown ear[20] across her lap. When the dogs is[21] leaving, Mabel looks so forlorn that even stingy old Brandy has[22] begun to think about making the friendship between Mike and Mabel official. Brandy usually wants two hundred dollar[23] for each dog, but now Mike and Mabel are[24] silently offering him a chance for an act of true generosity. The rest of us don't[25] think he'll be able to resist much longer.

1. _____	8. _____	15. _____	22. _____
2. _____	9. _____	16. _____	23. _____
3. _____	10. _____	17. _____	24. _____
4. _____	11. _____	18. _____	25. _____
5. _____	12. _____	19. _____	
6. _____	13. _____	20. _____	
7. _____	14. _____	21. _____	

Chapter 12 • Subject-Verb Agreement

Mastery Test

A. From each pair of verbs in parentheses, choose the one that agrees with its subject. In the space beside the sentence, write the letter (**a** or **b**) that corresponds to your choice.

_____ 1. All the people who work for the lumber company (**a.** are / **b.** is) covered by life insurance.

_____ 2. The height of those trees (**a.** are / **b.** is) awesome.

_____ 3. The grizzly bears that roam this country (**a.** are / **b.** is) dangerous.

_____ 4. The isolation of living in the wilderness (**a.** are / **b.** is) hard on some people.

_____ 5. Thoughts of home (**a.** were / **b.** was) weighing on their minds, so they didn't speak for several minutes.

_____ 6. The story that Bert Wibbley told about the lighthouse during storms (**a.** have / **b.** has) become exaggerated as other people repeat it.

_____ 7. Whenever the fish are biting, there (**a.** are / **b.** is) dozens of small boats out on the lake.

_____ 8. At times like that, there (**a.** are / **b.** is) nobody who loves being out there more than I do.

_____ 9. There (**a.** are / **b.** is) almost nothing that can keep me from collecting my gear and heading for the lake.

_____ 10. There (**a.** were / **b.** was) two reasons why you had to stay close to the phone.

_____ 11. I don't think there (**a.** were / **b.** was) any logic in what you said.

_____ 12. One of Mark's brothers (**a.** play / **b.** plays) professional football with a team down south.

_____ 13. In spite of what the newspaper says, there (**a.** are / **b.** is) still many people who vote on rainy days.

_____ 14. A few of his sisters (**a.** start / **b.** starts) on the high-school women's basketball team.

_____ 15. Nevertheless, nobody in our town (**a.** have / **b.** has) less athletic ability than Mark.

_____ 16. Some of Blane's classmates (**a.** think / **b.** thinks) that he is a genius just because he says such unexpected things.

Copyright © 1989 Houghton Mifflin Company

_____ 17. Everyone in his family (**a.** rely / **b.** relies) on his clarity of mind in an emergency, although in routine matters he's disorganized.

_____ 18. Most of the telephone repair work (**a.** need / **b.** needs) to be recorded on the spreadsheet.

_____ 19. Both wind and sea (**a.** wear / **b.** wears) these rocks down.

_____ 20. Neither TV nor radio (**a.** have / **b.** has) ever been seen or heard in this cabin.

_____ 21. The governor, along with his staff, (**a.** are / **b.** is) expected to arrive any minute.

_____ 22. I expect that both the basketball team and the baseball team (**a.** have / **b.** has) drafted him.

_____ 23. Probably the radio station or the newspaper office (**a.** know / **b.** knows) by now.

_____ 24. In this case, the parents and the child (**a.** appear / **b.** appears) before the probation officer every week.

_____ 25. A person who (**a.** listen / **b.** listens) well rarely misunderstands what people say.

_____ 26. I know four people who (**a.** play / **b.** plays) poker every Friday night, no matter what else happens during the week.

_____ 27. I can't find any more of those special three-inch nails that (**a.** do / **b.** does) not rust.

_____ 28. This is the computer that (**a.** have / **b.** has) taught me how modern technology can be useful.

_____ 29. The woman who (**a.** were / **b.** was) living upstairs had a baby.

_____ 30. That wood stove, which (**a.** were / **b.** was) rescued from the dump at Five Islands last year, can give off enough heat for several rooms.

B. In the following paragraphs, some of the underlined verbs agree with their subjects, and some do not. After each underlined verb is a number. If the verb it marks is correct, write **C** in the space beside the corresponding number in the list below the passage. If the verb is incorrect, write **I** beside the number in the list.

Everybody tells[1] stories about brilliant children who displays[2] outstanding talents at an early age. For instance, there is[3] the boy who star[4] in "Webster" on TV. Although the character in all those crazy episodes are[5] supposed to be in grade school, the actor who charm[6] everyone with all those bright innocent smiles is[7] actually a teenager. But even so, he's young, and most of his audience takes[8] pleasure in his success story. Then every year or so there is[9] newspaper reports about children who enter[10] graduate school at the age of fourteen or so. One of those kids were[11] written up in last week's paper. The amazing thing about this girl was[12] that she had never gone to elementary or high school. Her mother and father were[13] her teachers until she was ready for college. The superintendent of her town's schools were[14] embarrassed by the story. There were[15] a television interview last week with another child wonder — a ten-year-old pool champion. He and his uncle travels[16] all over the United States challenging the best pool players. The uncle rushes around managing the plans and finances while the boy, dressed in his little silk vest and perfectly pressed black trousers, calmly strokes[17] the colored balls into their soft green pockets. According to the TV report, not one of the full-grown pool experts has[18] beaten the ten-year-old yet.

Anybody who excels in an adult activity at such a young age has[19] earned respect and fame. But somebody older who tries to achieve something new deserve[20] even more admiration. I read recently about a sixty-three-year-old woman who have[21] just become an emergency medical technician. And yesterday I met a security guard who was[22] working his way through college at the age of forty-eight. Neither the medical technician nor the security guard inspire[23] doting parental feelings the way those wonderful kids do, but that spunky woman and that determined man inspire[24] something else in me. Learning about geniuses half my age reminds me of talents I'll never have, but the stories of adventurers twice my age make me wonder if there are[25] some hidden talents waiting to be uncovered in my own life.

1. _____   8. _____   15. _____   22. _____

2. _____   9. _____   16. _____   23. _____

3. _____   10. _____   17. _____   24. _____

4. _____   11. _____   18. _____   25. _____

5. _____   12. _____   19. _____

6. _____   13. _____   20. _____

7. _____   14. _____   21. _____

Chapter 13 • Pronouns

Mastery Test

A. From each set of words in parentheses, choose the correct word or group of words. In the space beside each sentence, write the letter (**a** or **b**) that corresponds to your choice.

_____ 1. Mr. Tseng gets terribly upset if a woman takes (**a.** her / **b.** their) bracelet off at bedtime.

_____ 2. After all, his daughters have worn something on (**a.** her / **b.** their) wrists since birth.

_____ 3. If a patient needs help, (**a.** he or she/ **b.** they) can press this buzzer, and a nurse will come.

_____ 4. In the old days, children didn't express (**a.** herself or himself / **b.** themselves) so freely.

_____ 5. A guest at one of those conferences has left the lights on in (**a.** his or her / **b.** their) car.

_____ 6. The Labor Department will release (**a.** its / **b.** their) unemployment report at noon.

_____ 7. Tim doesn't think that anyone will forget (**a.** his or her / **b.** their) book on Wednesday.

_____ 8. But just in case a few people do, here is an extra copy for (**a.** him or her / **b.** them) to consult.

_____ 9. Several of those women have complaints about (**a.** her / **b.** their) paychecks.

_____ 10. One of the women claims that (**a.** her / **b.** their) bank won't cash a check like that.

_____ 11. I doubt that either of those social workers knows what (**a.** his or her / **b.** their) caseload will be.

_____ 12. Among the Iroquois, everyone prepared (**a.** himself or herself / **b.** themselves) carefully for the gathering ceremonies.

_____ 13. According to Alvina and (**a.** he / **b.** him), this is the best math course you'll ever take.

_____ 14. Last week Linc said that (**a.** we / **b.** us) first-year students don't need to register yet.

_____ 15. The bus driver told me that he'd make change for you and (**a.** I / **b.** me) this time but never again.

_____ 16. Probably the captain doesn't expect any of (**a.** they / **b.** them) to show up on a day like this.

_____ 17. It sounds as if you're complaining whenever you and (**a.** she / **b.** her) talk that way.

_____ 18. Every winter Simon and (**a.** we / **b.** us) get together to look at each other's drawings.

_____ 19. This year Stan wants to paint you and (**a.** I / **b.** me) together.

_____ 20. Randy seems to think that there's some conflict developing between Jason and (**a.** he / **b.** him).

_____ 21. Those carrots are fresh and sweet, but I don't want to cook (**a.** they / **b.** them) and the squash for the same meal.

_____ 22. People expect something unusual to happen just because Blanche and (**a.** I / **b.** me) are in the same room at the same time.

_____ 23. Marion thought that you might know what (**a.** he / **b.** him) meant.

_____ 24. Whatever is going on between you and (**a.** she / **b.** her) does seem to take a lot of time.

_____ 25. I'll never forget that smug look on her face when (**a.** she / **b.** her) and Lisa walked in.

B. In the paragraphs below, some of the underlined pronouns are correct and some are not. After each underlined pronoun is a number. If the pronoun it marks is correct, write **C** by the corresponding number in the list below the passage. If the pronoun is incorrect, write **I** beside the number in the list.

When my brother Lou got a job on Cliff's lobster boat last fall, he knew that the fishermen spent much of their[1] time far from the harbor. Normally Lou would have liked that sense of adventure, but in October him[2] and Patty were expecting their second baby, and Lou wanted to be there when the baby was born. The lobster boats communicated with points onshore by CB radios, and everyone at sea kept their[3] radios on all the time. So Lou knew that Patty could get a message to Cliff and he[4] easily enough, but what if the boat and they[5] were far from shore? Whenever Patty and me[6] talked about it, we decided that this baby simply had to cooperate with all of us[7] grownups and be born at night, when Lou was safe at home.

Patty had just been laid off from her job, but that was fine with her[8] because she was eligible for unemployment benefits. Besides, their two-year-old son, Rod, and her[9] wanted to have some time together before the baby came. So the two of them[10] were out visiting the neighbors and letting everyone tell her[11] favorite pregnancy stories when Mrs. Giguere looked at Patty and announced, "I can always tell when a woman starts labor by the look in their[12] eyes. You'd better call Lou right now." Patty was too surprised to argue, and by the time Mrs. Giguere had dialed the number for the harbor store, labor had begun for sure.

When the message sputtered in on Cliff's radio, Lou and him[13] were out near the most distant traps. Cliff didn't even look at Lou. He just turned the boat square around and squeezed so much speed out of that old motor that nobody on a nearby cabin cruiser could believe their[14] eyes as the clumsy fishing boat plowed past them.[15] Meanwhile, Mrs. Giguere had Patty under control, giving Rod and she[16] a ride to the hospital and then waiting in the lobby with Rod. So when Lou burst into the lobby looking exactly like a fairy-tale sea monster with his[17] hair all matted from the salt and wind, it was Mrs. Giguere who swept him past the receptionist and led the way to Patty's room. Then she brought Rod home to my house and stayed with he[18] and me[19] to brag about baby Kate.

Lou was back on the boat by dawn the next morning, and he came home with more than a dozen lobsters that people had donated, one by one, from their[20] day's catches. No queen with a baby princess ever had a feast to match the one laid out for Patty on the day she brought Kate home.

1. _____   6. _____   11. _____   16. _____

2. _____   7. _____   12. _____   17. _____

3. _____   8. _____   13. _____   18. _____

4. _____   9. _____   14. _____   19. _____

5. _____   10. _____   15. _____   20. _____

Chapter 14 • Spelling

Mastery Test

A. From each set of words in parentheses, choose the correct word. In the space beside the sentence, write the letter (**a, b,** or **c**) that corresponds to your choice.

_____ 1. The Caspian Sea, on the border of Iran and the Soviet Union, is the (**a.** bigest / **b.** biggest) lake in the world.

_____ 2. A slot machine is called a one-armed bandit because it often (**a.** robs / **b.** robbs) people.

_____ 3. David is (**a.** ordering / **b.** orderring) a new set of dishes.

_____ 4. If anyone (**a.** catch's / **b.** catches / **c.** catchs') the volleyball, the other team gets the serve.

_____ 5. Chad is out sharpening his two new (**a.** ax's / **b.** axes / **c.** axes').

_____ 6. Whenever she's sick, she always (**a.** asks / **b.** askes) for ice cream.

_____ 7. Whenever Yadira (**a.** flies / **b.** flys / **c.** flyes) somewhere, she wears her silver chain for luck.

_____ 8. The Isle of Mull, off the Scottish coast, is the (**a.** foggiest / **b.** foggyest) place I've ever been.

_____ 9. The wild goose (**a.** obeies / **b.** obeys / **c.** obeyes) the laws of the season and heads south again with its clan.

_____ 10. I couldn't help (**a.** noticing / **b.** noticeing) that you use two fans in the living room.

_____ 11. She usually (**a.** prefered / **b.** preferred) to sit with her back to the windows.

_____ 12. Please bolt those (**a.** latch's / **b.** latches / **c.** latchs').

_____ 13. (**a.** Siting / **b.** Sitting) on the hill above the harbor, we lost track of time and were late to the party.

_____ 14. Only a few of your guests care about your (**a.** children's / **b.** childrens / **c.** childrens') baby pictures.

_____ 15. He claims that he can predict the weather from the (**a.** sky's / **b.** skys / **c.** skys') color at sunset.

_____ 16. All one hundred of the mailing (**a.** label's / **b.** labels / **c.** labels') were printed wrong.

———————— 17. When the alarm (**a.** ring's / **b.** rings / **c.** rings') these days, I get goose-bumps.

———————— 18. Eight (**a.** cat's / **b.** cats / **c.** cats') eyes stared down at us from the hayloft.

———————— 19. I want to see those two (**a.** acrobat's / **b.** acrobats / **c.** acrobats') routines.

———————— 20. My (**a.** sister's / **b.** sisters / **c.** sisters') thinking about applying to welding school.

———————— 21. (**a.** What's / **b.** Whats / **c.** Whats') so hard to understand?

———————— 22. Einstein was a hero of (**a.** her's / **b.** hers / **c.** hers').

———————— 23. The (**a.** women's / **b.** womens / **c.** womens') dressing room is always so crowded.

———————— 24. That (**a.** restaurant's / **b.** restaurants / **c.** restaurants') much cheerier since the renovations were done.

———————— 25. The past six (**a.** week's / **b.** weeks / **c.** weeks') of working have paid off.

———————— 26. She is out of town this week, but her (**a.** schedule's / **b.** schedules / **c.** schedules') going to be lighter after the beginning of the month.

———————— 27. Some whales are larger (**a.** than / **b.** then) the largest of the dinosaurs.

———————— 28. We left the harbor and (**a.** than / **b.** then) turned east.

———————— 29. Al agrees that he eats (**a.** two / **b.** to / **c.** too) much.

———————— 30. The marathon course leads out (**a.** two / **b.** to / **c.** too) the water tower and up Grunters Hill.

———————— 31. The Aztec and Mayan civilizations are famous, but there are other highly developed tribal cultures in ancient Mexico (**a.** two / **b.** to / **c.** too).

———————— 32. Adam didn't (**a.** no / **b.** know / **c.** now) a thing about building a house.

———————— 33. Probably the game will end (**a.** no / **b.** know / **c.** now) that the other team has earned so many penalties.

———————— 34. There's (**a.** no / **b.** know / **c.** now) milk in the refrigerator.

———————— 35. I can't tell (**a.** weather / **b.** whether) or not the furnace is running.

———————— 36. Some solar panels can function even in cloudy (**a.** weather / **b.** whether).

———————— 37. John was so excited that he nearly (**a.** passed / **b.** past) out.

———————— 38. Gwen talks to everyone who walks (**a.** passed / **b.** past) her porch.

———————— 39. Meet us (**a.** were / **b.** we're / **c.** where) the parade ends.

———————— 40. As long as the fire lasts, (**a.** were / **b.** we're / **c.** where) comfortable.

_____ 41. The reasons why the United States became involved in Vietnam (**a.** were / **b.** we're / **c.** where) complicated.

_____ 42. Close the windows; (**a.** their / **b.** they're / **c.** there) are too many mosquitoes.

_____ 43. You can trust them; (**a.** their / **b.** they're / **c.** there) good friends of mine.

_____ 44. Why are those people closing (**a.** their / **b.** they're / **c.** there) eyes?

_____ 45. (**a.** Your / **b.** You're) about to see something you'll never forget.

_____ 46. Sometimes I wonder what's happened to (**a.** your / **b.** you're) common sense.

_____ 47. The proverb says that virtue is (**a.** its / **b.** it's) own reward.

_____ 48. The shirt will fit perfectly after (**a.** its / **b.** it's) washed.

_____ 49. Is that the goalie (**a.** whose / **b.** who's) going to the Olympics?

_____ 50. Mr. Corder is the one (**a.** whose / **b.** who's) tests are so hard.

B. In the following paragraph, some of the underlined words are correct, and some are incorrect. After each underlined word is a number. If the word is correct, write **C** by the corresponding number in the list below the paragraph. If the word is incorrect, write **I** beside the number in the list.

Their[1] is going to be a huge fireworks show over the trucking companys'[2] field tonight. The paper says its[3] bound to be even bigger than[4] any of the other displaies[5] that we've seen over the past[6] year's,[7] including the special one too[8] years ago. At that show, there[9] was a child next to me who's[10] mother had gotten lost in the crowd, so he adoptted[11] me as his guardian and invited[12] me to sit down on his mother's[13] white raincoat. Then the worried[14] mother showed up, full of apologys[15] until she saw the crushed raincoat. Then, with blushes[16] coming and going all over her face, she tryed[17] to drag the boy off for a scolding. He didn't want to[18] leave me; even old grouchs[19] like me offer protection from an angry mother.

Anyway, your[20] coming with me now,[21] aren't you? Bring along a plastic ground cloth, because after whether[22] like this, we're[23] likely to need it. I know[24] the guy whose[25] going to be at the gate. He'll squeeze us in near the stands where[26] we can eavesdrop on the comments of the hotshot's.[27] They're[28] always good for a laugh or too,[29] and their[30] is always some good gossip being passed[31] around about life at City Hall. It's[32] sure to be entertaining if you keep you're[33] ears'[34] tuned to the sounds close by while your[35] eyes gaze innocently at the sparkling sky.

1. _____	10. _____	19. _____	28. _____
2. _____	11. _____	20. _____	29. _____
3. _____	12. _____	21. _____	30. _____
4. _____	13. _____	22. _____	31. _____
5. _____	14. _____	23. _____	32. _____
6. _____	15. _____	24. _____	33. _____
7. _____	16. _____	25. _____	34. _____
8. _____	17. _____	26. _____	35. _____
9. _____	18. _____	27. _____	

Chapter 15 • Consistency

Mastery Test

A. Some of the sentences below include sentence elements that are not parallel. Other sentences use inconsistent pronoun points of view or inconsistent verb tenses. If you decide that a sentence shows inconsistency among its elements, write **I** in the space beside its number. (Remember that the verbs in a sentence do not have to be in the same tense when the writer is using different tenses to show that the events being described occurred at different times.) If the sentence is correct, write **C** in the space.

_____ 1. The advertising agency has based this campaign on the theory that the sixties are gone but not forgotten.

_____ 2. Pets shed on your carpet, the upholstery, and in the car.

_____ 3. Discouraged but she was not defeated, Elise resolved to sing at one more audition.

_____ 4. My primary ambitions are a college education, to land a good job, and contributing to the community where I live.

_____ 5. Is it possible to complete these exercises quickly and accurately?

_____ 6. As they considered the matter and made their decision, they hoped that they were doing the right thing.

_____ 7. Are you here to compete officially or just for the experience?

_____ 8. Because Mario had trouble seeing things at a distance and gets headaches often, he goes to the eye doctor and got new glasses.

_____ 9. While Wally sits down and figures out how much we owe, we waited impatiently.

_____ 10. Before you returned to town last December, they had already finished all the sets for the play.

_____ 11. Even though Otis has memorized all his lines and is comfortable in his costume, he still feels uneasy about the play tonight.

_____ 12. Now that the school has been warned, the newspaper staff will be hesitant to print those articles.

_____ 13. I know how ill you are, so I had suggested that we should stay home.

_____ 14. When Laila saw the checkered flag, she starts imagining her victory celebration.

15. A woman who has not worked for many years may be surprised when she discovers that you have more opportunities for advancement now than women did before.

16. When people attend a birthday celebration for someone over fifty, you certainly don't expect to see a candle for every year.

17. When you are totally honest, most people admit that they fear painful illness more than death.

18. An individual should never assume that he or she can do this whole job alone.

19. We are sure that he will do his duty and live up to our high expectations.

20. One shouldn't leave any of this director's mystery films early, because you never know what tricks he will pull in the final scene.

B. In the paragraphs below, some of the underlined words and phrases are correct, and some are not. After each underlined word or phrase is a number. If the word or phrase it marks is correct, write **C** by the corresponding number in the list below the paragraph. If the word or phrase is incorrect, write **I** beside the number in the list.

Human beings have shared our[1] homes and hearths with dogs ever since they discovered what a good companion the dog makes. Many people who value loyalty and strength in their[2] canine companions chose[3] a puppy of the magnificent breed known as the Rottweiler.

Rottweilers are large dogs that excel in tracking, guarding their owners' homes, and to provide[4] personal protection. They are known for endurance, eagerness to work,[5] and fearlessness. When a Rottweiler stands at the door, alert and they have a businesslike expression,[6] few strangers, human or if they are dogs[7] come[8] closer. Rotts are also known for their agility, and they seldom wandered[9] far from home.

In deciding what kind of dog one wants in one's home, you[10] should consider the needs and expectations of all family members. When people who are very elderly or infirm try to handle Rottweilers, one[11] can be injured; a less powerful pet is better for them. Others who should choose a different breed are people who were[12] not able to offer their dog regular exercise outdoors. A woman who lives alone might select a Rottweiler as her pet because she knows you'll[13] gain a loyal and protective friend in this big black dog.

Occasionally stubborn but they have good tempers,[14] Rottweilers do need patient, consistent guidance in early obedience training. Gently but firmly,[15] the wise owner teaches the dog that obeying is less stressful than disobeying.[16] It is best to buy a puppy, because a Rott whose early training has been neglected[17] may be difficult to train later. Getting a puppy also gave[18] the owner more of a chance to help shape his or her dog's personality. The buyer pays around $350 for a pet-quality puppy or a show-quality adult can cost thousands.[19] But whatever the cost, one who decides a Rottweiler is right is not likely to regret your[20] choice.

1. _____   6. _____   11. _____   16. _____

2. _____   7. _____   12. _____   17. _____

3. _____   8. _____   13. _____   18. _____

4. _____   9. _____   14. _____   19. _____

5. _____   10. _____   15. _____   20. _____

Answer Key

The Answer Key includes answers for the Applications, Review and Practice exercises, and Pretests in *Sentence Sense.* The page number on which each exercise or test begins is given in parentheses.

Chapter 1: An Overview of the Sentence

Application (7)

Answers will vary. Compare yours with a classmate's.

Chapter 2: Verbs

Application 1 (13)

Answers will vary. Compare yours with a classmate's.

Application 2 (14)

1. intersection / is
2. We / should
3. state / is
4. complex / might
5. congestion / will

Application 3 (15)

had peaked, appeared
(x, mv, sv)

were pointing, explained, were seeing, was
(x, mv, sv, x, mv, sv)

were casting, was floating
(x, mv, x, mv)

look, will see
(sv, x, mv)

will show
(x, mv)

did watch, could see
(x, mv, x, mv)

must have been straining, could have put, would have called
(x, x, mv, x, x, mv, x, x, mv)

Application 4 (16)

1. is
2. should call
3. is building
4. might be completed
5. will become

Application 5 (17)

1. We're sending
2. She's enjoying . . . but she's been getting
3. I'd have spoken . . . but Jack's convinced . . . that she'll get (In conversation we sometimes say "I would've spoken," or even "I'd've spoken," but these contractions are not accepted in standard writing.)
4. I'm watching . . . that I've been
5. She's taught . . . that I'd forgotten

Application 6 (18)

1. will incur
   Will the hospital incur the risk of lawsuits?
   The hospital will not (or won't) incur the risk of law-
   suits.
2. could intervene
   In that case, could the mayor intervene?
   In that case, the mayor could not (or couldn't) inter-
   vene.
3. is meeting
   Is he meeting with his legal advisers now?
   He is not (or isn't) meeting with his legal advisers
   now.

Application 7 (20)

1. get → do get
   Do we get a bonus every six months?
   We do not get a bonus every six months.
2. waited → did wait
   Did we wait for two weeks between checks last
   month?
   We did not wait for two weeks between checks last
   month.
3. operates → does operate
   Does the business office operate more efficiently this
   year?
   The business office does not operate more efficiently
   this year.

Application 8 (20)

1. were
   Were the cookout and the party very successful?
   The cookout and the party were not very successful.
2. was
   Was Mom ecstatic about ~~them~~? *your friends*
   Mom was not ecstatic about ~~them~~. *your friends*
3. is
   Is there enough pie left for tomorrow?
   There is not enough pie left for tomorrow.

Application 9 (21)

Application 10 (22)

sang
will sing
am singing
was singing
will be singing
have sung
had sung
will have sung

Application 11 (23)

1. introduces → introduced
2. are practicing → were practicing, monitors → mon-
   itored
3. gather → will gather
4. stride → will stride
5. will attract → attracts, will amaze → amaze

Chart (24)

I yelled, I have yelled
I can dance, I am dancing
I dance
I am winking, I have winked
I stopped
I stop

Application 12 (25)

talk, offer
feel, depend, consider

Application 13 (25)

perform
ask, pass, believe
add, twirl, huddle, whistle

Application 14 (26)

turned
raced, spotted
called, answered
returned, ignored, lectured
sputtered, warmed, grinned

Application 15 (27)

expecting   baking
sitting   smelling
cooking

Application 16 (28)

begged, refused   talked
collapsed   joined

Application 17 (29)

spilled   appreciated
expected

Application 18 (30)

was   been
were   am, is
are, was   be
was

Application 19 (33)

threw   kept, were
brought, made, went   led, stole, ran, lay
paid, bought   grew, became, saw
rose

Application 20 (33)

have thrown
has brought, have made, has gone
have paid, have bought
have risen
have kept, have been
have led, have stolen, have run, have lain
have grown, have become, have seen

Application 21 (34)

1. <u>keeps</u>   4. <u>wake</u>
2. <u>loves</u>   5. <u>do(n't) want</u>
3. <u>was thinking</u>

Application 22 (35)

1. can buzz but not bite
2. tries yet fails
3. either eats my garbage or scatters it
4. not only bought herself a digital watch but also learned
5. surprised, delighted, instructed, and amused

Chapter 3: Subjects

Application 1 (41)

<u>children</u> <u>can learn</u>
<u>practice</u> <u>can humble</u>
<u>Strategy</u> <u>is</u>
<u>part</u> <u>is</u>
<u>veterans</u> <u>have developed</u>
<u>piles</u> <u>change</u>, <u>men</u> <u>know</u>
<u>they</u> <u>are</u>, <u>they</u> <u>show</u>
<u>speed</u> <u>can baffle</u>, <u>it</u> <u>can inspire</u>
<u>(You)</u> <u>come . . . see</u>

Application 2 (42)

1. She's slamming
   Is she slamming doors all over the house?
2. screen fell
   Did the porch door screen just fall off?
3. You could talk
   Could you talk to her about her temper?
4. She is
   Is she eager to please you?
5. You have
   Do you have a calming influence on her?

Application 3 (44)

Answers will vary. Compare yours with a classmate's.
The verbs in the printed sentences are

1. needs
2. loves, searches
3. knows
4. cooked
5. has been

Application 4 (44)

singer could cause
poet was renewing, he told
song could heal, chant could encourage
word was considered
It existed
(You) don't be, writers use
they may speak, power guides

Application 5 (45)

1–4. whales are racing
5–7. Everybody loves
8–10. answer reassured

Application 6 (46)

1. advice ~~about the care and treatment of leather~~ must have been
2. Some ~~of the gloves in the bin~~ were
3. few ~~of them~~ were
4. oil ~~for leather~~ has restored
5. rest ~~of the players~~ weren't

Application 7 (47)

1. The press and the police
2. Mosquitoes and blackflies
3. Either your dog or your cat
4. Neither Tara nor her boyfriend
5. The movie, the music, the popcorn, and the soda

Chapter 4: Completers and Modifiers

Application 1 (51)

women had established | tradition |

style evolved

This was | patchwork |

pioneers didn't discard | clothing |

Fabric was | precious |

they cut | clothes |, stitched | them |

women shared | patterns |, gave | names |, moved | craft |

Application 2 (52)

1. they're enjoying | themselves | *pronoun*
2. Soo-Yean will call | names | *noun*
3. whales can answer | her | *pronoun*
4. She has been training | them | *pronoun*
5. show is | popular | *describes subject*
6. act was | best | *describes subject*
7. aquarium is attracting | tourists | *noun*
8. You would enjoy | show | *noun*
9. afternoon is | time | *noun*
10. crowds have been | noisier | *describes subject*

Application 3 (53)

Coins were [sturdier]

they contained [metals], coins had [value], people
trusted [them]

Paper was [story]

It was [fragile], it was [vulnerable], it was [symbol]

bill represented [promise], people have been
[suspicious]

government issued [currency], people accepted [it]

countries adopted [custom], money spread

people pass [it]

Application 4 (54)

Answers will vary. Compare yours with a classmate's.

Application 5 (55)

1. Those fancy new forecasts amuse me.

2. Yesterday the reporters confidently predicted
snow.

3. Today they expect light rain.

4. They change every hour's forecast.

5. I am ignoring those fickle daily predictions.

6. My cows can usually interpret the changing
weather pretty accurately.

7. They sit still and face the humid wind.

8. My sinuses are becoming very reliable barometers.

9. Now I do not need any weather reports.

10. No scientific gadgets can beat my fine intuition.

Application 6 (58)

toward* every (stoplight)

under* the (bridge)

on* these (trips)

in* her steady good (humor)

until* the last (moment)

during* the train (ride)

like* (mine)

for* (her)

about* my best (friend)

from* a small (town)

of* some forgotten old (adventures)

Application 7 (59)

1. She has interests ⟨like mine⟩.

2. She'll love the ice cream shop ⟨under the bridge⟩.

3. She lives so intensely ⟨on these trips⟩.

4. ⟨During the train ride⟩, she didn't sleep a wink.

5. She was happily entertaining a homesick teenager
⟨from a small town⟩.

Application 8 (60)

1. watch the papers and the network news
2. impresses Ben but not me
3. eats my garbage or my flowers
4. loves your high little voice and the sound of your big old tuba
5. are neither new nor funny
6. sing beautifully and freely
7. buzz in the tent but not in the cabin
8. cooks spaghetti sauce in a wok or over her grill
9. easily with most people but not with children
10. to bed in the winter and even on chilly nights in the summer

Chapter 5: Embedded Thoughts

Application 1 (66)

Answers will vary. Compare yours with a classmate's.

Applications 2 and 3 (68) and (68)

1. ⟨Whatever you want⟩ is okay with me.
2. I can't understand ⟨why you are so upset about the new benefits package⟩.
3. You must report to the union ⟨before the managers call you⟩.
4. You should address your comments to the woman ⟨whom you met yesterday⟩.
5. The meeting ⟨that you will have with the negotiating team⟩ could make a difference to all of us.
6. ⟨Where the meeting will be held⟩ has been kept a big secret.
7. One or two managers may explain ⟨how they feel⟩.
8. You can judge their sincerity by ⟨whether or not they look at you⟩.

9. ⟨If I meet with the managers⟩, they'll just argue with me.
10. They'll probably like you better, ⟨because you're much calmer in these situations⟩.

Applications 4 and 5 (69) and (69)

1. ⟨ If I'm in a hurry⟩, that's ⟨how I go places⟩.
2. Our subways are just noisier ⟨than the ones in Washington are⟩ ⟨because our equipment is older⟩.
3. ⟨Unless you object⟩, I'll send Mark home on the subway ⟨after the party is over⟩.
4. ⟨Because he has spent so much time with me⟩, he'll know ⟨where he should transfer to the other line⟩.
5. ⟨Whether he eats supper or not⟩ can be his choice ⟨since we'll have plenty of food here⟩.

Applications 6 and 7 (71) and (72)

1. Nobody likes ⟨to wait⟩ in lines.
2. This workshop demonstrates new ways ⟨to concentrate⟩.
3. ⟨To survive⟩ on a minimum wage takes tremendous resourcefulness.
4. Out of the corner of her eye, Anuja glimpsed a ⟨shooting⟩ star.
5. ⟨Diving⟩ is not a good idea at this beach.
6. The cleaner will trim that ⟨dangling⟩ piece of lace.
7. Most students enjoy Ms. Burgess's ⟨teasing⟩.
8. The ball flew right between the ⟨astonished⟩ umpire's knees.
9. ⟨Frozen⟩ yogurt is becoming a fad in some cities.
10. The ⟨unemployed⟩ flight attendants are bringing pots and pans to the airport.

Applications 8 and 9 (73) and (73)

1. Some rock singers like (to go on tour).
2. They get a lot of money for (appearing live on stage).
3. They become inspired in front of audiences (cheering them on).
4. A star surrounded by fans) feels completely alive.
5. Sometimes adults in the audiences will squabble like two-year-olds (to get a good view of their idols).

Application 10 (74)

1. The child who was lost on the mountain rested on an old tree stump.
2. The stump forked in a short branch whose shape was like a chair.
3. The softness that the thick moss provided made the fork a perfect place for a nap.
4. He settled down and slept until a light rain started to fall.
5. When he woke up stiff and chilly, he realized that he was hungry.
6. Because he didn't have a watch, he wondered what time it was.
7. He wasn't worried although he was only nine years old.
8. The rangers would find him soon if he could stay in the open where they could see him.
9. He started singing loudly so that the moose at the nearby stream froze into stillness because she was both fascinated and afraid (or) He started singing so loudly that the moose . . .
10. The sky cleared as the boy cut sticks with a knife that he carried in his pocket (or) As the sky cleared, the boy . . .

Application 11 (76)

1. The soldiers avoided the sleeping children.
2. Singing quietly to herself, Talitha approached the troops.
3. Rosa and the twins shout in the rushing crowd.
4. Laughing about the meeting, they gesture with their hands.
5. The polished steel was sent to the die cutters.
6. The sample engraved with the machinist's initials went on display for a week.
7. Please clean up Billie Sue's dripping ice cream.
8. Rushed by the deadline, we're finally throwing out Dad's old gadgets.
9. Today I looked at my scratched fender.
10. I must have run into that car parked too close to my driveway.

Application 12 (77)

1. Even the president agrees that these weapons are a waste of money and that they may spoil our negotiating position.
2. People are asking how we got to this point and why we didn't stop before now.
3. You should lobby the legislators who are sympathetic or the ones who have strong arms-control pressure groups at home.
4. Politicians listen to people while any controversy is hot, when the news coverage is good, and before an election rolls around.
5. Learning about the political system and recognizing our power can give us hope.
6. Some people just don't have the energy to get involved or to make changes.
7. However, when I sit at home, I find myself getting depressed and feeling even more tired.
8. As a result, I have decided to rest often but not to give up.
9. Hoping for successes, failing often, yet making many small steps forward, I keep trying.
10. Sometime after my senator returns from Washington but before summer vacation slows things down, I will start a petition drive.

Chapter 6: Capitalization and Punctuation

Application 1 (84)

1. I, Canadians, Thanksgiving, November
2. David, *The Green Insects Return*
3. That, History 602
4. I
5. Since, Friday, German

Application 2 (84)

Throughout history . . . The ancient Greek dramatist, Sophocles . . . tragedy about Antigone . . . In modern times, Evelyn Waugh . . . *The Loved One* . . . Yet human beings . . . In Sociology 101 last Monday, Dr. Cummings . . . When I . . . I hardly expected . . . However, I find . . . the highway in October . . . massive African elephants . . .

Application 3 (85)

1. children.
   (*or*) children!
2. adults?
3. teenagers.
4. warnings?
5. yesterday.
   (*or*) yesterday!

Application 4 (86)

Watch out! The broken limb . . . is falling! Thank goodness . . . out of the way in time. Don't you think . . . cut that tree down? The electrician who lives on Brand St. . . . tree is dead. Sooner or later . . . will fall. It's a miracle . . . has been hurt yet. Besides, . . . the whole yard. Wouldn't you like . . . with the kids? I love trees . . . like a birch. That would please Mrs. Lowe . . . big old tree. What do you think?

Application 5 (86)

1. two aunts, two great-uncles, and all six
2. mother, oldest brother, and younger sister
3. A ham, a huge salad, baked sweet potatoes, and watermelon will be
4. two bedrooms, refinished the floors, replaced the light fixtures, and installed screens
5. the bathroom, the kitchen, and both hallways

Application 6 (87)

1. lottery, and that
2. business, but he
3. sailing, so he
4. car, but he
5. dream, yet he

Application 7 (88)

1. long winter, Mary
2. therefore, she
3. *no comma necessary*
4. Madeira, Mary
5. Africa, Madeira

Application 8 (89)

1. tulips, all members of the lily family, available
2. climates, however, and do not
3. popularity, to a great degree, to their use
4. bulbs, which are shaped like tear drops, need to be
5. bulbs, by the way, come

Application 9 (89)

1. "Well," he said, "that . . ."
2. reads, "And miles . . ."
3. hissed, "Stop crackling . . ."
4. phrase, "Fourscore and seven years ago," begins
5. ". . . dictionary," she

Application 10 (90)

1. November 19, 1919,
2. Zion National Park, Springdale, Utah.
3. May 14, 1930.
4. Carlsbad Caverns National Park, 3225 National Parks Highway, Carlsbad, New Mexico.
5. September 25, 1890.

Application 11 (90)

Aaron Copland, one of the grand old men of American music, came in with our century. He was born in Brooklyn, New York on November 14, 1900, and he began to study piano at the relatively late age of thirteen. He started composing soon after. Unlike many struggling artists, he met success early since he was only nineteen when he published his first piece. Although his earliest works show the influence of his studies in Europe, his later compositions are filled with American sounds. For example, he built symphonies around folk tunes, jazz rhythms, and hymns. Perhaps the familiarity of these sounds has helped to make his music popular with people who don't usually listen to orchestral music. At the same time, the clean and disciplined harmonies that link the horns and strings in his pieces have won Copland the reverence of music lovers. One critic said of him, "Copland, our own boy from Brooklyn, is able to please the person in the back seat of the taxi and the driver too."

Application 12 (91)

1. varieties: Mendel
2. remember: always
3. items: bone meal

Application 13 (92)

1. this morning; however,
2. the mail comes; the letter
3. in the last race; furthermore,
4. overflowing; therefore,
5. and gas companies; get our security . . . sink problem; and let

Application 14 (93)

In the twenty years between 1911 and 1931, second basemen dominated the National League roster of Most Valuable Players. Four men are responsible for this statistic: Larry Doyle, who played for New York in 1912; Johnny Evers, who won for Boston in 1914; Rogers Hornsby, who won the award for St. Louis in 1925 and then for Chicago in 1929; and finally Frankie Frisch, who returned the prize to St. Louis in 1931. In the American League during the same period, only Eddie Collins of Philadelphia brought the prize back to second base; his year was 1914. After that, second basemen nearly dropped off the MVP roster in both leagues; in fact, only five men represented the position through the next fifty years. Here are the names of those scattered stars: Charlie Gehringer (AL), Joe Gordon (AL), Jackie Robinson (NL), Nellie Fox (AL), and Joe Morgan (NL).

Application 15 (94)

1. "Give me liberty or give me death."
2. "Everything was going well," the mechanic said, "until we reached sixty miles per hour."
3. "Here come the blue jays,"
4. "A Good Man is Hard to Find,"
5. "Love Triangles."

Application 16 (95)

1. (I know you don't want to hear this)
2. (pencils, notebooks, tape recorders, even cups and spoons for coffee)
3. (yellow and purple with swirls)

Application 17 (95)

"I see you folks have an appetite for cholesterol,"
"Boiled cholesterol, cholesterol salad, fried cholesterol. Yum."
"You should read this article. It will change your life."
"Can You and Your Serum Lipids Live in Peace?"
(pages 56–58)
"Suicide!"
(believe it or not)

Chapter 7: Combining Sentences

Writing

Translated from La Rochefoucauld, a seventeenth-century writer:
"The accent of the country where you were born lives in your heart and spirit just as it does in your speech."

Application 1 (101)

1. Bud will be leaving by noon, so I'll call my mother then.
2. Baking bread every Saturday keeps Tillie happy, but eating it keeps her fat.
3. If you're sure, go ahead, or you may lose your chance.
4. The boy who got lost on the mountain settled down on an old tree stump, for he knew that he needed some rest.
5. My father loves TV, my fiancée loves football, my sister loves politics, and I love sleep.

Application 2 (102)

1. Bronson listens to dozens of records and imitates the quirks of his idols.
2. He's probably learning a lot just from talking with Bill and from watching Bill's rehearsals.
3. Bill and the drummer adopted Bronson in a good-natured way.

Application 3 (102)

1. He might just make it because he's throwing his whole soul into it.
2. His friends are supporting him in little ways although they're poking fun at him, too (*or*) Although his friends are supporting him in little ways, they're . . .
3. It's hard to believe that this is the same Bronson who hated jazz six months ago.

Application 4 (103)

1. Bronson loved that dented trombone immediately.
2. Working at night now, he's saving money to get it fixed.
3. Teased by his friends and family, Bronson moves steadily toward his dream.

Application 5 (103)

1. Bronson used to swear that jazz was nothing but noise, but look at him today.
2. I can't help laughing at his conversion, and I think even he will laugh with me eventually.
3. Meanwhile, he's enjoying his obsession, so let's leave him alone for now.

Chapter 8: Sentence Fragments

Application 1 (111)

These are suggested answers; other tenses of the auxiliary are also possible.

1. boys are thinking
2. hip was broken
3. goats are making
4. pan was leaking
5. mistake was forgotten
6. seeds are sprouting
7. she has given
8. people have taken
9. children have begun
10. Ted is spending

Application 2 (112)

Answers will vary. Compare yours with a classmate's.

Application 3 (112)

These are suggested answers; your phrases may be arranged differently. Check with a classmate or your teacher to be sure your phrases are modifying the words you want them to modify.

1. After the long, formal dinner, the graduates joked and sang loudly in their dignified academic robes.
2. Just like the coach's mother, Lourdes followed the action with passionate interest.

3. With fierce determination, Blake leaped toward the bright orange mat on the red tiled floor.

4. In the end, after all the crazy arguments, we always find ourselves joking about who washes the dishes.

5. On top of the world since his converstation with Gina, Matt drove all night through Ohio and on to Chicago without stopping to eat.

Application 4 (114)

Answers will vary. Compare yours with a classmate's.

Application 5 (114)

These are suggested answers; your phrases may be arranged differently. Check with a classmate or your teacher to be sure your phrases are as close as possible to the words you want them to modify.

1. Trying not to laugh at him, we watched poor Francis staring in innocent amazement at the escalator.

2. The gate was draped with rugs faded and tattered by the weather and drying after the storm.

3. Talking about nuclear war in a class full of eighth graders makes me realize how little I know.

4. Bored and irritated by the previews, we waited restlessly for the feature, stuffing ourselves with popcorn.

5. Relieved of her anxiety over Emmet, Sharon finally started trying wholeheartedly to let go of the past.

Application 6 (115)

Answers will vary. Compare yours with a classmate's.

Application 7 (116)

These are suggested answers; your clauses may be arranged differently. Check with a classmate or your teacher to be sure your clauses are as close as possible to the words you want them to modify.

1. Because Clyde was so wound up, no one wanted to argue when he insisted on that restaurant.

2. Although I kept putting in dimes whenever the dryer stopped, some of your clothes are still wet.

3. Because it's your birthday, this party is for you and for whoever else wants to come.

4. I'll run back to get you before the bus leaves so that you can work until the last minute.

5. If he doesn't call today before he leaves for work, I'm completely convinced that she'll give up on the whole plan.

Application 8 (117)

These are suggested answers; your clauses may be arranged differently. Check with a classmate or your teacher to be sure your clauses are as close as possible to the words you want them to modify.

1. The people who work in the shipping department will introduce you to Pablo's boss, who has lots of friends.

2. I was up until 2:00 A.M. watching the game that Red had taped for me on his VCR, which explains my crabby mood today.

3. I found the shoes that you lost in your closet, which looks like an abandoned shed.

4. She told me an amazing story that even your dad, who doesn't fool easily, will believe.

5. Those dazzling young dancers whose silver tunics are covered with feathers may be the reason for the show's success.

Review and Practice (118)

A.

1. Lonnie is coming
2. singer was featured
3. I have seen
4. you are traveling
5. teachers have begun
6. In the early hours of morning, the lions roar from their dark cages.
7. In the spring, they crave a special food with the taste and smell of African antelope.
8. Their food is shipped in huge crates on airplanes and trains.
9. It reaches the zoo on the other side of the world in less than a week.

10. Except in the spring, the zoo can't afford this extravagance for the demanding lions.

11. Lost in thought, I didn't hear my son slamming the front door.

12. Perfectly contented to continue my daydream, I ignored the stew burning on the stove.

13. My son rushed into the kitchen looking like a maniac.

14. He was yelling at the top of his lungs to warn me about the house filling up rapidly with smoke.

15. Swallowed up in the confusion of reality, my daydream fled.

16. You were Vivian's best friend when she got the divorce that she was so nervous about.

17. You were patient with her because you understood her shyness, although she never asked you for help.

18. Since she was embarrassed, she didn't talk to anyone until the court battle was over.

19. After she'd snubbed them for so long, her other friends were all mad at her, even though by then she needed support more than ever.

20. I often wonder what would have become of her if you hadn't been waiting and ready for her to talk at that point.

21. Those noisy people who are in the car that Gerry just bought want to get out.

22. They want to look for the movie star whose face is on the ad for the hotel that was recently built in this run-down town.

23. They have been traveling together for three weeks, which is a long time.

24. But Gerry, who has to get to the West Coast by Sunday, isn't happy about stopping.

25. On Monday, he'll sign up for the Army program that will train him in radio communications, which he has always wanted to study.

B. Several solutions are possible. Here is one:

The team started the season with skill and style, determined to prove to all the noisy critics that the new school could make the playoffs even in the big, tougher league. But in the past three weeks, something has been going wrong. The trainer is worried because the players have been gaining so much weight on their tours by eating all those steaks and drinking too much beer. They eat whatever they crave, like snacks, ice cream, or junk food. They're losing their self-discipline. The coach is getting pretty angry, too, especially after that great pep talk of his that should have inspired the team. He was really disgusted during the last game when they were so sluggish. It was hard to believe that they could have fallen so far so fast.

Chapter 9: Run-on Sentences

Application 1 (125)

1. The papers were all jumbled up, / therefore, we couldn't find the report (when) we needed it.

2. (Although) the patients thrive there, the hospital isn't perfect, / it seems awfully far from the center of town.

3. My boss has an idea (that) we should consider / it might solve our problems.

4. The application is due tomorrow, / could you type it up today, please?

5. These phone bills are puzzling me / I refuse to pay them (until) you explain them.

6. (Since) Coleman came along, the bouncers have left us alone, / they respect the reputation (that) he earned last fall.

7. It's dangerous to walk there alone / you shouldn't go without me.

8. The icicles were melting, / the tin bucket caught them.

9. Some household cleaners should not be mixed / for example, ammonia and bleach give off a poison gas (when) they're combined.

10. (You) look for hummingbirds around that tree /

they've been nesting.

Application 2 (126)

1. all jumbled up. Therefore, we
2. the hospital isn't perfect. It seems
3. we should consider. It might solve
4. is due tomorrow. Could you type
5. are puzzling me. I refuse
6. left us alone. They respect
7. there alone. You shouldn't go
8. icicles were melting. The tin bucket
9. should not be mixed. For example, ammonia
10. around that tree. They've been

Application 3 (128)

These are suggested answers; you may have selected different conjunctions. Compare your answers with a classmate's.

1. had better hurry or she's sure
2. to catch the oil; then you can
3. by the end of the day, so plan some
4. all jumbled up; therefore, we couldn't
5. gourmet foods, but hot dogs
6. on the beach, so try some
7. stretch your joints; that's what
8. is important, for the ozone layer
9. the wild turkey, but there are
10. in the spring, so take

Application 4 (129)

1. today, please since it is
2. under your sleeping bag when they
3. butterfly, which was emerging
4. eggshell water because it makes
5. Proxima Centuri although it is
6. Because it's dangerous to walk
7. a wartime president who was elected
8. custody suit that is being appealed

9. on her own unless she calls me
10. canceled even though the professor *or* Even though the professor

Application 5 (130)

Answers will vary; these are suggestions. Compare your answers with a classmate's.

1. I won't pay these puzzling phone bills until you explain them.
2. Be careful of those racing snowmobiles.
3. You'll love this old taped recording.
4. Mazie served us a platter of steamed biscuits.
5. I don't want to ride this crowded trolley.
6. Sitting on the shoulders of the road in the rain, the toads don't fear the cars.
7. I need to replace the blue sock that was lost in the washing machine.
8. Taking enormous risks, Marvin Hagler and Sugar Ray Leonard . . .
9. It's fascinating to watch the CIA changing its strategy in Central America.
10. Erected overnight in August of 1961, the Berlin Wall . . .

Application 6 (132)

These are suggested answers; you may have selected different conjunctions.

1. That woman is snoring. Give her a nudge.
2. That woman is snoring, so give her a nudge.
3. Since that woman is snoring, give her a nudge.
4. Give that snoring woman a nudge.

1. We were inspired by the news feature. We became organ donors.
2. We were inspired by the news feature and we became organ donors.
3. After we were inspired by the news feature, we became organ donors.
4. Inspired by the news feature, we became organ donors.

Application 7 (133)

1. beach. Try
2. day. Plan
3. for us. There's
4. cough. Avoid
5. on time. Don't

6. around. There's
7. floor. Take
8. door. I
9. flattery. Don't
10. soon. She

Application 8 (134)

1. enough. That's
2. sweepstakes. He's
3. window. It
4. Montgomery. This
5. hurry up. She's

6. bag. They
7. handle. It's
8. computers. He's
9. surfing. It
10. mother. She

Application 9 (136)

1. corn; meanwhile,
2. concert; besides,
3. shut; eventually,
4. quickly; however,
5. garden; nevertheless,

Application 10 (136)

1. oil. Next
2. cafeteria. For instance,
3. noisily. The whole
4. patch. However,
5. workshop. Otherwise,

Review and Practice (138)

A.

1. were laughing / they threw
2. was forgotten, / finally Jamaal
3. was rising / it gradually
4. were laughing. They threw
5. was forgotten. Finally Jamaal
6. was rising. It gradually
7. were laughing; they threw
8. was forgotten, but finally Jamaal
9. was rising, and it gradually
10. While the three friends were laughing, they threw
11. was forgotten until finally Jamaal
12. while the sun was rising, it gradually
13. The three laughing friends threw wads of newspaper at each other until they wore themselves out.
14. With a broom he found in the hallway, Jamaal finally decided to tackle the forgotten mess in the kitchen.
15. Meanwhile, the rising sun gradually lit up the gray windows.
16. hot dogs. Just
17. fixed, or
18. Since some candidates have behaved
19. Save the old rotting wood for landfill.
20. hurry; get
21. instruments. They
22. opinion, but
23. Although bubblebath is a frivolous
24. I got tired of listening to that bragging man
25. pocket while
26. strength. For example.
27. hand; however,
28. Pike's Peak, and then
29. wildly. Therefore,
30. The wealthy executives gathered around the delighted clown.

B.   One possible solution:

The two runners started out evenly. Then the tall one pulled ahead while the shorter one lagged behind, appearing discouraged already. The wind was harsh since this was October in Montana, so the spectators began to disperse. Suddenly the shorter runner put on speed, lengthening her stride until she was moving surprisingly fast. However, there were still twenty yards between her and the leader when the sun began to set. The runners leaned into the turn in the road. They seemed to shrink in the fading purple light, and finally they disappeared over the crest of the hill.

Chapter 10: Final -ed

Applications 1 and 2 (147) and (148)

Have you ever (walked²) across a dark, lonely, (deserted⁴) street or parking lot and for one reason or another become (scared⁴) because you thought you were going to be (mugged³) or (battered³)? If you've (answered²) "yes" to this question, don't feel (ashamed⁴) because you're in the great majority. I (asked) myself this same question about seven years ago and bravely (decided¹) to do something about the problem. I (wanted¹) to be able to control fear before it (controlled¹) me. I (learned¹) to control my fear and become more self-confident through the martial arts. . . .

I have now (earned²) my orange belt in Kenpo and my green belt in Shorin-Ryu. Looking back over the past seven years, I realize that I have (learned²) much more than I had first (wanted²) to. The philosophies of the martial arts can be (used³) for much more than just self-defense. To sum it all up, let me recall the words of my master, Eddie Parker: "I come to you with only karate, empty hands. I have no weapons, but should I be (forced³) to defend myself, my principles, or my honor, then here are my weapons: karate, my empty hands."

Application 3 (149)

1. When the singing waiter finished . . . woman pushed . . .
2. Angrily she whispered . . .
3. He glanced . . . and noticed . . .
4. As she stalked . . . he observed . . . walk seemed stiff.
5. He tried to understand what was wrong.
6. Normally she thrived . . .
7. Then it dawned . . . she hated . . .
8. . . . he apologized . . . and went . . .
9. . . . politely turned away and pretended . . .
10. But as the door closed . . . everyone began . . .

Application 4 (150)

The incident that ~~convinces~~ *convinced* me to learn martial arts ~~happens~~ *happened* when I ~~am~~ *was* in the Navy. Walking back to my ship with two friends one night, I ~~notice~~ *noticed* some guys ahead of us who ~~start~~ *started* making some stupid, drunken remarks. I ~~realize~~ *realized* immediately that these people ~~are~~ *were* fairly intoxicated, and I ~~try~~ *tried* to ignore their antics. But one of my buddies ~~is~~ *was* pretty drunk himself, and he ~~decides~~ *decided* not to let his friends be ~~badgers~~ *badgered* by anyone. So he ~~responds~~ *responded* with his own nasty comments. This ~~continues~~ *continued* as we ~~approach~~ *approached* our ship. Now the gentlemen ahead of us ~~stop~~ *stopped* and ~~wait~~ *waited* for us to reach them. They ~~begin~~ *began* to zero in on my drunken buddy who just ~~becomes~~ *became* more agitated. My sober friend and I ~~are~~ *were* trying to talk our drunken friend out of a confrontation when suddenly, out of the blue, I ~~feel~~ *felt* myself taking a couple of steps backward. I ~~have~~ *had* been sucker-punched for no reason! Of course, this ~~annoys~~ *annoyed* me and I ~~tackle~~ *tackled* my opponent. I'm not a good fighter, so I just ~~want~~ *wanted* to hold him back from hitting me again. The fight ~~is~~ *was* broken up by the quarterdeck personnel.

Application 5 (151)

1. I have listened . . . when I have waited
2. People have confessed . . .
3. Today one woman has described the diet she has used . . .
4. . . . man has explained why he has always left . . .
5. A tall teenager has bragged about how she has succeeded . . .
6. . . . someone has responded.

7. I haven't believed . . . I have enjoyed them.
8. I have jotted down . . .
9. I have tried to imagine . . .
10. . . . for my novel has entertained . . . waits that have bored . . .

Application 6 (152)

1. are measured	6. have been stored
2. is assigned	7. have been rinsed
3. will be completed	8. can be damaged
4. will be recorded	9. has been passed
5. have been finished	10. is now required

Application 7 (154)

Answers will vary. Compare yours with a classmate's.

Application 8 (154)

1. decorated	4. delighted and dazzled
2. finished	
3. pleased	5. prepared

Application 9 (155)

1. to fill the room.	4. to offer her congratulations.
2. to call to the baby.	
3. to shout for joy.	5. to act relaxed and casual.

Application 10 (156)

Suggested answers:

1. can save their outgrown	4. should talk about them
2. could collect several	
3. might line them up	5. may help them to recall

Application 11 (157)

1. Did Charlotte bait the hook?
   She didn't bait it.
2. Did she hate that job?
   She didn't hate it.

3. Did her line sail out over the water?
   It didn't sail out over the water.
4. Did the sinker drop neatly beside a marker buoy?
   It didn't drop there.
5. Did she settle down for a slow and satisfying afternoon?
   She didn't settle down.

Review and Practice (158)

A.

In the first five items, different students may put asterisks by different words. Compare yours with a classmate's.

1. At the forum, some people (claimed) * that inflation could be (reduced) * by wage and price controls.
2. The most (respected) researcher (insisted) that controls would hurt newly (hired) * trainees.
3. Most of the panelists (agreed) * to present their statements in the (published) * report.
4. When the forum (ended), the audience (applauded) for a long time.
5. Someone (asked) * if the discussion might be (continued) * later.

6. stayed, expected	17. am surprised, are swayed
7. warmed, talked	
8. remembered	18. is advertised
9. enjoyed	19. are prejudiced
10. showed	20. is predicted
11. have stopped	21. civilized
12. have asked, has happened	22. trusted
	23. closed
13. has shrugged	24. accepted
14. has evaded	25. tired
15. have convinced	26. to delivered
16. are influenced	27. to considered

28. to steer~~ed~~

29. to explain~~ed~~

30. to laugh~~ed~~

31. would nudge~~d~~

32. did not like~~d~~

33. might wreck~~ed~~

34. could remember~~ed~~

35. should not end~~ed~~

B.

As I thought about that fight the following day, I *realized* ~~realize~~ two things. First, I didn't enjoy being *punched* ~~punch~~. Second, I didn't know how to defend myself. Fortunately, one of my supervisors was highly *skilled* ~~skill~~ in karate, and after I *explained* ~~explain~~ what had *happened* ~~happen~~, he *suggested* ~~suggest~~ that I should learn karate. I eagerly *agreed* ~~agree~~ and we began exercising then and there. Every day he *demonstrated* ~~demonstrate~~ and I *practiced* ~~practice~~ the *assigned* ~~assign~~ techniques. After I *learned* ~~learn~~ the basics, we *discontinued* ~~discontinue~~ our class.

About two and a half years later I was *discharged* ~~discharge~~ from the navy. Upon returning to my hometown, I *decided* ~~decide~~ to pursue the martial arts beyond the basics. I *enrolled* ~~enroll~~ at the local Kenpo karate school and began learning the Kenpo style and its philosophy. It became very clear to me that there was more to the martial arts than just self-defense. I *learned* ~~learn~~ how to meditate, how to be more alert, and how to control pain through breathing techniques of the *Khi* (inner force).

Chapter 11: Final -s

Applications 1 and 2 (165) and (167)

Making money these (days)² (is)³ a real challenge. First you have to race with inflation. Every time you start to catch up, something (happens)³ to set you back. The price of food (seems)³ to go up whenever you go to the store, and your food (bills)² just get bigger every week.

Then there are the (gas)¹ and oil (bills)². They're all right in the summer, but when winter (comes)³ along, you either freeze or go broke. On top of all that (comes)³ paying the rent, which (is)³ just like burning money. The way (things)² look now, we won't ever see (prices)² going down — only up.

Another challenge (is)³ finding a good job that (pays)³ well. It (seems)³ you have to have either a college education or some kind of trade before you can apply, and that still (does)³ not mean you'll get hired. There are so many people who are looking for work and so few (jobs)² available that the competition (gets)³ fierce. (Lots)² of (times)² you just have to settle for a job that will get you by until you find something better. As long (as)¹ unemployment (stays)³ (this)¹ high, even those (jobs)² are hard to find.

The only way (things)² are going to change (is)³ for the government to get out of debt. Interest (rates)² can't go down until the government (gets)³ the deficit under control. And (as)¹ long (as)¹ interest (rates)² are high, (companies)² can't afford to borrow the money they need to stay in (business)¹. When (companies)² cut back on (business)¹ or fold, more people get laid off, and (jobs)² become even scarcer for everyone. Making enough money to live on will just get harder and harder until something (changes)³. I hope that (happens)³ soon.

Application 3 (168)

1. skills
2. computer schools
3. friends
4. jobs
5. interviews . . . people
6. women . . . classes
7. in chairs . . . screens
8. technicians . . . pleasures . . . computers
9. plans
10. courses . . . years . . . contracts

Application 4 (169)

At last the ~~engine~~ *engines* stopped idling. The ~~pilot~~ *pilots* couldn't see around the ~~hangar~~ *hangars*, but ~~his~~ *their* control ~~panel~~ *panels* reassured ~~him~~ *them*. The ~~seat~~ *seats* behind the ~~cockpit~~ *cockpits* held ~~a~~ plump ~~com-muter~~ *com-muters* sipping contentedly from ~~a glass~~ *glasses*. ~~This man~~ *These men* clearly thought ~~he~~ *they* deserved ~~his comfort~~ *their comforts*. ~~His face~~ *Their faces* reflected ~~his expectation~~ *their expectations* that ~~his journey~~ *their journeys* would be as mild and sweet as the ~~drink~~ *drinks* in ~~his hand~~ *their hands*. As the ~~wing~~ *wings* of the ~~plane~~ *planes* rounded the ~~bend~~ *bends* by the ~~searchlight~~ *searchlights*, the ~~pilot~~ *pilots* looked up from the ~~panel~~ *panels* and gasped. Toward ~~him~~ *them*, as if emerging from ~~a mirror~~ *mirrors*, taxied ~~an~~ identical ~~airliner~~ *airliners*, piloted by ~~an~~ identically gasping ~~captain~~ *captains*.

Application 5 (169)

1. machines
2. students
3. chips
4. menus
5. bolts

Application 6 (170)

1. One of the blossoms
2. one of the clothes-lines
3. the last of the kids
4. either of the girls
5. one of the storms

Application 7 (171)

1. watch
2. watch
3. watches
4. watches
5. watch
6. hope
7. hope
8. hopes
9. hopes
10. hope

Application 8 (171)

droops, sags
rises
falls
tremble, face
fascinates, draws

Application 9 (172)

are
are
am
are, are

is
is
is, is

Application 10 (173)

have
have, have
has

has, has
has(n't)

Application 11 (173)

do
does

(You) do, does, does
does

Application 12 (174)

1. are singing
2. am singing
3. is singing
4. is singing
5. are singing
6. am dancing
7. is dancing
8. is dancing
9. is dancing
10. are dancing

Application 13 (174)

is drooping, is sagging
is rising
is falling
am trembling, am facing
is fascinating, is drawing

Application 14 (175)

1. have worked
2. have worked
3. have worked
4. has worked
5. has worked
6. have begun
7. has begun
8. have begun
9. has begun
10. have begun

Application 15 (176)

has drooped, has sagged
has risen
has fallen
have trembled, have faced
has fascinated, has drawn

Application 16 (176)

1. do not watch (*or*) don't watch
2. does not watch (*or*) doesn't watch
3. does not hope (*or*) doesn't hope
4. do not hope (*or*) don't hope
5. does not hope (*or*) doesn't hope
6. Does she hope
7. Does the caged bird sing
8. Do you sing
9. Do they dance
10. Does that cranky old gentleman dance

Review and Practice (178)

A.

1. (This) shopping mall (shows) * a lot of (class).
2. Very few of the (stores) * make a (fuss) when you return (items) * that don't fit your (kids).*
3. Don't (miss) the big (sales) * that the mall (sponsors) * during the two (weeks) * before Thanksgiving.
4. My favorite (dress) shop (faces) * the fountain near the (escalators).*
5. (Across) from the doughnut (counters),* Santa (Claus) (sets) * up (his) throne each year.

6. tickets
7. dollars
8. things, eggs
9. gifts
10. presents, treats
11. speaks, blushes
12. know, means
13. guesses, feels
14. pleases, admits
15. look, sit
16. is ending, is waving
17. is trying
18. are screaming
19. is coming, are noticing
20. is jumping
21. has received
22. have been
23. has warned, has gone
24. has offended
25. has inspired
26. Does Roz earn money
27. Roz doesn't earn
28. does she wear
29. she doesn't wear
30. Do the views delight
31. views from there don't delight
32. Do the ships on the river look
33. ships on the river don't look
34. Does she spy
35. She doesn't spy

B.

Paragraph with plurals:

When I was two *years* ~~year~~ old, there was a certain tree my two *brothers* ~~brother~~ would climb. Sometimes I went with them, not to climb but to watch. I sat right under these *branches* ~~branch~~ and looked up, watching them climb. They would go one by one and jump from limb to limb. They would climb all the way to the top of the tree and yell how many *miles* ~~mile~~ they could see. Some of those *days* ~~day~~ they could even see New Haven.

Paragraph in present tense:

Anyway, this day as they *are* ~~were~~ going up, they *see* ~~saw~~ a dead branch. One of my brothers *decides* ~~decided~~ to pull it down. Well, when the branch *breaks* ~~broke~~, it *is* ~~was~~ coming straight for me. I *don't* ~~didn't~~ get out of the way fast enough, and the branch *comes* ~~came~~ to rest on my head. When my brothers *see* ~~saw~~ this, they *come* ~~came~~ out of the tree faster than squirrels. My brother Skip *picks* ~~picked~~ me up and *runs* ~~ran~~ home to show my mom. She *takes* ~~took~~ me to the clinic and I *have* ~~had~~ twenty stitches put on the cut.

Chapter 12: Subject-Verb Agreement

Application 1 (185)

1. gigantic pancake reminds
2. daughter is wolfing
3. friend is always asking
4. ingredient has remained
5. cousin does not know
6. brothers have given up
7. neighbors have prayed
8. open windows are imposing
9. Do the complaints . . . matter
10. brothers don't care

Application 2 (187)

were
was, was
were
was
were, were

Application 3 (187)

was, were
were
were, was
were, was
were
were

Application 4 (188)

1. was returning
2. student was putting
3. relative was laughing
4. bird was singing
5. janitor was relieved
6. strangers were trying
7. they were calling
8. army buddies were recommending
9. organizers were hoping
10. officers were consulted

Application 5 (189)

1. is
2. are
3. is
4. are
5. are
6. is
7. was
8. were
9. was
10. were

Application 6 (190)

1. mailboxes are
2. mailbox is
3. librarian reminds
4. librarians remind
5. marshal has issued
6. marshals have issued
7. partners have left
8. partner has left
9. Don has left
10. phones are ringing
11. phone is ringing
12. students are teasing
13. student is teasing
14. report is going
15. reports are going

Application 7 (192)

1. truck needs
2. trucks need
3. tenants yell
4. tenant yells
5. grower makes
6. Growers make
7. uncle loves
8. uncles love
9. phones were ringing
10. phone was ringing
11. student was teasing
12. students were teasing
13. reports were going
14. report was going
15. shadow was bringing

Application 8 (194)

1. several ask
2. Anyone knows
3. Neither spends
4. Everybody wants
5. few increase
6. Nobody has worked
7. many have basked
8. neither has tried
9. few have contradicted
10. each has developed

Application 9 (195)

1. All looks
2. All look
3. Some smell
4. Some smells
5. None show
6. None shows
7. Most needs
8. Most need
9. Any belong
10. Any belongs

Application 10 (196)

1. win
2. wins
3. puts
4. put
5. burns
6. burn
7. earn
8. earns
9. are
10. is

Application 11 (197)

1. freckle identifies
2. freckle, scar identify
3. insect grows
4. insect, centipede grow
5. Marisa dances
6. Marisa, Leonard dance
7. Cleaning improves
8. Cleaning, painting improve
9. diver reaches
10. diver, equipment reach

Application 12 (198)

1. watch, clocks keep
2. clocks, watch keeps
3. Andra, boys look
4. boys, Andra looks
5. kids, Lillie goes
6. Lillie, kids go
7. cake, cookies appear
8. Cookies, cake appears
9. father, friends talk
10. friends, father talks

Application 13 (199)

1. Toan, brother work
2. Either works
3. Either makes
4. motion make
5. Neither breaks

Review and Practice (200)

A.

1. seedlings grow
2. stems have doubled
3. plant is progressing
4. vine does not thrive
5. window offers
6. was
7. were
8. was, was
9. was
10. were, was
11. are
12. is
13. is
14. is
15. are
16. loves
17. teaches
18. hope
19. encourage
20. claims
21. knows
22. report
23. seem
24. remembers
25. wants
26. shows
27. appear
28. belongs
29. promise
30. feel
31. stick
32. happens
33. takes
34. study
35. are
36. welcome
37. rushes
38. hammer
39. irritates
40. appreciate

B.

goes   *has*
Everyone who ~~go~~ to horror movies ~~have~~ some reason for spending good money on a bad experience. And nobody denies that those two hours in the theater *feel* ~~feels~~, in fact, perfectly ghastly. Most of the people who *come* ~~comes~~ out looking dazed and paranoid eagerly *agree* ~~agrees~~ that the movie *was* ~~were~~ really awful and that they can't wait for the next one. Why do they do this to themselves?

come
Some of the people ~~comes~~ just for the physical sensation of fear, a sensation that a wild ride at an amusement park also *provides* ~~provide~~. But these rushes of excitement *respond* ~~responds~~ to nothing but illusions of danger. Everybody *knows* ~~know~~ that neither the movie's monsters nor the peril of the amusement park ride *is* ~~are~~ real. In either case, a customer buys five bucks' worth of fear and *confronts* ~~confront~~ it heroically in complete security.

give
Most of the viewers ~~gives~~ other reasons for loving these movies. Many simply like the fantasy of them. The characters and plot of one movie *aren't* ~~isn't~~ much different from the characters and plot of another one, so the *stays* horror ~~stay~~ within predictable limits, even when its subject is completely unreal. In addition, the simplicity *is* of the stories ~~are~~ appealing. Neither the good guys nor *forgets* the monster ever ~~forget~~ what's good or what's bad, so there is no gray area in the viewer's value judgments. And finally, horror movies are relaxing. After all, a *is* monster or a demon ~~are~~ easier to cope with than the arms race or job insecurity, and all that screaming and shaking over horror movies help to relieve other tensions, too. So even though such movies may force people to check under their beds and bolt all their windows *were* for a few days, while they ~~was~~ sitting in the theater,

their minds were resting in some deeper way. So why have people always laughed at me when I've told them I wish that life could be as safe, simple, and restful as a good horror movie?

Chapter 13: Pronouns

Application 1 (210)

See Application 4.

Application 2 (211)

The new tractor had a big scratch on *its* side. Mr. Larsen said *he* thought the Bradley boys had been driving *it*, but *they* denied that *they* had been anywhere near *it*. *Their* mother, of course, angrily defended *her* boys. Mr. Larsen eventually gave up *his* accusation, but not until the argument had run *its* usual boring course.

Application 3 (211)

Answers will vary; compare yours with a classmate's.

Application 4 (212)

NA
Dave brought (me) a chart clipped from (his) evening newspaper (It) showed the responses of American executives to the question "How many hours should there be in an average workday?" The majority of the executives interviewed favored the status quo; 57 percent of (them) voted for the eight-hour day. However, Dave was excited because 10 percent favored a seven-hour day (That) was enough to get (him) started on a *NA* fantasy about how fifty years from now (everyone) will consider an eight-hour day a violation of human rights. *NA* But when (I) asked (him) to add up the numbers farther

down the chart, (he) stopped gloating. A significant portion of the executives — 11 percent of (them), in fact — thought (everyone) [NA] should buckle down to nine- and ten-hour workdays. Dave and (I) [NA] decided not to pay attention to the vote of (anyone) [NA] (who) could show such ignorance of human nature, and (we) [NA] used the clipping to light (our) barbecue.

Application 5 (213)

1. I
2. She
3. she
4. You
5. we
6. I
7. they
8. he
9. he
10. I

Application 6 (214)

1. I
2. she
3. she
4. you
5. we
6. I
7. they
8. He
9. He
10. I

Application 7 (215)

1. him
2. you
3. her
4. them
5. me
6. her
7. them
8. us
9. him
10. her

Application 8 (216)

1. him
2. you
3. her
4. them
5. me
6. her
7. them
8. us
9. him
10. her

Application 9 (217)

1. I
2. I
3. We, him
4. him
5. them
6. them
7. me, he
8. me, he
9. them
10. them

Application 10 (218)

1. woman . . . *her* ~~their~~ neighbors
2. administration . . . *it* ~~they~~ promised
3. The human race . . . *itself* ~~themselves~~
4. boy . . . *his* ~~their~~ parents
5. woman . . . *she* ~~they~~ had

Application 11 (220)

1. customer . . . *him or her* ~~them~~
2. child's . . . *him or her* ~~them~~
3. student . . . *his or her* ~~their~~
4. minor . . . *he or she* ~~they~~
5. person . . . *him or her* ~~them~~

Application 12 (220)

1. individual . . . *his or her (your choice)* ~~their~~
2. person . . . *his or her (your choice)* ~~they~~
3. student . . . *his or her* ~~their~~ . . . *himself or herself (your choice)* ~~themselves~~
4. person . . . *his or her (your choice)* ~~their~~
5. kid . . . *he or she (your choice)* ~~they~~

Application 13 (221)

1. ~~an adolescent~~ *adolescents* . . . they . . . their
2. ~~a young person~~ *young people* . . . they
3. ~~A news announcer~~ *News announcers* . . . their
4. ~~doctor~~ *doctors* . . . they
5. ~~parent~~ *parents* . . . they

Application 14 (222)

1. somebody . . . ~~they~~ *he/she (your choice)*
2. anybody . . . ~~they~~ *he/she (your choice)*
3. anyone . . . ~~they~~ *he/she (your choice)*
4. each . . . ~~their~~ *her*
5. anyone . . . ~~they~~ *he/she (your choice)*

Application 15 (222)

Answers may vary: *people* works each time.

1. ~~Everybody~~ . . . their   *All soap opera fans*
2. ~~anybody~~ . . . them   *The students*
3. ~~Everybody's~~ . . . their   *People's*
4. ~~everyone~~ . . . their   *All the guests*
5. ~~someone~~ . . . their   *individualists*

Review and Practice (224)

A.

1. and ~~the cable TV station~~ devoted   *it*
2. ~~the woman's~~ struggle to keep ~~the woman's~~ home   *her* ... *her*
3. to sell ~~the owners'~~ land   *their*
4. and ~~the woman in the report~~ claims the land is ~~the woman's~~   *she* ... *hers*
5. but ~~taking the issue to court~~ may be   *it*
6. people . . . (they) learn faster than (they)
7. going to college at the age of forty has (its)
8. ~~Molly~~ . . . (her) classmates made (her)
9. students . . . (their) strengths
10. (Nobody), (me)   *NA NA*
11. I, us
12. she
13. them, us
14. we, us
15. he, she
16. ~~their~~   *his/her (your choice)*
17. ~~they~~   *he/she (your choice)*
18. ~~their~~   *his/her (your choice)*
19. ~~A winner~~   *winners*
20. ~~nobody~~   *none of the people*

B. One possible solution:

~~A person's~~ vision is adapted to their environment. *People's*
The Pygmies provide one good example. They live in
forests where trees limit ~~his~~ field of view to about fifty *their*
yards, but within that space, ~~he~~ must make shrewd ob- *they*
servations. ~~A person~~ in that situation can develop a *People*
very accurate sense of the relationships among objects
near to them. However, when ~~a Pygmy is~~ taken to a *Pygmies are*
hill in another part of Africa where they can suddenly
see for miles, they look out at elephants on the plain
ten miles away and act as if the elephants are nearby
and only about the size of lizards. ~~He doesn't~~ perceive *They don't*
the distance and the distortions of perspective.

The inversion-glasses experiment provides another
example of how ~~anybody's~~ vision shapes itself to their *people's*
needs. In this experiment, volunteers were asked to
wear special glasses that showed them everything up-
side-down. ~~Nobody was~~ allowed to take off their *None of the volunteers were*
glasses for a week. ~~Everybody~~ went around for a few *They*
days tripping over their own feet and having a terrible
time, but then they began to see things right side
up again without ever taking off their glasses. Then
the researchers removed the glasses. Suddenly
~~each volunteer~~ saw everything upside-down again, *the volunteers*
and it took several days for their vision to return to normal.

When my friends and ~~me~~ learned about that, we be- *I*
gan to think it might be fun to participate in a vision
experiment. My professor told Willie and me that we
should go over to the psychology department at the
university and see if any researchers could use us. In
fact, when ~~him~~ and I got there, somebody was looking *he*
for volunteers, but it didn't sound appealing to him

and *me* ~~I~~. The researcher wanted the other volunteers and us to sit in a chair and guess what word was being held up on a card behind us. If we all guessed wrong, we would get a little electric shock. If someone guessed right, *he or she* ~~him~~ and the rest of us would be rewarded with a little rocking motion in our chairs. Willie and *I* ~~me~~ decided that although human vision may be very adaptable, he and *I* ~~me~~ didn't have eyes in the backs of our heads. I wonder who volunteers for experiments like that. You have to admire people like *them* ~~they~~ and others who are willing to suffer a little for the sake of science.

Chapter 14: Spelling

Application 1 (231)

1. reddest
2. quieter
3. omitted
4. napping
5. benefiting

Application 2 (232)

1. are running
2. are getting
3. are beginning
4. are costing
5. are planning
6. stopped
7. waited
8. nagged
9. developed
10. submitted

Application 3 (233)

1. wishes
2. echoes
3. stereos
4. kisses
5. churches

Application 4 (233)

1. watches
2. munches
3. teaches
4. fixes
5. misses
6. walls, posters, heroes
7. pitches
8. friends, passes, games
9. successes, waxes
10. flashes, camera

Application 5 (234)

1. funniest
2. implied
3. frying
4. magnifies
5. inventories

Application 6 (235)

1. hurried
2. steadied, played
3. carried
4. cried, enjoyed
5. ferried
6. amplifies
7. says, destroys
8. stays
9. qualifies
10. pays, justifies

Application 7 (236)

1. the wind's sound
2. your friend's face
3. the women's votes
4. the geese's wings
5. the sea's smell
6. the child's faith
7. the children's energy
8. the car's seats
9. Grady's radio
10. the city's money

Application 8 (237)

1. the coach's hopes
2. the media's predictions
3. the team's victory
4. my children's dreams
5. our family's pride

Application 9 (237)

1. the leaves' sounds
2. your friends' faces
3. those two sisters' talents
4. the robins' wings
5. the gases' smells
6. those mothers' faith
7. those kids' energy
8. the buses' seats
9. his roommates' radio
10. the cities' money

Application 10 (238)

1. the coaches' hopes
2. the reporters' predictions
3. the short guys' victory
4. my kids' dreams
5. our relatives' pride

Application 11 (239)

1. talks, smokes
2. has, borrows
3. is (or) 's, helps, breaks
4. breaks, supervisors, brothers
5. adventures, homelands
6. spirits, families
7. hers
8. his
9. its
10. theirs

Application 12 (240)

1. than
2. then, then
3. than
4. then
5. then

Application 13 (241)

1. to, two, to
2. to, too, to
3. to, two
4. to, two, too, to
5. two, too

Application 14 (242)

1. Now
2. no
3. now, know
4. no, know
5. no

Application 15 (243)

1. weather
2. whether
3. whether
4. whether
5. weather

Application 16 (243)

1. past
2. passed
3. past
4. passed
5. past

Application 17 (244)

1. were
2. we're
3. where
4. Were
5. We're, where

Application 18 (245)

There once were two women who'd wear
Their necklaces wrapped round their hair.
  With their chains on their heads
  They're supposed to have said,
"They're less weight on our poor necks up there."

Application 19 (245)

1. you're, your
2. your, your, you're, your
3. You're, your, you're
4. your, your
5. your, your

Application 20 (246)

1. It's
2. its
3. it's
4. its
5. It's

Application 21 (247)

1. who's
2. who's, whose
3. whose
4. who's
5. whose, Who's

Review and Practice (251)

A.

1. trotting, swooped
2. flatness, controlling
3. started running
4. students, grasses
5. patches, scorches, scalps
6. stashes, hoboes, treasures
7. relies, heavily
8. cloudier
9. stayed, implied
10. Josie's
11. television's, baby's
12. children's
13. Aunt Julia's
14. branches'
15. parks', kids'
16. years'
17. parents'
18. seems
19. legs, lungs
20. wants
21. than
22. then
23. then
24. to
25. too
26. two
27. now
28. know
29. no
30. weather
31. whether
32. Whether, weather
33. passed
34. passed, past
35. past
36. where
37. We're, where
38. were, were
39. there
40. their
41. they're
42. you're
43. your
44. you're
45. it's
46. its
47. its, its
48. who's
49. whose
50. who's

B.

When Lavinia and I got ~~too~~ *to* the stadium, the weather was pretty bad, so the bleachers ~~we're~~ *were* much less ~~crowdded then~~ *crowded than* we expected. We sat down behind some cheerful ~~lookking~~ *looking* fans ~~who's~~ *whose* T-shirts showed that ~~there~~ *their* team was the wrong one. We joked with them a bit about the standings of our teams during the past season, and then Lavinia and I settled down to business.

"~~Whose~~ *Who's* pitching?" she ~~askked~~ *asked*.

I ~~past~~ *passed* my eyes over the newspaper ~~cliping~~ *clipping* I'd brought to see ~~weather~~ *whether* it said who the starting players ~~where~~ *were* going to be. "~~Their puting~~ *They're putting* in a rookie." I groaned.

She ~~stoped~~ *stopped* smiling, amazed. "Oh, ~~know~~ *no*, not today! They should ~~no~~ *know* better by now. A rookie at a time like this always ~~implys~~ *implies* a desperate strategy in the dugout. ~~Were~~ *We're* going to lose our chance for the pennant."

We continued with our usual ~~commentting~~ *commenting* while the team went through its warm-up ~~play's~~ *plays*, and then it started to drizzle. The two people in front of us immediately hauled out gigantic ~~umbrella's~~ *umbrellas*. The point on the top of the big ~~guys~~ *guy's* umbrella hovered right by my ear ~~were~~ *where* it blocked my view completely. We asked them to lower the umbrellas a little, at least. They just ~~shruged~~ *shrugged* and said, "But ~~its~~ *it's* raining. If you can't see, ~~than~~ *then* that's ~~you're~~ *your* problem."

Lavinia always ~~trys~~ *tries* to be patient. "You shouldn't treat your rival ~~fans'~~ *fans* that way," she teased, and sweetly passed them some popcorn.

But I was mad. "These bleachers are ~~geting~~ *getting* even ~~nastyer~~ *nastier* than the subways," I roared. The fellow ~~who's~~ *whose* umbrella blocked my view of left field just smirked while the other ~~happyly~~ *happily* took some ~~sandwichs~~ *sandwiches* out of his ~~friends'~~ *friend's* pocket. By then, the rain was ~~comming~~ *coming* down hard, so we got up and headed for shelter. The ~~whether~~ *weather* was so bad that the officials called a rain delay in the game.

As we stood inside the door eating our steaming hot dogs and french ~~fryed potatos~~ *fried potatoes*, I was ~~mader~~ *madder* than ever about those creeps. But Lavinia was ~~begining~~ *beginning* to giggle. She nudged me and pointed out at the drenched bleachers. "You're not going to believe this," she whispered, "but those ~~guy's~~ *guys* are still crouching there under ~~they're~~ *their* silly umbrellas." Lavinia always ~~breaks'~~ *breaks* through even the worst of my moods, and pretty soon I was laughing, ~~two~~ *too*.

Chapter 15: Consistency

Application 1 (263)

1. ⟨Quickly⟩ but ⟨quietly⟩
2. ⟨to climb the telephone pole⟩, ⟨to find the broken wire⟩, and ⟨to fix it⟩
3. ⟨loved wiring⟩ and ⟨trusted his new skill⟩
4. ⟨climbing the pole steadily⟩ and ⟨shifting his weight perfectly⟩
5. ⟨that Sung had ever been afraid of heights⟩ or ⟨that courage was his biggest challenge in this job⟩

Application 2 (264)

Suggested answers:
1. Some people fear both failure and success.
2. I like to watch the news and to listen to the radio at night.
3. You can get to the caves either by taking a special train or by hiking.
4. We want you to check in with us when you finish your training program and after you get your first job.
5. Ruth says that the statistics prove her point and that we should get the paper to publish them.

Application 3 (265)

Suggested answers:
1. The three places where people learn are at home, at play, and at work.
2. You should try to gather as much knowledge as you can, because knowledge will help you to solve problems and to cope with life.
3. The charm costs $8.00 in gold and $3.50 in silver.
4. The techniques for getting good grades are to study course material thoroughly, to test your understanding, to have confidence, and to relax.
5. I meet people at work because I answer phone calls, fix bulletin boards, and make posters.

Application 4 (266)

Lorna took promises very seriously. She never forgave anyone for breaking one. In addition, she considered the slightest little agreement to be a full-fledged promise, so people often found Lorna counting on them to do things they had no intention of doing. She filled her life with trumped-up promises and then made a huge fuss when most of those promises fell through.

Application 5 (267)

1. Once the astronauts ~~were~~ in orbit, they ~~relaxed~~. They ~~had not been able~~ to think their own thoughts for several hours, and they ~~needed~~ a chance to sit back and to absorb what was happening to them. Below them the Pacific Ocean ~~edged~~ into view. Above them the moon ~~looked~~ as distant as ever. We like to cover every detail of these space ventures in the news, but most of us will never know what goes on in the minds of people who are beyond the pull of their own world's gravity. What we do know is that finally the astronauts ~~ate~~ their rations quietly and ~~slept~~.
2. simple past tense

3. **was happening** — describes an action continuing during past time
like — shows our present feelings
will (never) know — looks ahead to the future
goes — describes something that happens in general, at almost any time
are — same as **goes**
do know — describes our present state of mind
is — present state

Application 6 (268)

1. but then his whole personality changed when his girlfriend left him
2. the man behind him does
3. and everyone broke out laughing
4. so they aren't spending much time with me
5. and my father was walking toward us carrying a bucket.

Application 7 (269)

In this part of the country, if you want those little Mexican tomatoes called tomatillos, you have to grow them yourself. You can't expect to find them in the supermarkets. So instead, you order the seeds from a catalogue and plant them in flats right in your own kitchen. When the weather warms us, you keep them on the balcony. In a few months they're just as juicy as the sweet little balls your mother used to put in dozens of fillings and sauces.

Application 8 (270)

1. and they usually end up making fools of themselves
2. consider what one has been experiencing
3. we are often surprised at how our actions reflect our hidden values
4. they can become . . . because they can't just learn it all
5. responded well when its survival . . . and it will do so again now

Review and Practice (272)

A.

The fruit of success in all these tasks would present the world with ⟨the greatest task⟩, (and) ⟨the greatest opportunity⟩ of all. It is this: the dedication of ⟨the energies⟩, ⟨the resources⟩, (and) ⟨the imaginations⟩ of all peaceful nations to a new kind of war. This would be declared a total war, not ⟨upon any enemy⟩ (but) ⟨upon the brute forces of poverty and need⟩.

The peace we seek, founded upon decent trust and cooperative effort among nations, can be fortified not ⟨by weapons of war⟩ (but) ⟨by wheat and by cotton⟩, ⟨by milk and by wool⟩, ⟨by meat and by timber and by rice⟩. These are words that translate into every language on earth. These are needs that challenge this world in arms.

(Look for some smaller and larger parallel elements within or around the ones marked here.)

Tense consistency passage:

Barry unfolds his legs and leaves the couch. The top of the door frame dents his wrinkled hat as he ~~stepped~~ *steps* out onto the grass. From his shoulders, his binoculars ~~had swung~~ *swing*, bumping his hip with each stride. Ignoring them, he ~~turned~~ *turns* his bare eyes toward the tree where something rustles — a goldfinch. He stands as still as a stick for a moment, and then slowly ~~fumbled~~ *fumbles* in his pocket for a brown, dog-eared notebook in which he ~~scratched~~ *scratches* something while the bird poses on an open branch and ~~stared~~ *stares* toward the sea. The smell of pine needles after a hard rain stings in the breeze that brushes unevenly from the shore.

Pronoun consistency passage:

The story of Tarzan succeeds for ~~you~~ *us* only if ~~we're~~ *you're* willing to accept the possibility of a human baby being raised by apes. If you can allow yourself that little flight of fancy, you'll probably enjoy the movie *Greystoke*. It takes the old Tarzan story and entices ~~the viewer~~ *you* into its fantasy by presenting ~~him or her~~ *you* with beautiful images and haunting sounds of the jungle. ~~We~~ *You* soon stop worrying about whether any of it is realistic and you find yourself wondering how young John (Tarzan) will adjust to the human world. When John feels himself torn between his human and his animal natures, ~~many viewers~~ *you* can sympathize almost as if this had actually happened in ~~our~~ *your* own ~~lives~~ *life*. Perhaps in some symbolic way it has.

B.

We are often fascinated by the harmless eccentrics in our hometowns. ~~You~~ *We* become used to seeing someone like the local hat lady, who ~~wore~~ *wears* a different set of strange rags on her head every day, or the dancing man ~~because of his~~ *whose* feet ~~which~~ move all the time. ~~One~~ *We* ~~doesn't~~ *don't* envy these people. After all, ~~you realized~~ *we realize* that they are usually struggling just to survive. But ~~you~~ *we* can't help admiring the way they ~~coped~~ *cope* with life on their own terms. Sometimes watching such people teaches ~~one~~ *us* to see society in a new way and ~~paying~~ *to pay* attention to some of life's unexpected possibilities.

Chapter 16: Techniques for Writing

4B (285)

Circle the following: 2, 4, 7, 8

4C (286)

Possible supporting facts for each topic sentence:

1. ABC has sponsored twelve of the top thirty-five shows.

   The last episode of ''Roots'' is rated number three, and the other episodes take up positions 16, 19, 22, 26, and 28.

   ''The Day After'' and ''The Fugitive'' stand at positions 15 and 16.

2. Eight out of the first fourteen positions are filled by Super Bowls.

   Even games from ten years back still hold high standings (#9 & #10).

   The 1982 and 1983 games were even more popular than the more recent ones (see #4 & #5).

3. ''Fugitive'' was particularly successful (#16).

   Certain of the Ed Sullivan shows stand as classics (#20 & #28).

   Two episodes of ''Beverly Hillbillies'' attracted large audiences (#27 & #34)

6A (290)

1. hammer
2. diamonds
3. washing machine
4. overscheduling the first year of college
5. buying a car

7 (292)

The first words of each paragraph in the original version:

Some people think

I was four years old

However, everything changed

Now, looking back,

Other paragraph breaks are also possible. Explain your reasons for making other choices.

8A (294)

(For example) I remember

(Besides) I was scared

(Then) my mother

(At the same time) , the teacher

(However,) everything changed

(First) I was quiet

(Then) I began to understand

(For instance) there was a time

(Soon) I began to make friends

(Meanwhile) I learned to make arrangements

(Finally,) I walked in and out

(Now,) looking back

(In addition) it opened

(In fact,) though, they all look

8B (294)

Answers will vary. Compare yours with a classmate's.
Here are some possible transitions:
For example, a friend of mine
As a result, he was accepted
Eventually, he received
However, he was unable
Finally, he was forced
Consequently, I have become convinced

9A (295)

1. I see making money these days as a real challenge.
2. Laughter is an age-old elixir that modern healers should both practice and prescribe, a growing number of humor-oriented health professionals maintain.

NOTE: A thesis statement is not necessarily the first sentence in the essay.

9B (296)

Answers will vary. Compare yours with a classmate's.
Here are some possible thesis statements:
1. Sylvia was a slave to her superstitions.
2. Companies should have the right to conduct drug tests on their employees.

Chapter 8: Sentence Fragments

Pretest (315)

A.	B.
1. C	1. C
2. I	2. I
3. I	3. I
4. I	
5. C	
6. I	
7. C	

INCOMPLETE VERBS:
Review your work on verbs in Chapter 2. Then complete this chapter, paying particular attention to p. 111.

A.	B.
8. I	4. I
9. I	5. C
10. C	6. I
11. C	
12. I	
13. I	
14. C	

DISCONNECTED PREPOSITIONAL PHRASES:
Review your work on prepositional phrases in Chapter 4. Then complete this chapter, paying particular attention to pp. 112–113.

A.	B.
15. C	7. I
16. I	8. C
17. I	9. C
18. I	10. C
19. C	11. I
20. C	
21. I	

DISCONNECTED VERBAL PHRASES:
Review your work on verbal phrases in Chapter 5. Then complete this chapter, paying particular attention to pp. 113–115.

A.	B.
22. I	12. I
23. C	13. C
24. C	14. C
25. I	15. C
	16. I
	17. I
	18. I
	19. C
	20. C

DISCONNECTED DEPENDENT CLAUSES:
Review your work on dependent clauses in Chapter 5. Then complete this chapter, paying particular attention to pp. 115–117.

Chapter 9: Run-on Sentences

Pretest (317)

A.	B.
1. I	1. I
2. C	2. C
3. I	3. C
4. I	4. I
5. I	
6. C	
7. C	
8. I	
9. I	

COMMAND in one of the independent clauses:
Complete pp. 125–132. Then concentrate on p. 133 before going on to the Review and Practice at the end of the chapter.

10. I	5. I
11. I	6. C
12. C	7. I
13. C	8. I
14. I	9. C
15. C	10. I
16. I	
17. C	
18. I	

PRONOUN in one of the independent clauses:
Complete pp. 125–132. Then concentrate on p. 134 before going on to the Review and Practice at the end of the chapter.

19. C	11. C
20. C	12. I
21. I	13. I
22. I	14. C
23. I	15. I
24. I	
25. C	

TRANSITIONAL EXPRESSION in one of the independent clauses:
Complete pp. 125–132. Then concentrate on pp. 135–137 before going on to the Review and Practice at the end of the chapter.

Chapter 10: Final -ed

Pretest (319)

A.	B.
1. b	1. C
2. a*	4. I
3. b	5. I
4. b	8. I
5. a*	12. C
6. a*	13. I
7. b	16. I
	20. I

SIMPLE PAST form of a regular verb:
Complete pp. 147–148. Then pay particular attention to pp. 149–151 before going on to the Review and Practice at the end of the chapter.

8. a*	10. C
9. b	14. I
10. b	18. I
11. b	19. C
12. a*	
13. b	
14. b	

PAST PARTICIPLE form of a regular verb used in the PERFECT TENSE:
Complete pp. 147–148. Then pay particular attention to pp. 151–152 before going on to the Review and Practice at the end of the chapter.

15. b	15. C
16. b	21. I
17. a*	23. C
18. b	24. I
19. a*	
20. b	
21. b	

PAST PARTICIPLE form of a regular verb used in the PASSIVE VOICE:
Complete pp. 147–148. Then pay particular attention to pp. 152–153 before going on to the Review and Practice at the end of the chapter.

22. b.	3. C
23. a*	6. I
24. b	7. C
25. b	22. I
	25. I

PAST PARTICIPLE form of a regular verb used as a MODIFYING VERBAL:
Complete pp. 147–148. Then pay particular attention to pp. 153–155 before going on to the Review and Practice at the end of the chapter.

*If	2. I
you	9. C
made	11. I
mistakes	17. C
in	
any	
starred	
items	

-ed endings that are not needed:
Complete pp. 147–148. Then concentrate on pp. 155–157 before going on to the Review and Practice at the end of the chapter.

Chapter 11: Final *-s*

Pretest (321)

A.	B.	
1. b	1. C	
2. a	2. I	
3. b	16. I	
4. b	18. I	
5. a	22. I	**PLURAL NOUN:**
6. b	23. C	Complete pp. 165–167. Then pay particular attention to pp. 167–170
7. b	24. I	before going on to the Review and Practice at the end of the chapter.
8. a	25. C	
9. b		
10. a		

A.	B.	
11. b	3. I	
12. b	4. I	
13. a	5. C	
14. b	6. I	**Present tense verb with a SINGULAR SUBJECT that is not *you* or *I*:**
15. a	14. I	Complete pp. 165–167. Then pay particular attention to pp. 170–171
16. a	15. C	before going on to the Review and Practice at the end of the chapter.
	17. C	
	21. I	

A.	B.	
17. b	7. C	**IS in the PRESENT PROGRESSIVE TENSE:**
18. b	8. I	Complete pp. 165–173. Then concentrate on pp. 174–175 before going
19. a	9. I	on to the Review and Practice at the end of the chapter.
20. b	10. I	**HAS in the PRESENT PERFECT TENSE:**
21. a	11. C	Complete pp. 165–173. Then concentrate on pp. 175–176 before going
22. b	12. C	on to the Review and Practice at the end of the chapter.
23. a	13. C	**DOES in a present tense question or negative statement:**
24. a	19. I	Complete pp. 165–173. Then concentrate on pp. 176–177 before going
25. b	20. C	on to the Review and Practice at the end of the chapter.

Chapter 12: Subject-Verb Agreement

Pretest (323)

A.	B.
1. a	1. C
2. b	12. I
3. b	17. I
4. a	19. I
5. a	
6. a	

Clauses beginning with THERE IS, THERE ARE, THERE WAS, or THERE WERE:
Complete pp. 185–189. Then concentrate on pp. 189–190 before going on to the Review and Practice at the end of the chapter.

7. b	4. I
8. a	5. C
9. a	8. C
10. b	9. C
11. b	10. I
12. b	16. C

MODIFYING PHRASES or CLAUSES between subject and verb:
Complete 185–189. Then concentrate on pp. 190–193 before going on to the Review and Practice at the end of the chapter.

13. b	11. I
14. a	13. I
15. b	18. C
16. a	
17. b	
18. a	

INDEFINITE PRONOUNS that act as subjects:
Complete pp. 185–189. Then concentrate on pp. 193–196 before going on to the Review and Practice at the end of the chapter.

19. a	2. I
20. a	3. C
21. b	7. I
22. b	14. C
23. b	
24. b	

WHO, WHICH and THAT acting as subject:
Complete pp. 185–189. Then concentrate on pp. 196–197 before going on to the Review and Practice at the end of the chapter.

25. a	6. I
26. b	15. I
27. a	20. C
28. a	
29. b	
30. a	

COMPOUND SUBJECTS:
Complete pp. 185–189. Then concentrate on pp. 197–199 before going on to the Review and Practice at the end of the chapter.

Chapter 13: Pronouns

Pretest (327)

A.	B.
1. b	1. C
2. a	2. I
3. a	3. C
4. a	4. C
5. b	5. I
6. b	6. C
7. b	7. I
8. a	8. I
9. b	9. I
10. a	10. C
11. b	
12. a	
13. b	

SUBJECT or OBJECT form:
Complete pp. 209–212. Then pay particular attention to pp. 212–217 before going on to the Review and Practice at the end of the chapter.

A.	B.
14. b	11. I
15. a	12. C
16. a	13. C
17. b	14. I
18. a	15. C
19. a	16. I
20. a	17. C
21. b	18. I
22. a	19. C
23. a	20. C
24. b	
25. a	

Pronouns antecedent AGREEMENT:
Complete pp. 209–212. Then pay particular attention to pp. 218–223 before going on to the Review and Practice at the end of the chapter.

Chapter 14: Spelling

Pretest (331)

A.	B.
1. a	2. I
2. b	3. C
3. b	7. I
4. b*	9. C
5. a	10. I
6. b*	19. C
7. b	21. I
8. b	34. I
9. a	
10. b	
11. a	
12. a	
13. b	
14. b	
15. b	

Changes before an ADDED ENDING:
Start your spelling chart (pp. 247–250), and then pay particular attention to pp. 231–235 before going on to the Review and Practice at the end of the chapter.

A.	B.
16. a	20. I
17. b*	22. I
18. a	31. C
19. c	
20. b*	
21. c	
22. a	
23. b*	
24. a	
25. a	
26. a	

POSSESSIVE NOUNS:
Start your spelling chart (pp. 247–250), and then pay particular attention to pp. 236–238 before going on to the Review and Practice at the end of the chapter.

27. b	1. C
28. a	4. C
29. b	6. I
30. c	8. I
31. a	12. I
32. b	13. C
33. a	14. C
34. c	15. I
35. b	16. I
36. a	17. I
37. a	18. I
38. b	23. C
39. a	24. I
40. c	25. I
41. b	26. C
42. a	27. C
43. c	28. C
44. b	29. I
45. b	30. C
46. a	32. I
47. a	35. I
48. b	
49. b	
50. a	

Words that SOUND ALIKE:
Start your spelling chart (pp. 247–250), and then pay particular attention to pp. 240–247 before going on to the Review and Practice at the end of the chapter.

*If	5. I
you	11. I
made	33. I
mistakes	
in	
any	
starred	
items	

Apostrophes that are not needed:
Start your spelling chart (pp. 247–250), and then pay particular attention to pp. 238–239 before going on to the Review and Practice at the end of the chapter.

Chapter 15: Consistency

Pretest (335)

A.	B.
1. I	4. I
2. I	5. C
3. C	6. C
4. I	8. C
5. C	12. I
6. I	16. C
7. C	17. I

Consistency of PARALLEL ELEMENTS:
Pay particular attention to pp. 263–265 before going on to the Review and Practice at the end of the chapter.

A.	B.
8. I	2. I
9. I	9. C
10. C	10. I
11. I	15. I
12. C	18. C
13. I	19. C
14. I	

Consistency of VERB TENSE:
Pay particular attention to pp. 266–269 before going on to the Review and Practice at the end of the chapter.

A.	B.
15. I	1. I
16. C	3. I
17. I	7. I
18. C	11. I
19. I	13. I
20. C	14. C
	20. I

Consistency of PRONOUN POINT OF VIEW:
Pay particular attention to pp. 269–271 before going on to the Review and Practice at the end of the chapter.

Index

Added endings, 231–235
Addresses, commas with, 89
Adjectives
   defined, 56
   see also Modifiers
Adverbial conjunctions, *see* Transitional
   expressions
Adverbs
   defined, 56
   see also Modifiers
although, as dependent word, 65–66
Antecedents
   defined, 211
   to personal pronouns, 211–223
Apostrophes
   avoidance of incorrect, 238–239
   in contractions, 17
   with possessive nouns, 236–238
Auxiliaries to verbs, 14–18
   defined, 14
   with base form of verb, 25
   contractions, 17–18
   forms of *to be,* 111
   forms of *to have,* 111
   within verb strings, 16

Base form of verb, 24–26
   examples, 24
   of irregular verbs, 30–32
   as simple present tense, 25
   in verb strings, 25

Capital letters, 83–84
Character sketch, as writing topic, 301–302
Clauses
   defined, 65
   dependent, 65–70, 74–77
   embedded, 67–70, 102
   independent, 65–67, 70
Clustering, 282–283
Colons, 91
Commands
   hidden subject in, 41

in run-on sentences, 133
Commas
   in compounding clauses, 127
   summary of usage, 90
   with transitional expressions, 88, 135–136
   usage, 86–91
Comma splice, 125
Complements, *see* Completers
Completed action tenses, *see* Perfect tenses
Completers, 51–62
   clauses as, 67–68
   compound, 59–61
   as different from subjects, 53–54
   modifiers as, 52, 54–62
   role in sentence, 7
   words that act as, 52
Complex sentences, 75
Compound completers, 59–61
Compounding
   defined, 35, 46
   completers, 59–61
   embedded thoughts, 77–78
   independent clauses, 125–127
   modifiers, 59–61
   pronouns, 216–217
   sentence parts, 102
   subjects, 46–47
   verbs, 35–36
   whole sentences, 101, 103
Compound subjects, 46–47, 197–199
Compound verbs, 35–36
Conjunctions
   for compounding independent clauses, 87, 127
   in partnership with other words, 46
   for subjects, 46–47
   for verbs, 35
Conjunctive adverbs, *see* Transitional expressions
Consistency, 261–275
   defined, 261
   mastery test, 359–361
   of parallel sentence elements, 263–265
   pretest, 335–337
   of pronoun point of view, 269–271

Consistency, (continued)
    of verb tenses, 266–269
Contractions
    as auxiliaries, 17–18
    list of common, 18
Controversial stand, as writing topic, 304
Coordinating conjunctions, *see* Conjunctions

Dates, commas with, 89
Definition of an emotion, as writing topic, 303
Dependent clauses
    combined with independent clauses, 74–77
    and dependent words, 65–67
    disconnected, 115–120
    embedded clauses, 67–70, 74–75
    as sentence fragments, 115–120
    and subject-verb agreement, 192–193
Dependent words, 65–69
    defined, 65, 67
    common, listed, 65
    and embedded clauses, 67–69
Description of a place, as writing topic, 302
Direct objects, *see* Completers
Disconnected clauses, 115–120
Disconnected phrases, 112–115
does, with present tense verb, 180
Drafts, 279

-ed ending, *see* Final -ed
Embedded clauses, 65–70
    in combined sentences, 102
    to correct run-on sentences, 129, 132
    recognizing, 67
    see also Dependent clauses
Embedded thoughts, 63–79
    defined, 63
    dependent clauses, 65–70
    verbal phrases, 72–77, 103
    verbals, 75–77, 103
Embedded verbal phrases, 72–77, 103
Embedded verbals, 75–77, 103
Emotion, definition of, as writing topic, 303
Endings, added, 231–235
Essays
    defined, 295
    thesis statements for, 295–296
Examples, as writing technique, 288–289
Exclamation points, 85
Explanations, as writing technique, 288–289

Final -ed, 145–162
    avoidance of incorrect, 155–157
    with completed action, 151–152

    mastery test, 343–344
    with modifying participle, 153–155
    with passive voice, 152–153
    pretest, 319–320
    in simple past tense, 148–151
    in speech, 148
    summary of usage, 148
    when not to use, 160–161
Final -s, 163–182
    mastery test, 345–346
    natural -s, 166–167
    plural -s, 167–170
    present tense -s, 166–167, 170
    present tense of irregular verbs, 172–177, 179–
        181
    pretest, 321–322
    recognizing, 165–167
    in speech, 165–166
    spelling with added -e, 232–234
    spelling of possessives, 236–239
Final -y, spelling of added endings, 234–235
First person, 269
Fragments of sentences, *see* Sentence fragments
Freewriting, 281
Future time, and verb tense, 21–23

Gender, 219–222
General language, 290–292
Gerunds, 71–72

I, 83
Incomplete verbs, 111, 118
Indefinite pronouns
    and gender agreement, 221–222
    listed, 194, 209
    as subjects, 193–194
Independent clauses
    beginning with pronouns, 134
    combined with dependent clauses, 74–77
    in run-on sentences, 123–143
    standing alone, 65
    with transitional expressions, 135
    turned into dependent clauses, 67
Indirect objects, *see* Completers
Infinitives
    defined, 34
    role of, 34
    as verbals, 70
Interruptions, 88
Introductory phrase or clause, 87
Irregular plurals, 167
Irregular verbs, 29–33
    defined, 29

list of common, 30–32
to be, 29–30
Items in series, *see* Series
it is — it's, 246

Language
general, 290
specific, 290–291
Limiting a topic, 283–284

Main clause, *see* Independent clause
Main verb, 14
Modifiers, 54–62
defined, 54
adjectives, 56
adverbs, 56
clauses as, 67–68, 190–191
as completers, 52
compound, 59–61
prepositional phrases, 57–58
role in sentence, 7
single-word, 55–56, 58
Modifying clauses, 67–68, 190–191
Modifying participles, 153–154
Modifying phrases, 190–193

Natural *-s,* 166–167
Negative statements
present tense of *to do* with, 176
verb splits in, 18–21
no — know — now, 241–242
Non-verb forms, 34
Nouns
defined, 43, 52
common, 83
as completers, 52
final *-s* with plurals, 166–167, 178
person of, 269
plural, 167, 169
possessive, 236–239
proper, 83
as subjects, 43–44

of prepositional phrases, with plural nouns, 169
Objects
personal pronouns as, 212–217
see also Completers

Paragraph breaks, 292–293
Paragraphs
defined, 284
topic sentences for, 284–287

Parallel elements in sentences, 263–265
Parentheses, 94–95
Participles
non-verbal role, 34
as parts of verb strings, 34
see also Past participles; Present participles
Passed — past, 243–244
Passive voice, 28–29
defined, 28
final *-ed* with, 152–153, 159
Past participles
defined, 27–29
-ed endings with, 148–155
gerunds, 71–72
of irregular verbs, 30–32
as modifiers, 153–155
of *to be,* 29
as verbals, 71
Past tense, *see* Simple past tense
Past time, and verb tense, 21–23
Perfect tenses
defined, 28, 151
-ed with, 151–152, 159
present perfect, 175–176
Periods, 85
Person
defined, 269
and pronoun point of view, 269
Personal pronouns
antecedents to, 211–223
listed, 209
subject vs. object forms, 212–217
Phrases
prepositional, 57–59, 112–113
verbal, 72–77, 113–115
Place description, 302
Plural nouns
final *-s* in, 166–167, 178
irregular, 167
with prepositional phrases, 169
Point of view, and pronoun consistency, 269–271
Possessive nouns, spellings of, 236–239
Predicative adjectives, *see* Completers
Predicative nominatives, *see* Completers
Prepositional phrases
defined, 57
as modifiers, 57–59
with *of,* 169
as sentence fragments, 112–113, 118
and subject-verb agreement, 190–192
Prepositions
chart of common, 57–58
relationships shown by, 57–58

Present participles
  defined, 27
  of *to be*, 29
  as verbals, 71
Present perfect tense, 175–176
Present progressive tense, 174
Present tense
  final *-s* with, 170–181
  simple, 15, 25, 29
  subject-verb agreement, 185–186
  of *to be*, 29, 172
  of *to do*, 172
  of *to have*, 172
Present time
  and base form of verb, 25
  and verb tense, 21–23
Progressive tenses, 27, 174
Pronouns, 207–228
  defined, 43, 52, 209
  agreement with antecedent, 219–222
  antecedents to, 211–212
  at beginning of independent clauses, 134
  as completers, 52
  in compounds, 216–217
  consistent point of view, 269–271
  indefinite, 193–194, 209
  lists of, 209–210
  mastery test, 351–354
  object form of, 215–216
  person of, 269
  personal, 209, 219–223
  pretest, 327–329
  subject forms of, 213–215
  as subjects, 43–44
  with unclear gender antecedents, 219–222
Proper nouns, 83
Punctuation, 85–96
  comma, 86–91
  colon, 91
  exclamation point, 85
  parentheses, 94–95
  period, 85
  question mark, 85
  quotation marks, 93–94
  semicolon, 91–93

Question marks, 85
Questions
  to do with, 176
  verb splits in, 18–21
Quotation marks, 93–94
Quoted words, commas with, 89

Relationships shown by prepositions, 57–58
Round robin story as writing topic, 300–301
Run-on sentences, 123–147
  defined, 123
  avoidance of, 133–137
  correction methods, 126–132
  spotting, 125–126
  mastery test, 341–342
  pretest, 317–318

-s ending, *see* Final *-s*
Second person, 269
Semicolons, 91–93
  in compounding clauses, 91–92
  with items in series, 92
  with transitional expressions, 135–136
Sentence fragments, 109–122
  defined, 109
  dependent clauses, 115–117
  incomplete verbs, 111
  mastery test, 339–340
  prepositional phrases, 112–113
  pretest, 315–316
  tips for finding, 117
  verbal phrases, 113–115
Sentences
  combining, summary, 100–105
  combining with compound completers, 59–61
  combining with compound modifiers, 59–61
  combining with compound subjects, 46–47
  combining with compound verbs, 35–36
  combining by embedding thoughts, 74–78
  compared to growing plants, 6–8
  complex, 75
  compounding parts of, 102
  compounding whole sentences, 101, 103
  fragments of, 109–122
  overview of, 3–10
  parallel elements in, 263–265
  parts of, 7–8
  run-on, 123–143
  topic, 284–287
Series
  commas with, 86
  semicolons with, 92
Simple past tense
  defined, 26, 149
  final *-ed* with, 148–151
  of irregular verbs, 30–32
  one word verbs as, 15
  of *to be*, 29

Simple present tense
  one word verbs as, 15
  of *to be*, 29
  as verb base form, 25
  see also Present tense
Simple subject, 45–46
Single-word modifiers, 55–56
Single-word verbs, 14–18
Sound-alike words, spellings of, 240–247
Space relationships, and prepositions, 57
Specific language, 290–292
Speech
  final *-ed* in, 147
  final *-s* in, 165–166
Spelling, 229–259
  added endings, 231–235
  chart of own problems, 247–250
  mastery test, 355–358
  possessive nouns, 236–239
  pretest, 331–334
  sound-alike words, 240–247
Split verbs
  with negatives, 18–21
  with questions, 18–21
  subject of, 42
Subject complements, *see* Completers
Subordinate clauses, *see* Dependent clauses
Subordinating conjunctions, *see* Dependent words
Subjects, 39–48
  compound, 46–47, 197–199
  with compound verbs, 35
  as different from completers, 53–54
  identification of, 41
  nouns as, 43–44
  placement of, 42
  pronouns as, 43–44, 212–217
  in seeds of sentence, 7
  simple, 45–46
  verb agreement with, 183–206
Subject-verb agreement, 183–206
  compound subjects, 197–199
  indefinite pronouns, 193–194
  mastery test, 347–350
  with modifying phrases or clauses, 190–193
  with *or* or *nor*, 198–199
  present tenses, 185–186
  pretest, 323–325
  that as subject, 196–197
  with *there is*, 189–190
  with *was* and *were*, 186–189
  with *which*, 196–197
  with *who*, 196–197

Summaries
  defined, 304
  as writing topic, 304–308

Techniques for writing, *see* Writing techniques
Tense of verbs, 21–28
  defined, 22
  consistency of, 266–269
  perfect, 28
  progressive, 27
  simple past, 26
  simple present, 25
that
  in dependent clause, 116, 120
  and subject-verb agreement, 196–197
then — than, 240
there are, and subject-verb agreement, 189–190
there is, and subject-verb agreement, 189–190
there — their — they're, 244–245
there was, and subject-verb agreement, 189–190
there were, and subject-verb agreement, 189–190
Thesis statements, 295–296
Third person, 269
Time of event, and verb, 21–23
Time framework, and tense, 266–269
Time line for verbs, 21
Time relationships with prepositions, 58
Titles
  capitalization of, 83
  quotation marks with, 94
to be
  as auxiliary to verbs, 15, 16, 27
  forms of, 29, 111
  as irregular verb, 29–30
  in negatives, 20–21
  with passive voice, 28
  present tense forms, 172, 174, 179
  in questions, 20–21
  simple past tense forms, 187
  as single-word verb, 20–21
  and subject-verb agreement, 186–189
to do
  as auxiliary to verbs, 16
  with negatives, 176
  present tense forms, 172
  with questions, 176
  with split verbs, 19–20
to have
  as auxiliary to verbs, 15, 16
  forms of, 111
  with perfect tenses, 28, 151, 175–176
  present tense forms, 172

Topics
  limited, 285–286
  limiting, 283–284
  starting, 284
  for writing, 297–309
Topic sentences, 284–287
to — too — two, 240–241
Transitional expressions
  defined, 135
  commas with, 88
  common, listed, 135
  punctuation for, 88, 92, 135–136
  semicolons with, 92
  using in writing, 293–295

Verbal phrases
  defined, 72
  embedded, 72–77, 103
  independent clause changed to, 130, 132
  as sentence fragments, 113–115, 119
  and subject-verb agreement, 192–193
Verbals, 70–77
  embedded, 75–77, 103
  gerund, 71
  independent clause changed to, 130, 132
  infinitives, 70
  kinds of, 70–71
  past participle, 71
  present participle, 71
  verbal phrases, 72–73
Verbs, 11–37
  agreement with subjects, 183–206
  auxiliaries to, 14–18
  base form, 24–26
  being, 13
  compound, 35–36
  consistency of tenses, 266–269
  doing, 13
  final *-s*, 166–181
  forms of, 24–29
  incomplete, 111, 118
  irregular, 29–33, 172–181
  main, 14
  non-verb forms, 34
  passive voice, 28–29
  past participle, 27–29
  present participle, 27
  present tense forms, 166–181
  in seeds of sentence, 7
  simple past form, 26

single-word, 14–18
  split, 18–21
  string of, 14–18
  tenses of, 21–23, 266–269
  and time of event, 21–23
  tip for finding, 14, 18
  verbals from, 70–72
Verb strings, 14–18
  defined, 14
  auxiliaries within, 16
  base form in, 25
  do, does, or *did* with, 19–20
  with negatives, 19, 176
  participles as parts of, 34
  in progressive tenses, 27
  with questions, 19, 176
  split, 19
Verb-subject agreement, *see* Subject-verb
  agreement

was, subject-verb agreement with, 186–189
weather — whether, 242–243
were, subject-verb agreement with, 186–189
were — we're — where, 244
which
  in dependent clause, 116, 120
  and subject-verb agreement, 196–197
who
  at beginning of dependent clauses, 116, 120
  and subject-verb agreement, 196–197
whom, at beginning of dependent clauses, 116, 120
whose, at beginning of dependent clauses, 116, 120
whose — who's, 246–247
Words that sound alike, spellings of, 240–247
Writing techniques, 279–296
  clustering, 282–283
  examples, 288–289
  explanations, 288–289
  freewriting, 281
  limiting topic, 283–284
  paragraph breaks, 292–293
  specific language, 290–292
  thesis statement, 295–296
  topic sentences, 284–287
  transitional expressions, 293–295
Writing topics, 297–309

y at end of word, 234–235
your — you're, 245–246

To the student:

Some of the valuable information for authors and publishers comes from you, the student. Your reactions and suggestions will help me in writing future editions of *Sentence Sense*. After you have finished this course, please answer the questions below. Then tear out this page and mail it to:

Evelyn Farbman
c/o Marketing Services
Houghton Mifflin Company
College Division
One Beacon Street
Boston, Massachusetts 02108

1. Which chapters did you find especially helpful? Why?

_____

_____

_____

_____

2. Which chapters did you find least helpful? Why?

_____

_____

_____

_____

3. Do any chapters need more explanation or practices? Which ones and why?

_____

_____

_____

_____

4. Were any chapters too difficult or too easy? Which ones?

_____

_____

_____

_____

_____

5. Did you complete any chapters by yourself? Which ones?

_____

_____

_____

_____

_____

6. Do you have any other suggestions, criticisms, or reactions to *Sentence Sense*?

_____

_____

_____

_____

_____

Your name (optional): _____

School (optional): _____